SACCO-VANZETTI

SACCO-VANZETTI

THE MURDER
AND THE MYTH

BY

ROBERT H. MONTGOMERY
OF THE MASSACHUSETTS BAR

THE DEVIN-ADAIR COMPANY, NEW YORK

1960

PREFACE

THAT GREAT *cause célèbre* of the 1920s, the Sacco-Vanzetti case, is for the extremists a judicial murder engineered by a decadent ruling class ("hangmen in frock-coats") to eliminate two innocent radicals ("goddam agitators") who were menacing the Old Order in Massachusetts. A variant of this extreme interpretation acquits the ruling class of murder with malice prepense, but finds in the Massachusetts of the 1920's a hatred of aliens, a fear of radicalism, and a sadistic fury which made it impossible for anyone from juror to Governor, from policeman to university president, to act sanely, decently, or humanely when a radical was accused of crime.

On the other hand, there are those who, like Mr. Justice Holmes, interpreted the case as an ordinary murder made into a text by the Reds.

Because of the great and continuing influence upon the world of the belief that Massachusetts executed two innocent men because of their radical opinions, the case remains an event of importance with which historians must deal.

This book is an attempt to tell the truth about the case and to answer two questions—"Were they guilty?" and "Did they have a fair trial?"

I am not young enough to believe that telling the truth about the case will demolish a myth so dear to the credulous who have deified Vanzetti and so valuable to the powerful influences here and abroad who still use it for propaganda and mass agitation.

Yet the truth should be told, and by one who lived in Massachusetts at the time, knew many of the principal actors and after thirty years had the time and inclination to examine the whole record and all the documents and to consider every criticism of the trial and the conviction.

I am very much aware of my obligation to scores of persons who have during the writing of this book sent me information, opened their files, submitted to interviews, answered my letters, and read my first drafts. I am grateful to them all and will someday make due acknowledgment by listing them in a supplementary volume in which I intend to publish reports of my interviews, much of the correspondence, and other off-the-record evidence.

In the meantime, as an expression of gratitude, I am sending a copy of the book to all who have given me aid.

ROBERT H. MONTGOMERY

Cambridge, Massachusetts
February 12, 1960

REFERENCE NOTE

THE PRINCIPAL SOURCE is *The Sacco-Vanzetti Case, Transcript of the Record of the Trial of Nicola Sacco and Bartolomeo Vanzetti in the Courts of Massachusetts and Subsequent Proceedings, 1920-7,* New York, Henry Holt & Company, 1928, five volumes. To these volumes there was added in 1929 a Supplementary Volume which includes the Bridgewater Case and "Available Material."

References in this book to the first five volumes of the Holt Transcript are by page number enclosed in parentheses in the text as, for example, (1001), and to the Supplementary Volume are by page number after the Roman numeral VI, so enclosed, as, for example, (VI, 101).

CONTENTS

SACCO-VANZETTI

1   THE ARREST

In the Sacco-Vanzetti case there were two crimes, an unsuccessful holdup in Bridgewater, for which Vanzetti (but not Sacco) was tried at Plymouth, and the South Braintree murders, for which both were tried at Dedham.

The attempted holdup occurred on Wednesday, December 24, 1919, at about 7:30 A.M. A payroll amounting to $33,113 was being carried from the Bridgewater Trust Company to the L. Q. White Shoe Factory in a Ford truck manned by the driver (Earl Graves), the paymaster (Alfred E. Cox, Jr.), and the paymaster's guard (Benjamin F. Bowles). Graves and Bowles were sitting on the front seat, and Cox was sitting behind them on the box in which the money had been placed. En route, three men got out from a parked car, rushed at the truck with weapons in their hands, and started firing. The guard and the paymaster returned the shots. No one was hit, nothing was stolen, and the truck moved on while the assailants got back into their car and quickly went away.

One of the would-be bandits carried a shotgun which he fired twice, and almost immediately after the affray Dr. John M. Murphy picked up near the scene a common Winchester 12-gauge shotgun shell which had been discharged. Until the arrest of Vanzetti on May 5, 1920, the man with the shotgun was not identified.

Within a few minutes of the attempt, Michael E. Stewart, Chief of Police of Bridgewater, came to the scene and took charge of the investigation.

There was a light dusting of snow or frost on the roads which, with some wayside evidence, enabled Stewart to track the bandit car from the scene of the crime through Stoughton to Randolph, but he lost it there. Searches were made in Bridgewater and neighboring towns, but the car was not found at this time. Nor until the arrest did investigations by the Pinkertons, the State Police, and Stewart solve the crime.

THE SOUTH BRAINTREE MURDERS

During the afternoon of April 15, 1920, Frederick A. Parmenter, paymaster of the Slater & Morrill Shoe Factory, and his guard, Alessandro Berardelli, while carrying a payroll of $15,776 in two large black boxes from one factory building to another along Pearl Street in South Braintree, were shot and killed by two men who had been leaning on a fence waiting for them. Immediately after the shooting a large dark-colored car moved up the street; the two murderers picked up the boxes and with a third man got into the automobile, which left the scene of the murder and made its getaway.

The car was abandoned the same day. On Saturday, April 17, it was found by horseback riders in the woods off Manley Street in West Bridgewater and brought by the Brockton police to the Brockton police station. Later it was identified as the bandit car used in the Bridgewater crime. Although this discovery connected the two crimes, it did not solve them.

THE COACCI HOUSE SUSPECTS

During World War I, an alien anarchist named Feruchio Coacci lived in Bridgewater. Stewart had arrested him there under a warrant of the Department of Labor, the charge being that Coacci was spreading literature advocating overthrow of the government by force and violence. Stewart, as a police officer of Bridgewater, had had to do with several other deportation cases initiated by the Immigration authorities. His connection with deportation cases was, however, limited to arrests of persons living in Bridgewater upon warrants sent to him by the Department for purposes of arrest. He had nothing to do with the investigation of these cases or with any proceedings following the arrests, and his communication was with the Immigration Department and not with the Department of Justice.

In November 1919, Michael Boda (Buda) had come to live with Mr. and Mrs. Coacci in what came to be known as the Coacci house at the corner of Cochessett and Elm Streets in West Bridgewater, about eight hundred feet from the corner of Lincoln and Elm Streets and less than two miles from where the bandit car was found.

Soon after this, Coacci was ordered deported and was out on bond and due to surrender himself in Boston on April 15, 1920. Coacci failed to appear in Boston, and on April 16 Inspector Root of the Immigration Department, who had charge of the deportation, telephoned to Stewart and asked him to find out if Mrs. Coacci was ill; her illness had been used as an excuse for Coacci's failure to appear the day before in Boston. When told by Root that Coacci was living in West Bridgewater, which was not in his bailiwick, Stewart suggested that Root make the inquiry himself and offered to send a police officer to accompany him to the Coacci house.

Root decided to do this, and on the evening of April 16 he came to the Bridgewater Town Hall and took a police officer with him to the Coacci house. The next day Stewart learned from his officer that Coacci's wife was not ill, her pretended illness was an excuse for more time, and Root had taken Coacci with him. The day after this, Coacci was sent to New York, and on April 18 he was put on board a ship for Italy, but Stewart did not know this until later.

These circumstances aroused Stewart's suspicions and led him to visit the Coacci house several times over the weekend, with officer Albert L. Brouillard of the State Police, to interview Boda. What they saw and heard put Boda himself under suspicion, and Stewart told me in July 1958 that he thinks he made a mistake in not arresting him then and there, for when he returned within a day or so, Boda had left the Coacci house and Stewart never saw him again. He did, however, set a trap for him.

THE TRAP

During the interview with Boda, Stewart learned that on April 19, 1920, Boda had had an old Overland car towed for repairs from the Coacci house to the garage in Elm Square, West Bridgewater, operated by Simon E. Johnson and his brother. This car was not the car used in either crime. Johnson and his wife lived in a house a short distance from the garage, and Stewart arranged to have the Johnsons telephone the police when the car was called for.

During the evening of May 5, Boda, Sacco, Vanzetti, and a man named Ricardo Orciani came from Sacco's house in Stoughton to the Johnson house and asked for the Boda car. They had no 1920 number plates, and for that reason Johnson either refused to deliver it or advised them against taking it. While they were talking, Mrs. Johnson went to a neighbor's house and, as prearranged, telephoned to the West Bridgewater police. The arrest was a consequence of this telephone call.

Shortly after Mrs. Johnson's telephone call the four men left without the car; two of them, Boda and Orciani, on a motorcycle, Boda in the sidecar; the other two, Sacco and Vanzetti, walked away and took a streetcar going toward Brockton.

At this point Boda disappears from the case. He was next heard of in Italy.

Orciani, who rode off with Boda, was arrested on May 6 but was never brought to trial for either crime. His time clock had been punched on December 24, 1919, which gave him an alibi for the Bridgewater crime, and there was not sufficient identification evidence to charge him with the South Braintree murders. He was in and about the courthouse during the Dedham trial but was not called as a witness by either side.

The telephone message from Mrs. Johnson was relayed to Michael J. Connolly, a Brockton policeman who that night was in the station at Campello. Within a few minutes Connolly boarded the streetcar from Bridgewater and on it arrested Sacco and Vanzetti. At the next stop, the police car met them, and the prisoners were taken to the Brockton police station, where they were booked and searched. Stewart was sent for and took charge of the interrogation of the prisoners.

Stewart could not know it then, but the arrest he had planned solved both crimes.

GUNS, BULLETS, AND SHELLS

When arrested, Sacco had on his person a .32-caliber Colt pistol containing nine bullets and in his pocket twenty-three additional .32-caliber bullets. The fatal bullet found in Berardelli's body had been fired from a .32 Colt, and proof was to come that it had been fired from Sacco's pistol.

Moreover, as it developed, several of the bullets were of such a rare type that no duplicates could be found for ballistic-test purposes. Yet the mortal bullet found in the dead guard's body matched these bullets. Years after the Dedham trial all but one of the surviving jurors were interviewed and all said that in their minds this was the single most damning piece of evidence. The Governor's Advisory Committee[1] relied heavily on this extraordinary coincidence.

When arrested, Vanzetti had in his pocket a Harrington & Richardson .38-caliber revolver, fully loaded. This revolver was

[1] On May 3, 1927, a Petition for Clemency was signed by Vanzetti and transmitted to Governor Alvan T. Fuller with a letter signed by William G. Thompson and Herbert B. Ehrmann, then counsel for both defendants. Sacco refused to sign the Petition, but it was regarded as if made by both defendants. Governor Fuller instituted an investigation in which he was assisted by his personal counsel, Joseph Wiggin, and the Attorney General's office. On June 1, the Governor announced that Robert Grant, then a judge of the Probate Court for the County of Suffolk, President Abbott Lawrence Lowell of Harvard University, and President Samuel W. Stratton of the Massachusetts Institute of Technology had consented to serve as an Advisory Committee in connection with the Governor's investigation of the case. The Advisory Committee interviewed many persons, on July 11 and 12 held hearings at which counsel were present, and on July 17 filed its Report with the Governor. There is no transcript of the Governor's investigation; his decision is printed in full in the Holt Transcript (5378c-h). There is a transcript of the Advisory Committee's hearings of July 11-12 (4949 *et seq.*) and their Report is printed in full in the Holt Transcript (5378i-z).

not used in the murders, but since it was of the same make and caliber as the revolver customarily carried by Berardelli, and since his revolver was not found on his person or at the murder scene, it could be inferred that it had been taken from his person during the shooting and carried away. As we shall see, the evidence that the gun found in Vanzetti's pocket belonged to Berardelli was very strong, and Vanzetti's attempts to explain his possession of it were far from satisfactory.

Vanzetti was also carrying four 12-gauge shotgun shells in his pocket. The finding of these shells put Vanzetti for the first time under suspicion of the Bridgewater crime, and the eyewitnesses of that crime were sent for within a day. Identification of Vanzetti as the man with the shotgun was followed by similar identification at the preliminary hearing and at the Plymouth trial.

Except for the circumstances of the arrest—the guns, bullets, and shells and the men's conduct during and after the arrest— Sacco and Vanzetti in all probability would never have been suspected of either crime.

NO LITERATURE

At the time of the arrest a draft in Italian of a notice of a public meeting to be held in Brockton early in May at which Vanzetti was to speak was found on Sacco's person, but unless that is literature, no literature was found.

On July 12, 1921, near the close of the defendants' case at Dedham, a translation of the draft was read to the jury by one of the defendants' attorneys. It was agreed that the word *padrone* was subject to three interpretations, and so in the translation this word had a triplicate sense. This is what was read:

> You have fought all the wars. You have worked for all the "capitalists," or "all the owners," or, "all the employers." You have wandered over all the countries. Have you harvested the fruits of your labors, the price of your victories? Does the past comfort you? Does the present smile on you? Does the future promise you anything? Have you found a

piece of land where you can live like a human being and die like a human being? On these questions, on this argument, and on this theme, the struggle for existence, Bartolomeo Vanzetti will speak. "Hour"—blank—"day"—blank—"hall" —blank. "Admission free. Freedom of discussion for all. Take the ladies with you." (2120)

THE INTERROGATIONS

Shortly after their arrest, Sacco and Vanzetti were interrogated separately by Stewart at the Brockton police station. During the interrogation several police officers were present and also Simon E. Johnson, from whose house Sacco and Vanzetti had walked to the streetcar an hour or two before.

The Stewart interrogation has been criticized on two grounds. It is said, first, that Stewart by his initial questions led the defendants to believe that their radical activities were involved in their arrest and, second, that at no time were they confronted either with the Bridgewater or the South Braintree crime. This, say the critics, explains the falsehoods told to Stewart by both defendants.

Stewart's initial questions to Vanzetti and *all* that related to his political or social opinions or radical activities and Vanzetti's answers were as follows:

Q. Are you a citizen?

A. No.

Q. Do you belong to any clubs or societies? [The answer does not appear. Judge Thayer at both trials excluded the question.]

Q. Are you an Anarchist?

A. Well, I don't know what you call him. I am a little different.

Q. Do you like this government?

A. Well, I like things a little different.

Q. Do you believe in changing the government by force, if necessary?

A. No.

Q. Do you subscribe for literature or papers of the Anarchistic Party?

A. Sometimes I read them.

Q. How do you get them, through the mail?

A. A man gave one to me in Boston.

Q. Who was the man?

A. I don't know him.

Q. Did he know you?

A. I don't think so.

Q. Why do you think he gave you a paper?

A. Well, he was an Italian man and maybe he know I am.

[Vanzetti testified that he was also asked whether he was a Socialist, an I.W.W., a Radical, or a Black Hand. Vanzetti was not asked if he was a Communist.] (2110-2112)

Sacco was asked the following questions and gave the following answers:

Q. Are you a citizen?

A. No.

Q. Do you belong to any clubs or societies? [The answer does not appear, and Judge Thayer excluded the question.]

Q. Are you an Anarchist?

A. No.

Q. Are you a Communist?

A. No.

Q. Do you believe in this government of ours?

A. Yes, some things I like different.

Q. Do you believe in changing the government by force, if necessary?

A. No. (2110-2112)

Sacco was not asked about Anarchistic literature or papers, nor did he testify that additional questions about radicalism had been asked.

Neither prisoner was asked about draft dodging.

The rest of the questions put to Vanzetti were about the re-volver in his pocket, his occupation, his reason for being in West Bridgewater that night, his friend Vittorio Papa ("Poppy"), when he left Plymouth, his visit to Sacco's house, the trip from Stoughton to Brockton, whether he saw a motorcycle that night, whether he knew Boda, Coacci, or Parochi, and whether he had ever been in Hyde Park or Needham. Sacco was also asked about the doings of the evening, the motorcycle, Boda, and Coacci.

It is true that Stewart did not that evening charge either pris-oner with banditry or murder or refer specifically to December 24, 1919, or April 15, 1920, but there were good reasons for this. Stewart at the time of the arrest had nothing to do with the South Braintree crime. South Braintree is in Norfolk County, about twenty miles from Bridgewater. Braintree, of which South Brain-tree is a part, had its own police department. It was not until July 2, 1920, after the conviction of Vanzetti at Plymouth, that Frederick G. Katzmann, District Attorney for a district which in-cluded Norfolk and Plymouth Counties, called upon Stewart to take charge of the investigation and gathering of evidence to be used in the trial for the South Braintree murders. At the time of the arrest and until July 2, 1920, Stewart's only official interest was in the Bridgewater case.

Nor was he ready to charge either of them with either crime. The trap he had set for Boda had caught two men he had never heard of. They were armed, but he could not know that the pistol Sacco was carrying was the one which the Commonwealth would claim had killed Berardelli or that obsolete bullets in his pockets matched the bullet in Berardelli's body. Nor could he know that the Commonwealth would claim that the .38 Vanzetti was carry-ing was the one Berardelli had carried. The shotgun shells sug-gested a connection with the Bridgewater crime but surely, with-out other evidence, only a tenuous one. For Stewart to have said to them that they were being held for the South Braintree mur-ders or the Bridgewater holdup would have been premature, unfair, and somewhat absurd. As it turned out, Sacco was never charged with the Bridgewater crime, and Vanzetti was not charged with the South Braintree crime until after July 20, 1920. On this date John W. Faulkner went to the Plymouth jail and, from five men lined up for him to look at, picked Vanzetti as the man who, on the morning of April 15, had left the Plymouth-Boston train at the East Braintree station.[2]

It is impossible to believe that this very gentle "grilling" and Stewart's failure to mention banditry or murder misled Sacco and Vanzetti into thinking that they had been arrested because of their radical opinions or activities or draft dodging, even if we concede that the two men were confused and had difficulty with the English language. But, however all that may be, these points lost their importance the next day when, after thirty or thirty-five eyewitnesses of the two crimes had been brought to Brockton to look at the prisoners, they were interrogated at much greater length by Katzmann, who was accompanied by an interpreter and by a stenographer whose transcript of the questions and answers was used at the Dedham trial. By the time Katzmann questioned them, Sacco and Vanzetti knew that the flock of witnesses who had looked at them were not interested in whether they read Proudhon or Tolstoi or had dodged the draft but were interested in murder and banditry. Katzmann, who did not ask a single question about political or social opinions, radical affiliations or activities, or draft dodging, certainly made it clear to them that he was interested in specific crimes and what happened on December 24, 1919, and April 15, 1920. It was the questions Katzmann asked and the falsehoods they told him that made their conviction at Dedham inevitable.

No claim was made in either trial that the answers made to Stewart and the next day to Katzmann were not free and voluntary. At the Plymouth trial, where Vanzetti did not take the stand, the admission that he had talked freely and had had every consideration was made by his counsel, and at the Dedham trial both

[2] See Chapter 9 ("The Eyewitnesses") for Faulkner's testimony.

defendants admitted that they had been duly warned and had talked voluntarily. (1742)

It is true that, when he was on the stand in the Dedham trial, Vanzetti did attempt to prove police brutality on the evening of May 5, 1920, (1725) but this did not stand up well under cross-examination (1739-1747) and was not relied upon by the defense as an explanation of his falsehoods or in any of the posttrial maneuvers as evidence of unfairness. He made no claim that he had been badly treated by Katzmann the following day; on the contrary, he admitted that Katzmann had treated him "as a gentleman ought." (1742) Sacco did not narrate the incidents of the arrest or complain of police brutality or corroborate Vanzetti's account of the brutality.

MYTHICAL VERSION OF THE ARREST

The award for the most untruthful account of the arrest by a writer claiming historical objectivity goes to Professor Arthur M. Schlesinger, Jr., for this flight of fancy:

> In May 1920, following the murder of a paymaster in South Braintree, Massachusetts, Brockton police picked up two Italians in an *automobile filled with the innocent and febrile literature of anarchistic propaganda.* (My italics.)[3]

After an extended correspondence I succeeded in having Professor Schlesinger forget the automobile as the place of arrest, but he will not forget the literature nor will he add a mention of the streetcar or the guns, bullets, and shells. His revised account reads:

> In May, 1920, following the murder of a paymaster in South Braintree, Massachusetts, Brockton police picked up two Italians who had been seeking an automobile in order to dispose of a bundle of anarchistic literature.

[3] Arthur M. Schlesinger, Jr., *The Age of Roosevelt—The Crisis of the Old Order 1919-1933*, Boston, 1957, pp. 139-140.

The bundle exists only in Schlesinger's imagination and is his own contribution to the Myth. The important deception in his account is the failure to mention the guns, bullets, and shells, which put the two men under suspicion and led to their trial and conviction.

2 THE PLYMOUTH TRIAL FOR THE BRIDGEWATER CRIME

THE TRIAL of Vanzetti for the Bridgewater holdup was held at Plymouth, June 22–July 1, 1920.

Upon the return of a verdict of guilty, Vanzetti was sentenced by Judge Webster Thayer to serve twelve to fifteen years in the State Prison at Charlestown and was serving that sentence when the Dedham trial for the South Braintree murder started in the following May. The Bridgewater case created no great stir in the press or among the people. Vanzetti went quietly to State Prison and no one accused John P. Vahey (Vanzetti's counsel) of treachery, Thayer of prejudice, or Katzmann of misconduct. The defense did not appeal to the Supreme Judicial Court, which is the court of last resort in Massachusetts. It was an ordinary criminal trial, and Vanzetti's failure to take the stand was the only unusual feature. Edmund M. Morgan's summary is a just one:

> The available record shows a rather long but ordinary trial for assault with intent to rob and murder. The defendant's failure to take the stand coupled with the impeachment of the alibi witnesses explains and justifies the verdict. There is nothing to support a charge of unfairness or prejudice on the part of the trial judge.[1]

[1] G. Louis Joughin and Edmund M. Morgan, *The Legacy of Sacco and Vanzetti*, New York, 1948, page 56. Chapters II to VI, inclusive, for which Morgan is solely responsible, are cited as Morgan, the rest as Joughin.

If the radicals who had come to Vanzetti's defense had expected to make anything of the Plymouth trial except an ordinary criminal case, they were disappointed, for radicalism had not been mentioned, the trial was admittedly fair, there was no evidence of class prejudice, the jury except for two "clerks" was made up entirely of industrial workers, the public was not inflamed for or against Vanzetti, and worst of all he had not gone on the stand himself to assert his innocence or to make the witness stand a soapbox. Certainly he had not carried into the courtroom the determined militancy which radicals prescribe for the defense of a comrade brought into a court of the capitalist class justice.

The case against Vanzetti at Plymouth consisted of uncontradicted identification of him as the man with the shotgun, the shotgun shells, identification of his cap, and consciousness of guilt as proved by the falsehoods told to Stewart.

IDENTIFICATION

Benjamin F. Bowles, the paymaster's guard, described the man with the shotgun and identified him positively as Vanzetti, the man he saw in the dock. Bowles's description of the man with the shotgun included a "short croppy moustache," and much was made of this later. The meaning of the word "croppy" and its application to Vanzetti's moustache became one of the issues, and four moustache witnesses were produced by the defense, one of whom appeared before the Advisory Committee. (5106)

Alfred E. Cox, Jr., the paymaster, described the man with the shotgun and felt that he had seen him since in the Brockton police station and in the police court, and that he was the man in the dock; he would not positively identify him but was pretty sure. Cox was one of the witnesses interviewed by Governor Fuller in 1927. In his offer of proof in the Canter case,[2] William G. Thomp-

---

[2] On November 3, 1928, a young Communist named Harry J. Canter led about twenty-five others marching in a single line in front of the State House in Boston. Canter carried a placard bearing the words "Fuller—Murderer of Sacco and Vanzetti." Canter was arrested, charged with the crime of criminal libel,

son, who in November 1924 became counsel for Sacco and Vanzetti, said that the Governor had told him that he knew the witness Cox in former days and had placed considerable reliance on him, "and I think he said that Mr. Cox had gone farther with him, the Governor, than he had on the witness stand, where he expressed some doubts as to Vanzetti."

Frank W. Harding, a garage employee who was walking to work at the time of the crime, identified the man with the shotgun as the man in the dock and the man he saw in the Brockton police station.

Earl Graves, the driver, had died in February 1920.

Mrs. Georgine F. Brooks, who was walking to a train about 7:25, passed the bandit car before the shooting (which she did not see) and "judged" that the man sitting at the wheel of the stopped car was the man she had seen at the Brockton police station and was the man in the dock. Mrs. Brooks probably was mistaken in placing Vanzetti at the wheel, and part of her other evidence (that is, what she said she saw and heard after reaching the railroad station) was impeached.

Maynard Freeman Shaw, fourteen, a newsboy on his paper route, identified the man with the shotgun as the man in the dock and as the man he saw with Stewart in the Brockton police court. In describing the actions of the man with the shotgun, Shaw said he "knew by the way he ran he was a foreigner." Frankfurter in the footnote he devotes to the Bridgewater case makes fun of this and because of it characterizes all the identification evidence as

---

tried before a jury, convicted, and sentenced to a year in prison. At his trial one defense was that, although Governor Fuller was not a murderer in the ordinary sense, he was morally responsible for the death of Sacco and Vanzetti. In support of this the defense offered several witnesses to testify about conversations with Governor Fuller. The Court excluded the testimony, but in the absence of the jury the witnesses were heard, their testimony going in as offers of proof. The principal witness was William G. Thompson, who testified about several conversations he had had with Governor Fuller and his arguments to him when the plea for clemency was heard. In this "offer of proof" Thompson included as a part of the conversation a long, comprehensive, detailed, and elaborated restatement and reargument of the Sacco-Vanzetti case itself and of the charges against Judge Thayer and Katzmann.

bordering on the frivolous.[3] But Shaw on the stand did not identify Vanzetti by a statement that he ran like a foreigner. Face to
face with Vanzetti, he recognized the man sitting in the dock as
the man he saw running. Frankfurter's exclamation: "Vanzetti
was a foreigner, so of course it was Vanzetti!" misstates the major
premise of the Shavian syllogism, which ran thus: The man in the
dock is the man I saw running with the shotgun; since the man
in the dock is Vanzetti, it must follow that the man I saw running
with the shotgun was Vanzetti.

In mid-August of 1920 Fred H. Moore was put in complete
command of the legal defense. Moore's primary interest was in
the South Braintree crime, but he did not neglect the Bridgewater
case. In the latter case his first effort was to obtain new evidence,
and in September 1920 he employed a man named George Norman Woodbury as an investigator to "find something in Bridgewater to reopen the Vanzetti case."

Before the Advisory Committee, Woodbury testified that he
had found two eyewitnesses, John Barry, who was in an electric
car near the scene, and Elden Thompson, who watched the affray
from behind a tree, both of whom told him that Vanzetti was
not the man with the shotgun. Neither ever testified or gave
Woodbury a statement. Woodbury blamed this on pressure from
some unidentified source. (5213-5215)

It seems probable that Woodbury and perhaps others tried to
find further eyewitnesses, but of this I find no evidence. Certainly
none was brought forward or mentioned.

In the spring of 1927, when the plea for clemency was before
the Governor, the Pinkerton reports about the Bridgewater case
had been made available to the defense, and upon them Thompson and Ehrmann based what amounted to a reargument of the
identification of Vanzetti. Graves, the driver of the truck, died in
February 1920, before the arrest, and so he was never called
upon to identify Vanzetti. He had, however, described the man
with the shotgun to the Pinkerton detective. Bowles and Harding

---

[3] Felix Frankfurter, *The Case of Sacco and Vanzetti: A Critical Analysis for
Lawyers and Laymen*, Boston, 1927, p. 7, fn.

had also been interviewed before the arrest, and discrepancies between their descriptions of the man with the shotgun were elaborately discussed to impeach the identification at the trial.

Fraenkel,[4] quoted with approval by Herbert B. Ehrmann,[5] a defense lawyer in 1926-1927, states that there can be little doubt that if the Pinkerton reports had been available to the defense at the trial in Plymouth, the identification testimony against Vanzetti would have been discredited, so great are the discrepancies between the statements made to those detectives and the testimony given at the trial.

I cannot agree. The reports would doubtless have been of assistance to the cross-examiner, but it is unlikely that the face-to-face identification of Vanzetti in the courtroom by the eyewitnesses would have been impeached by mistaken description or discrepancies in the reports. Governor Fuller heard the eyewitnesses himself in the company of his personal counsel, Joseph Wiggin, a lawyer of great experience and wisdom, and had the benefit of the Pinkerton reports and of Thompson's analysis of them. In spite of the discrepancies, he believed that the eyewitnesses told the truth to him and at the trial.

THE SHOTGUN SHELLS

Michael J. Connolly, a police officer of Brockton, who testified about the arrest of Sacco and Vanzetti on the streetcar on May 5, 1920, and the finding of the shotgun shells in Vanzetti's pocket, identified the shells and they went into evidence.

Dr. John M. Murphy identified a common Winchester shell, twelve gauge, which had been discharged; he had picked it up on the street immediately after the holdup.

After the trial it was learned that a debate had taken place in the jury room on whether Vanzetti could be found guilty of assault with intent to *murder*, when his weapon was a shotgun presumably loaded with birdshot. The jury then went back to the

---

4 Osmond K. Fraenkel, *The Sacco-Vanzetti Case*, New York, 1931, p. 159.
5 *The Untried Case: the Sacco-Vanzetti Case and the Morelli Gang*, New York, 1933, p. 25, fn.

courtroom and asked Judge Thayer to instruct them whether, instead of a verdict of assault with intent to murder, they could return a verdict of assault with a dangerous weapon under the count of assault with intent to murder. Judge Thayer said they could. Upon their return to the jury room, however, one of them improperly opened two of the shotgun shells and found that they were loaded with buckshot and not, as was supposed, with birdshot. The difference between buckshot and birdshot as lethal missiles was enough to convince the jury that there had been an intent to *murder* as well as an intent to *rob,* and so they agreed on a verdict of guilty on both counts. The opening of the shell was improper, but no harm came of it, because Judge Thayer imposed the sentence on one count only, assault with intent to *rob,* and did not impose sentence on the other count, assault with intent to *murder.*

As a result of the jury's improper action, only two of the shotgun shells got into evidence at the Dedham trial, and by agreement the jury was told that the failure to produce the other two was the fault of neither side.

When the Bridgewater case came before the Governor in 1927 Thompson and Ehrmann in a letter to the Governor accused Stewart of substituting shotgun shells for those taken from Vanzetti's person.

This charge against Stewart was modified somewhat, but the claim of Thompson and Ehrmann that the shotgun shells were false exhibits, in that, while the shells were in the possession of the police, *someone* had either tampered with them and substituted buckshot or had substituted new shells, was never withdrawn although never supported by anything except assertion and suspicion.

It is noteworthy that, in the last stages of the Sacco-Vanzetti case, whenever Thompson and Ehrmann tried to meet the evidence of the bullets and the shells, they resorted to the desperate claim that there had been a substitution of a false exhibit by some highly improper person. They applied this accusation to the shotgun shells in the Bridgewater case and, as we shall see, to the mortal bullet found in Berardelli's body. In neither case did they present any evidence, hearsay or otherwise, to substantiate their suspicions.

VANZETTI'S CAP

Richard Grant Casey, who was leaving his house at about 7:20, said the man sitting at the right of the driver was taller than the driver, or at least appeared so while sitting, and "noticed that he had on a cap that appeared to be a brown cap." About a week before the trial, Stewart had asked him to pick from seven caps a cap that resembled the one he saw. A cap was produced which the witness identified as the one he saw in Stewart's office, and it appeared to be "on this man in the machine on the right of the driver." Stewart testified that this was the cap that on May 11, 1920, he had found in Vanzetti's closet at 35 Cherry Street, Plymouth.

CONSCIOUSNESS OF GUILT

It is a rule of law that untruths told upon arrest are evidence of consciousness of guilt and can be used against a defendant when such consciousness relates to the crime with which he is charged. At the Plymouth trial the Commonwealth relied upon the falsehoods told by Vanzetti to Stewart.

Stewart testified about his interrogation of Vanzetti the evening of the arrest. The entire interview was read to the Court in the absence of the jury, and the Court, with the acquiescence of Katzmann, excluded all that related to Vanzetti's political opinions, all that related to the .38-caliber revolver, and all that related to Sacco. All that got in is summarized by Morgan as follows: (1) he went to Bridgewater to see his good friend Papa, (2) he didn't know whether he had reached Bridgewater, for he had never been there before, (3) he did not see a motorcycle in West Bridgewater, (4) he had never been in Hyde Park or Needham, and (5) he did not know Mike Boda.

There was uncontradicted evidence which could be accepted by the jury as proof that these answers to Stewart's questions were false, and from this the jury could infer a consciousness of guilt and relate it to the crime. The more important falsehoods were proved by evidence that he had been in Bridgewater before, that he did see a motorcycle in West Bridgewater, and that he did know Mike Boda. This came in through several witnesses, notably Mr. and Mrs. Johnson, who described what happened at their house on the night of the arrest, and Austin C. Cole, the conductor on the streetcar at the time of the arrest, who testified that he had seen Vanzetti either Wednesday or Thursday before April 19 (April 14 or 15) on his car going from Bridgewater to Brockton with Sacco.

Katzmann's interrogation of Vanzetti, which counted so heavily against the defense at Dedham, would have supplied additional evidence of consciousness of guilt and, if Vanzetti had taken the stand, would presumably have been used. To introduce it as a part of the Commonwealth's case would have been time consuming, because to prove the falsity of the answers it would have been necessary to call several other witnesses and open up several collateral issues. With Vanzetti on the stand at Dedham, the question and answer were read by Katzmann, the falsity of the answer was admitted by Vanzetti, and the reason or lack of reason for the untruth ascertained from him at once.

3   VANZETTI'S ALIBI AT PLYMOUTH

AT THE Plymouth trial, Vanzetti's sole defense was an alibi, the principal testimony coming from a group of his close friends who had rehearsed their stories together. The most important witness was an attractive thirteen-year-old boy, Beltrando Brini, who testified that on December 24, 1919, he was helping Vanzetti deliver eels from early morning until early afternoon. This testimony was impeached by his own admissions. In cross-examination, Katzmann had him repeat his story; there were significant variations, and the little boy candidly admitted that he had told his story twice to Vahey and five times to his parents; that if he had omitted anything, his papa would tell him and next time he would be sure to put it in.

Q. You learned it just like a piece at school?
A. Sure. (VI, 266)

The testimony of the next-most-important witness, Mrs. Mary Fortini, Vanzetti's landlady, was impeached by her own admission that she had told the police a day or two after the arrest a story different in several important particulars from that told on the stand, omitting among other items mention of the little Brini boy, the horse, and Balboni. (VI, 233)

The testimony of the other witnesses also suffered in cross-examination, and the whole alibi seems to have been thoroughly impeached. Certainly the jury and Governor Fuller, when the

23

case was reviewed by him, did not believe it. But many do, and in all fairness a detailed review is in order.

Although the critical time was a period of a few hours in the morning of December 24, Vanzetti's alibi witnesses undertook to place him in Plymouth continuously from 6:00 P.M. on December 23 to the morning of Christmas Day.

The evidence about the night of December 23 came from Mrs. Fortini and two members of the Brini family.

The Fortinis lived at 35 Cherry Street, Plymouth. Vanzetti had boarded with them since October 1919 and had an upstairs room in their house.

Mrs. Fortini testified that Vanzetti had supper at her house on December 23, 1919, at 6:00 P.M., that he left about 6:30 and came back at about 8:00; that from 8:00 to midnight he was in her kitchen preparing eels for delivery by putting them in packages and that she awakened him the next morning at 6:15.

From 6:30 P.M., when Vanzetti left the Fortini house after his supper, we do not see him again until he reached the Brini house in Suasso's Lane between 7:00 and 7:30 P.M. The Brini household consisted of the father, Vincenzo Brini, who was working on the night shift at the Plymouth Cordage Company; his wife, Alfonsine Brini, who was working on the day shift; their thirteen-year-old son, Beltrando Brini, and two daughters, one of whom was older than Beltrando. Mrs. Rose Forni, who worked in the Puritan Mill, had an upstairs room in the Brini house. The father was at work and did not see Vanzetti that evening or until the evening of December 24. The girls were not called as witnesses. Mrs. Forni was called, but she did not see Vanzetti that evening or the next day until the evening. Vanzetti had boarded with the Brinis before going to the Fortinis' and was a frequent visitor to their house. The Brini house was not far from the Fortinis', a few minutes' walk.

The story that the little boy told on the stand about this evening was substantially this: On the night of December 23, at about 7:30, Vanzetti came to the Brini house. The family had finished supper and the table had been cleared. The father had left for work. At about the time that Vanzetti entered the house, two American men brought half a pig to the house and put it down cellar, and then came up for a drink in the kitchen. Vanzetti did not drink with them; he never drank. Vanzetti asked the little boy to go with him to peddle fish the next day, saying he would borrow a horse.

The half pig has no significance except that its delivery was the reason given by the Brinis for remembering that it was on December 23 and not on another evening that the arrangement with Vanzetti was made to have the little boy deliver fish the next day. This would have been a telling point, except that the date and time of the pig delivery were never fixed, other than by the assertion of the Brinis; this failure took from the pig story its corroborative effect, for if the Brini version had been the correct one, the two Americans who delivered the pig could have testified that they saw Vanzetti at the Brini house at the time of the delivery. This would have supplied the defense with two corroborating alibi witnesses who were not Italians. No explanation of the failure to call them was given.

Mrs. Brini's testimony about the evening visit of Vanzetti on December 23 was substantially the same as her son's, with the addition that Vanzetti delivered eels to her at the same time the pig came and she salted them to prepare them for eating the next day.

Now we come to the morning of December 24. Vanzetti's presence in Plymouth the night before was important only because it showed that he was preparing to spend the next day peddling eels in Plymouth. So far as the crime was concerned, he could have spent the evening and night of December 23 exactly as Mrs. Fortini and the Brinis testified and still been in Bridgewater at 7:30 A.M. on December 24.

At 6:00 A.M. on December 24, Carlo Balboni, a night fireman at the Cordage, left his work and walked to the Fortini home to get some eels which he had ordered from Vanzetti on his way to work the day before. He found Mrs. Fortini in the kitchen fixing breakfast for the men to go to work. She went into the hall and called Vanzetti, who was asleep in his upstairs room. In a few minutes he came down dressed in a green sweater, no jacket, stockings and no shoes, and gave Balboni two pounds of eels. *They were not in a package and Balboni did not see any packages.* Balboni never bought fish from Vanzetti except on this occasion. He remembered it was December 24 because that is the day Italians eat eels, and he fixed the time at 6:15 or 6:20 because he had left work at 6:00.

When Balboni left with his eels in a basket he had brought with him, Vanzetti put on his shoes while Mrs. Fortini warmed the milk which constituted his breakfast. Then, at about 6:30 A.M., he left the house, and Mrs. Fortini did not see him again until about 8:00 A.M., when he returned with the little Brini boy. Mrs. Fortini remembered that all this happened on December 24 because it was the day before Christmas, a fast day upon which Italians eat eels.

After Vanzetti left the Fortini house about 6:30 A.M. on December 24, we see no more of him until he brought eels to Mrs. Terese Malaquci at 48 Cherry Street, "after" 7:00 o'clock in the morning. This witness fixed the date because it was the day before Christmas, and the time because she heard the 7:00 (not the 8:00) o'clock whistle blow shortly before the eels were delivered. After testifying in cross-examination that she had ordered the eels the Friday before, she changed her testimony and said that she had ordered them the day before. She also testified that she had ordered them delivered on December 23.

We have two witnesses for 7:05 A.M. Mrs. Rosa Balboni, wife of Joseph Balboni, not of Carlo, lived at 14 South Cherry Street. She had ordered her eels of Vanzetti on Sunday, December 21, and got delivery at her house on Wednesday, December 24, after dinner, about 3:00 or 4:00 o'clock. She had, however, taken her bread to Bastoni, the baker, whose bakeshop was on Cherry Street, early in the morning, and at about 7:05 she saw Vanzetti delivering fish to a woman on Cherry Street. She placed the date because it was the day before Christmas and a "holiday" (holy day?) for Italians.

Vincent Louis Longhi, a weaver in the Puritan Mill, was also a

7:05 A.M. witness. Vanzetti, he testified, came to his house at 42 Cherry Street on December 24 and delivered some eels to his mother. He fixed the date by the eel custom and said that the eels were eaten about 5:30 that day. At the time of the trial his mother was ill and could not testify, so he had been sent for at the mill on the day he testified. Although this was the first time the matter had been called to his attention, he instantly remembered the day and fixed the time by the time that the streetcar he took to work left the foot of Cherry Street. Longhi did not do well on cross-examination.

John DiCarli kept a shoe-repair store at 301 Court Street, about eight minutes' walk from Vanzetti's boardinghouse, and lived nearby with his son. He always opened his store at 7:00 A.M. and started to clean at 7:15. While he was cleaning on December 24, Vanzetti brought him a little bundle of eels done up in a newspaper. He had ordered them the Sunday before and they were eaten on December 24. He fixed the date because of the custom of eating eels on Christmas Eve, and the time by the time that he swept up every morning.

The little boy's father, Vincenzo Brini, left his work at the Cordage at 5:00 A.M. on December 24. He came home, went downstairs to see if the half pig had come, went upstairs, lighted the stove, washed himself, and made the bread. At about 7:00 he took the bread dough to the bakeshop, almost opposite the place where he lived. About half an hour or thirty-five minutes later he came out of the bakeshop and then he saw the boy coming to meet him. This was about 7:25 or 7:35. The little boy wanted to go selling fish. The father sent him home for his rubbers and did not see him again during the morning. He did not see Vanzetti at this time or at all during the day until late in the evening. He did see people going to work about 7:30.

Mrs. Alfonsine Brini, the little boy's mother, left for work at 6:45 A.M. on December 24 and did not see her son or Vanzetti until the evening.

The little boy does not tell us when he arose. Suddenly we find him on Court Street near Maxwell's drugstore, where between

7:25 and 7:35 he saw and talked with Vanzetti. He thought he also saw John DiCarli (the shoemaker who was a witness) and Mr. Ferrari, who had a store on Court Street, and an unnamed lady. Ferrari did not testify nor was the lady ever named. Afterward he talked with his father and then went back to the house to find his rubbers, which after a search of "maybe half an hour or less" he found under the cellar steps.

On direct examination he said that the encounter with his father was at the end of Suasso's Lane, but when on cross-examination Katzmann, to show that the story was a rehearsed one, asked him to repeat it, he said, "I brought a bundle of fish into Mr. Ferrari's store [on Court Street] and my father was also in the store when I went up to him and told him I was going to Mr. Vanzetti's. He looked at my feet and said 'Go home and get your rubbers.'" (VI, 259, 264)

His father testified that the meeting was on the street as he, the father, was coming out of the bakeshop.

After the half-hour hunt for his rubbers the little boy put them on and went to 35 Cherry Street, arriving "maybe past eight," fixing the time by the Cordage whistle (there were three in the morning—one at three minutes to seven, one at seven, and one at eight) and by the fact that he had not eaten his breakfast.

At 35 Cherry Street, Vanzetti was putting packages of fish in the wheelbarrow. The packages had the names of customers on a white paper with the price to collect. The boy asked Vanzetti about the horse, and Vanzetti said he had not been able to borrow it. So they set off delivering fish, Vanzetti with a wheelbarrow, afterwards replaced by the pushcart, the little boy with a basket.

The boy remembered that he delivered fish to Mrs. Bonjonanni at 15 Cherry Street, because when he brought fish to her she gave him a two-dollar bill for the fish, which cost $1.20, and since he did not have the right change, she came down and paid it to Vanzetti at the steps. He also remembered Mrs. Christophori, who also did not have the right change.

The rest of the names he did not remember, nor did he remember how many deliveries he made or how often he replenished his basket. He did remember that he got through between 1:00 and 2:00 in the afternoon after four hours' work or more, that he saw Vanzetti again in the evening at the Brini house, and that he received a present of two silver half dollars from him in his Christmas stocking.

After the encounter with the Brini boy at 7:25 or 7:35, we see no more of Vanzetti until about 7:50 or 7:55 when, as Enrico Bastoni testified, he came into Bastoni's bakeshop on Cherry Street to borrow a horse. Bastoni fixed the date by the fact that it was the day the Italians celebrate, and the exact time by the Cordage whistle. After he had tried unsuccessfully to borrow a horse, Vanzetti left the bakeshop. He delivered Bastoni's eels after noonday dinner on December 24.

Returning to Mrs. Fortini's testimony, we find Vanzetti back about 8:00 A.M. ("before") in her kitchen, talking with her about a horse. After this talk he left the house with fish, taking the little Brini boy with him.

Vanzetti's activities from 8:00 A.M. to 9:00 A.M. depend on the testimony of the little Brini boy. At 9:00 ("after"), Mrs. Fortini testified, Vanzetti came back to get more fish, then she saw him no more until 12:00 when he came for the noonday meal, leaving again in half an hour with more fish. At 5:00 or 5:30 he was back for the evening meal, leaving shortly after.

It was between 9:00 A.M. and 10:00 A.M., maybe 9:55, that Mrs. Adeladi Bonjonanni, of 3 South Cherry Street, bought her eels and saw Vanzetti, who had to make change. She had ordered the eels Sunday, December 21, for delivery the twenty-third, but Vanzetti did not come until the twenty-fourth. She wanted them on the twenty-third so that she could salt them. She fixed the time of day by the fact that she was making polenta when she went down to get her change.

Mrs. Margaretta Fiochi, of 1 South Cherry Street, a next-door neighbor of Mrs. Bonjonanni, also got her eels after 9:00 and before 10:00. She had ordered them on Sunday and got them on the twenty-fourth, a date she remembered because of the custom of eating eels on Christmas Eve. She would have liked to salt them the day before, because "if I kept them in salt longer it would be more delicious to eat."

Mrs. Emma Borsari, of 6 South Cherry Street, who lived near Mrs. Bonjonanni, got her eels from Vanzetti between 10:30 A.M. and 10:45 A.M. ("no more") on December 24. She had ordered them on Sunday but remembered they were not delivered until the fast day. This was the only time she bought eels from him.

About 11:00 A.M. Miss Esther Esteno G. Christophori, of 7 Suasso's Lane, saw the little Brini boy when he brought the eels to her mother, but she did not see Vanzetti. Miss Christophori, American born, had one year more to go in the high school and did not care very much for eels herself. She fixed the day because it was a fast day, and the time because the little boy brought the fish into the kitchen when she was there getting some furniture polish.

Except for the unspecified deliveries generally described by the little boy, there were no further deliveries until between 3:00 and 4:00 ("after dinner"), when Mrs. Rosa Balboni got eels from Vanzetti himself. She had ordered them on Sunday and remembered the day because it was a fast day.

At 3:30 or 4:00 Enrico Bastoni, the baker, whose bakeshop was on Cherry Street, got eels from Vanzetti and sometime during the afternoon saw him on the street.

And that is all, until about 5:00 or 5:30, when Vanzetti came back to the Fortini house and had supper. He left soon thereafter but came back much later and was in his bed on Christmas Day morning. Meanwhile he had been at the Brini house, arriving about 7:30 or 8:00 and staying late. The little boy, who afterward was to become an accomplished orchestra leader, spent the evening playing his violin and talking with his sisters.

The alibi witnesses undertook to remember without the aid of any record what they did and saw on a day six months in the past, and to place Vanzetti at a certain place within a narrow range of minutes with a degree of particularity (7:05 exactly, 7:15, 7:25 to 7:35) far beyond the ability of most humans. Until his arrest on May 5, 1920, over four months after the crime, they would have had no occasion to associate the day of the crime or any particular time of that day with Vanzetti. Associating their glimpse of Vanzetti with the Cordage whistle or a streetcar stop or sweeping up the store or polishing the furniture or making polenta or hunting for a pair of rubbers was obviously no help. Why should one associate the sight of Vanzetti selling a package of eels with a whistle which blew several times a day every day?

December 24 was Christmas Eve and a fast day upon which it was customary for Italians to eat eels at the midday or evening meal. For this reason, purchases and deliveries of eels to them by Vanzetti, the fish peddler, were associated with December 24 in the minds of several of his customers, but in cross-examination this proved to be dangerous ground, because it was also the custom of Italians to salt the eels a day or so before eating. This made it more likely that the eels were delivered on December 22 (Monday) or 23 (Tuesday). The *eating of eels* and Christmas Eve were reasonably associated, but the *buying of eels* was more reasonably associated with December 22 or December 23.

In this connection, it is noteworthy that Vanzetti, in giving his alibi testimony at the Dedham trial, explained that he went on a certain day to Kingston "because the Americans, they like to buy the fish the same day, they buy the same day they eat, and the Italians like better to buy the fish the day before and put the salt on top, on fish." (1701)

When the case came before the Governor, he interviewed several of the alibi witnesses, among them the little Brini boy, by then a college student, and Mrs. Fortini, and also called in Mr. Fortini. On July 28, 1927, Vanzetti wrote the Governor a long letter, of which the following is the last paragraph:

I don't understand what your Excellency meant by telling me what the Fortini's said to you. Mrs. Fortini certainly saw me early in the morning of December 24th in her house and called me down-stairs, as she testified. None of the other Fortinis testified at Plymouth. Mrs. Fortini's testimony was true. The same was true at Dedham. Mrs. Fortini testified that I was in Plymouth selling fish.[1] The only man member of the Fortini family that has any brains is Tony Fortini [Venuste], the nephew, who now lives with James Caldera in Plymouth. He saw me on December 24, 1919 and I think he saw me April 15th in Plymouth. The youngest Fortini boy is simple-minded. The father is alcoholic. The oldest Fortini boy is a domestic tyrant, and I have told him many times that if I were his brother I would throw him out of the window for the way he treated his mother. The other boy is a good boy, but not very intelligent. The father and three sons usually left the house before seven o'clock in the morning to work, and I should be surprised if they saw me on April 15th; but I think that some of them must have seen me, as the mother did, on the early morning of December 24th.[2]

From this we may infer that Mr. Fortini and perhaps Mrs. Fortini did not support the alibi when questioned by the Governor.

THE AMERICAN EXPRESS COMPANY RECEIPT

It would have helped the alibi immeasurably if the supply of eels had been delivered to Vanzetti on but not before December 23. Morgan thinks that, if the American Express Company receipt had been in evidence, it would have been strong corroboration of Mrs. Fortini's story that Vanzetti spent the evening of December 23 in her kitchen packaging the eels and started delivering them the next morning.

In 1927 Governor Fuller, after reading the record, noted and told the defense that there was no documentary evidence showing delivery of eels to Vanzetti. Ehrmann thereupon made a search and found that the express-receipt book of the Corso & Canizzo Company of Boston contained an American Express Company receipt showing receipt by the American Express at Boston on De-

---

1 Vanzetti is in error here if he meant to say that Mrs. Fortini testified at Dedham. She did not.

2 *The Letters of Sacco and Vanzetti*, Edited by Marion Denman Frankfurter and Gardner Jackson, New York, 1928, Appendix II, p. 397.

cember 20, 1919 (Saturday), of one barrel of eels for delivery C.O.D. to B. Vanzetti at Plymouth. This receipt had not been introduced at the trial, but Mrs. Fortini had testified that at about 9:30 A.M. on December 22 (Monday) or 23 (Tuesday) a barrel of eels was delivered by express to Vanzetti at her home. Vanzetti was away when the expressman first called, and she had no money. "After one Monday Vanzetti and the express came back."

Morgan's comment is that, if Mrs. Fortini's "After one Monday" meant "Tuesday," the receipt, coming from an unimpeachable source, would have furnished strong corroboration of her story of Vanzetti's work in her kitchen on the twenty-third and of the testimony of the numerous witnesses that the delivery of the eels to his customers occurred on the twenty-fourth, the day of the Bridgewater crime.

But why should we assume that "After one Monday" meant "Tuesday," or anything else than "After one o'clock Monday"? The expressman came first at about 9:30 A.M. or 10:00 A.M. on a day Mrs. Fortini did not know, but either Monday or Tuesday, and took back the eels. He returned and made the delivery "After one Monday." A shipment of eels from Boston delivered to the express company on Saturday, December 20, would ordinarily be delivered not later than Monday, December 22, and if so, Vanzetti's delivery of eels to his customers would have occurred that day or on the twenty-third, thus giving time for a day or so of salting before their use on December 24.

It would seem that, if the delivery by the Express Company had actually been made on the twenty-third, this important point would have been proved by the testimony of the expressman (who was not a witness) or by his records, and not left, as Mrs. Fortini left it, as something which might have happened on December 22 or 23. The actual express receipt would not have been helpful on this point; in fact it hurt, because of its date, which made likely a delivery by the express company on Monday the twenty-second and not on Tuesday the twenty-third.

In his footnote about the Bridgewater case, Frankfurter devotes two sentences to the alibi:

> More than twenty people swore to having seen Vanzetti in
> Plymouth on December 24, among them those who remem-
> bered buying eels from him for the Christmas Eve feasts. Of
> course all these witnesses were Italians.

The first of these two sentences is inaccurate in the count of
the witnesses. More than twenty people did not swear to seeing
Vanzetti in Plymouth on December 24; the number was fourteen.
The defense produced twenty-one witnesses in all. One of these
was Vittorio Papa of East Bridgewater, who was produced to
prove that there was a man of this name known to Vanzetti living
in one of the Bridgewaters. Papa was not an alibi witness and had
not seen Vanzetti in Plymouth for years. Four other witnesses
(Vernazzano, Christophori, Gault, and Schilling) testified about
Vanzetti's moustache and were in no sense alibi witnesses. This
leaves sixteen. The witness Andrew Sassi did not see Vanzetti on
December 24; he testified about the pig. We must also exclude
Miss Christophori, who saw the little Brini boy when he delivered
fish to her mother on December 24, a little past 11:00, but did not
testify about Vanzetti at all. This leaves fourteen. Of these, there
were three (Mr. Brini, Mrs. Brini, and Mrs. Forni) who saw Vanzetti on December 24, but none of them saw him until the evening, twelve hours after the crime. Literally, Frankfurter may
count them, but there were only eleven witnesses who positively
testified that Vanzetti was in Plymouth on the morning or afternoon of December 24.

No great importance is to be attached to this careless miscount,
but one shudders to think what would have happened to Thayer
or Katzmann or Lowell or Wigmore if one of them had made a
similar mistake about numbers.

4 VANZETTI DID NOT TAKE THE STAND AT PLYMOUTH

In the Plymouth trial, Vanzetti did not take the stand. This was his right, and the jury was told that they must not infer guilt from his failure to testify. This counsel of perfection the jury may have followed—the Commonwealth's case was strong enough and the defense weak enough to justify the verdict without benefit of the inference—but it is surely common sense for us to infer that a defendant who does not take the stand in his own behalf has no confidence in his innocence.

At the conclusion of the Commonwealth's case, several witnesses had identified Vanzetti as the man with the shotgun. It is inconceivable that an innocent defendant would not have gone on the stand and denied that testimony.

It also appeared that at the time of the arrest Vanzetti had in his possession four shotgun shells. An innocent defendant would have wanted to explain his possession of them. Frankfurter says that the innocent possession of them was accounted for at the Dedham trial. Why not at the Plymouth trial? Vanzetti knew then as well as later how they came into his possession.

Similarly, part of the case against the defendant was the consciousness of guilt to be inferred from Vanzetti's untruthful answers to Stewart during the questioning immediately after the arrest. The evidence clearly showed that some of the answers were untruthful. An innocent defendant would have wanted to explain why he had told these untruths.

35

And, finally, an innocent defendant whose only defense was an alibi would have wanted to help his alibi witnesses by telling all he knew about his actions between 7:00 and 8:00 on the morning of December 24, 1919. He, if anyone, knew what he was doing then and where he was.

But he did not take the stand and an excuse had to be found. The first version came from his own lips in the interview upon which John Nicholas Beffel based his article "Eels and the Electric Chair," published in the *New Republic* of December 29, 1920:

> . . . his attorneys, for instance, would not let Vanzetti take the witness stand in his own defense unless he would agree to conceal that he held radical beliefs about the economic conflict. He refused to make that pledge; he is a philosophical anarchist, and wanted to explain why. But the attorneys kept him from testifying, and thus the jury never heard Vanzetti's own story. . . . Other attorneys, who are not afraid to let Vanzetti express his real philosophical opinions before the world, have now taken charge of his defense. . . .

But this was too foolish even for the mythmakers, and by 1927 the exact opposite had become the authorized version. Says Frankfurter:

> The circumstances of the trial are sufficiently revealed by the fact that Vanzetti, protesting innocence, was not allowed by his counsel to take the witness stand for fear his radical opinions would be brought out and tell against him disastrously." [1]

This statement interested me so much that I initiated a correspondence with Frankfurter. In my first letter, dated February 4, 1958, I quoted the foregoing sentence from his footnote and asked him if he would please tell me the source of the information upon which he based the statement.

[1] Frankfurter, *op. cit.*, p. 7, fn.

Under date of February 20, 1958, I had in reply a letter of which I quote the opening sentences:

> Perhaps you will not charge me with crass immodesty if in reply to your inquiry of February 4 I vouch to warranty President Lowell for the accuracy of what I wrote in "The Case of Sacco and Vanzetti." In the fall of 1927, President Lowell said to Norman Hapgood, a Harvard friend, "Wigmore was a fool! Wigmore was a fool to enter into controversy with Frankfurter. He should have known that Frankfurter would be accurate." Now, of course, such a general statement does not give you chapter and verse for the accuracy of what I said about the Bridgewater trial. I do not know whether in the great mass of my materials touching the case I would find a reference to the source of my statement. I cannot possibly undertake to go through those materials; it would involve an amount of time that is not at my disposal. But I have not the slightest doubt that what you quote as the reason given by me for Vahey's advice to Vanzetti not to take the stand in the Bridgewater trial was a fact, the truth of which I had ascertained at the time on unimpeachable evidence.

This did not satisfy me. President Lowell may have told Norman Hapgood that Wigmore could expect accuracy when Frankfurter quoted a record, but that remark did not seem to me to establish an infallibility which would make a Frankfurter assertion conclusive proof of a fact without production of the evidence upon which he relied. So, in search of that evidence, I wrote a letter of considerable length in which I argued the improbability of a Massachusetts lawyer advising Vanzetti to keep off the stand because of his radical opinions. A Massachusetts lawyer, I wrote, would have known, on the authority of the cases collected in *Jones v. Commonwealth*, 327 Mass. 491, that Vanzetti's radical opinions could not have been introduced by cross-examination or otherwise unless he himself introduced them, as he did in the

Dedham trial.[2] A Massachusetts lawyer would also have known
that in a serious case a defendant who does not take the stand
has little if any chance of acquittal. So, I argued, staying off the
stand damaged Vanzetti's chances much more than any possible
reference to radicalism could have done. My letter ended with
the following paragraph:

> Under these circumstances it seems inconceivable that Vahey
> would have advised Vanzetti to keep off the stand for the
> reason that you give, but if there is an unimpeachable source
> for your statement I cannot urge you too strongly to find it.

But Frankfurter had tired of our correspondence. His next letter read:

> This is in acknowledgment of your letter of February 25.
> Since Dean Wigmore published his two blasts immediately
> after what I wrote on the *Sacco and Vanzetti* case, I deemed
> it, of course, my duty to vindicate what I had written. Since
> then, and particularly since coming on the Court, I have
> steadfastly refused to enter upon any discussion about my
> book or otherwise to express comment on the case. I must
> adhere to that policy and leave my book to whatever fate
> may befall it at the hands of future commentators. Perhaps
> I may be allowed to add that no one was better placed than
> President Lowell to attest to the accuracy of what I wrote.

While I quite agreed that no one was better placed than President Lowell to attest to Frankfurter's accuracy, I could not give
his remark to Norman Hapgood the sweeping consequence that
Frankfurter claimed for it. Rather I was inclined to limit that remark to its context and to find Lowell's appraisal of Frankfurter's
accuracy about matters of fact in the following passage in a letter
to Chief Justice William Howard Taft written by President Lowell
on November 1, 1927:

> We [the Governor's Advisory Committee] certainly started
> with no prejudice against Sacco and Vanzetti. Indeed, all I

2 See Chapter 16 ("Radicalism at the Trial").

had read was Frankfurter's article in the Atlantic, which, though partisan argument, I supposed stated the facts correctly; and that naturally left the impression that something was wrong with the trial; but on reading all the facts, none of us had the least question about the men's guilt. The proof seemed to be conclusive. On the other hand, there was gross misstatement in the propaganda in their favor. . . .[3]

So, still in search of evidence, I sent the correspondence to James M. Graham, who was with Vahey in the Plymouth trial and was also Sacco's attorney at the time. On March 13, 1958, he wrote me this letter:

I have your letter of March 7th enclosing some correspondence in reference to the Sacco-Vanzetti case, and I am directing my attention particularly to the footnote referred to in your letter to Justice Frankfurter, dated February 4, 1958, in which it is said that Vanzetti, protesting his innocence, was not allowed by his counsel to take the witness stand, for his radical opinions would be brought out and held against him disastrously.

There were only three people who ever knew whether Vanzetti's failure to take the stand in the Bridgewater trial was on the advice of counsel or his own decision. They were Mr. Vanzetti, Mr. John P. Vahey, and myself. We spent considerable time with him at the Plymouth County Jail as the case was drawing to a close when it had to be decided whether he would take the stand or not. The situation as it stood at that time was gone over carefully with Mr. Vanzetti by Mr. Vahey and myself. Mr. Vahey was senior counsel in the case and I was associated with him in this case by reason of the fact that I represented Sacco in another case.

After a lengthy discussion with Mr. Vanzetti, at either his suggestion, or with his approval, I went to the Dedham

[3] Henry Aaron Yeomans, *Abbott Lawrence Lowell* (biography), Cambridge, 1948, pp. 494-495.

House of Correction and talked with Sacco, and then came back to Plymouth and met with Vahey and Vanzetti in the Jail, and the three of us, for a considerable time, discussed the question of Vanzetti taking the stand. He was carefully and thoroughly advised as to the evidence that had gone in as to what inference the Jury might draw if he failed to take the stand despite what the Judge would tell them in his charge, and as to what information might be elicited from him if he did take the stand.

I do not think it proper to discuss the subject matter of the pros and cons as it might trespass upon the duty of non-disclosure of an attorney, but I do recall very distinctly because of the impression it made on me, the fact that toward the very end of the discussion, Mr. Vahey said to Vanzetti, in substance, "I can advise you as to what the District Attorney may inquire about and the effect of your failure to take the stand, but you are the one who has got to make the decision as to whether you will testify or not," and it was after that that Vanzetti wanted me to go up to Dedham and talk to Sacco.

After I came back from Dedham and reported my conversation with Sacco to Vanzetti, and the case was further discussed, he said, in substance, "I don't think I can improve upon the alibi which has been established. I had better not take the stand." Incidentally, there was no fear that his radical opinions, if he had any, might be brought out during that trial because his connection with "Bolshevism," as it was called in those days, did not ever enter into the trial.

Hoping that this would surely settle the question, I sent Frankfurter a copy of Graham's letter and a letter of my own in which I asked Frankfurter to permit me to include a correction of his footnote in my book.

But my hopes were ill founded. All I got was the following letter, dated March 25, 1958:

You ask me to permit you to include the following sentence in your projected book:

"Mr. Justice Frankfurter authorizes me to say that he was in error in stating that Vanzetti, protesting innocence, was not allowed by his counsel to take the stand because his radical opinions would have been brought out and told against him disastrously. He has learned that the decision not to take the stand was made by Vanzetti himself after discussion with his counsel and that his radical opinions had nothing to do with it and formed no part of the discussion."

Under no circumstances can I authorize you to make any such statement on my behalf. My article in the Atlantic Monthly and its slight enlargement in book form, published early in 1927, was, as I have already stated to you, the product of the most minute care for securing accuracy. President Lowell surely had the amplest means and reason for testing the accuracy of what I wrote, and I have already told you that he attested to my accuracy in emphatic language. The only person who publicly contemporaneously challenged any of my statements was Dean Wigmore and it becomes appropriate for me to say that Wigmore's classmate, Professor Williston, told me at the time that my replies to Wigmore "pulverized him." My book was written more than thirty years ago and is, for purposes of this case, a historic document. As such, it must, of course, share the fate of all historic documents, namely, be subject to the scrutiny and the reexamination of others. But since I have no doubt whatever that the statement which you now call into question I took great pains to verify at the time, of course I cannot say that I was in error.

I do not mean to question the good faith of Mr. Graham. I do say that the time for Mr. Vahey or Mr. Graham to have challenged the accuracy of my statement was at the time that I made it and not for Mr. Graham to do so more than thirty years later. Let me say again that I do not of course question the good faith of Mr. Graham, but we all know how treacherous even the most honest memory can be.

In my next letter I was rather free in telling Mr. Justice Frankfurter what his duty was, but I thought it was unfair to Vahey and Graham, and even to me as an author seeking the truth about an important fact, for Frankfurter to take advantage of the prestige his book enjoyed as a historic document written by a law professor who had become a Justice of the Supreme Court and been honored throughout the academic world for his scholarly achievements. Should he not acknowledge his error or furnish the "unimpeachable evidence"? *Noblesse oblige,* quoth I.

But this appeal also failed and the reader must choose between the *ipse dixit* of the infallible Frankfurter on the one hand and Graham's letter and all the probabilities on the other. Frankfurter's final letter read as follows:

> Since you make free to tell others of their duty, your letter of March 31 leads me to say that I assume that in case you will ever be publishing anything pertaining to the Bridgewater trial and, in connection with it, publish Mr. Graham's recent letter to you, you will also publish, and in full, my letter to you under date of March 25 in regard to the matter.

In *The Atlantic Monthly* for February 1928 there is an article by William G. Thompson entitled "Vanzetti's Last Statement, Monday, August 22, 1927." In the article, Thompson, who became defense attorney for Sacco and Vanzetti in 1924, tells of his interview with Vanzetti during the evening before the execution:

> I had heard that the Governor had said that if Vanzetti would release his counsel in the Bridgewater case from their obligation not to disclose what he had said to them the public would be satisfied that he was guilty of that crime, and also of the South Braintree crime. . . . I then asked Vanzetti if he had at any time said anything to Mr. Vahey or Mr. Graham which would warrant the inference that he was guilty of either crime. With great emphasis and obvious sin-

cerity he answered "no." . . . I asked Vanzetti whether he would authorize me to waive his privilege so far as Vahey and Graham were concerned. He readily assented to this, but imposed the condition that they should make whatever statement they saw fit to make in the presence of myself or some other friend . . .

It nowhere appears that this offer to waive the privilege was ever communicated to Vahey and Graham, and in fact Graham did not know about it until I told him in 1958. Whether he or Vahey would have made public statements in 1928 may well be doubted. A lawyer's reputation for fidelity and secrecy even where there is no legal obligation to remain silent is an invaluable possession of the individual lawyer and of the bar at large. If the public disclosure would have helped the client, of course it should and would have been made.

MOORE BIDS FOR A CONFESSION OF THE BRIDGEWATER CRIME AND THE "OUTLOOK" BUYS ONE

ON December 4, 1920, a Boston Italian whose real name was Frank Silva but who was called Martini in the affidavits quoted below, was convicted under the name of Paul Martini in the United States District Court for the Southern District of New York. The charge was a conspiracy to steal money from post office boxes, and there were two co-defendants, Jacob Luban and Adolph G. Witner. After the execution of Sacco and Vanzetti, Martini, using his real name, sold a confession of the Bridgewater crime to *The Outlook and Independent,* which published it on October 31, 1928.

Witner, in the course of the trial and after he had testified falsely, withdrew his plea of not guilty and pleaded guilty. He then testified for the Government against Luban and Martini, who were convicted and sent to Atlanta for a long sentence. Witner got 30 days.

During the week of April 21, 1922, Moore (Sacco and Vanzetti's attorney) visited the United States Penitentiary at Atlanta, with Witner, and had at least five or six interviews with Luban and Martini.[1]

After Moore and Witner left, Luban, who was a stool pigeon or decided to become one, communicated with William J. Burns,

---

[1] The visit of Moore and Witner and the five or six interviews with Luban and Martini were certified by the Record Clerk of the Penitentiary on December 21, 1922, in a letter in the files of the Attorney General of Massachusetts.

then Director of the Bureau of Investigation of the Department of Justice, giving an account of the interviews.

Sometime later, Burns sent an agent to Atlanta to interview Luban and Martini, and on November 28, 1922, he wrote to his Boston agent, Lawrence Letherman, giving an account of that interview and suggesting that Letherman communicate with the Attorney General of the State of Massachusetts and advise him of this matter. "If he is desirous of having any of his representatives interview Luban, I shall be very glad to facilitate the arrangements. . . ."

A copy of Burns's letter to Letherman was sent to the Attorney General of Massachusetts. A few days later, Albert Hurwitz, an assistant attorney general, went to Atlanta and on December 14 got the affidavits of Luban and Martini from which the account of the Moore visit found below has been gathered.[2]

After preliminary questions and answers, Luban testified as follows:

> On or about April 18, 1922, I was called to the Warden's office for a visit, which is very unusual, because every visit a prisoner gets in the Federal Penitentiary a guard must be present.
>
> When I came into the Warden's office I found Martini and another one, a man whom I later learned to be John Jocomo, of Boston, working for the defense of certain two men by the name of Vanzetti and Sacco. Martini introduced me to this John Jocomo, and told me that John Jocomo came to see Martini to find out if he had anything to do at any time with the crime at Bridgewater, Mass., committed by Vanzetti and Sacco.
>
> During the conversation with Jocomo he told me while he personally knew that Martini had nothing to do with it, he had to come here to speak to Martini for two reasons. One of the reasons was he was getting paid for coming over, and

---

[2] The correspondence and the affidavits are in the files of the Attorney General of Massachusetts.

the second reason was to cover himself and brother, because of money taken during the Braintree holdup which was deposited by his brother. Jocomo said that his brother deposited a certain amount of money that was equal with the amount taken at Braintree, Mass., and his brother could not afford to tell where he got it to deposit; he agreed to help along and do whatever counsel for the defendants Sacco and Vanzetti wanted him to do.

He then tried to induce Martini to speak to a certain lawyer by the name of Fred H. Moore. Upon my advice Martini consented to talk to Moore. . . .

On the next day Martini and I was called to the Warden's office again. On the second day Gacomo [*sic*] introduced us to another man by the name of Fred Moore, who neither one of us had never seen before. Mr. Moore started to speak to us about Sacco and Vanzetti case, and we told him we didn't know the first thing about it. He then asked if we would like to talk to Adolph G. Witner, the man who testified against us during our trial.

I was very much surprised to learn of any connection between Witner and Moore, and I asked Mr. Moore how does he come to be connected with a low life like this Witner was, and here is what he explained to Martini and myself. Witner was brought to Boston from Philadelphia by several indictments that were pending against Witner in Boston for forgery and mail robbery. It was at the police headquarters Moore happened to meet Witner, and Witner made a proposition to Mr. Moore that if he will help him get out of his troubles he will be a great help to Mr. Moore in Sacco and Vanzetti case.

I don't know exactly what arrangements were made between Mr. Moore and Witner, but as Mr. Moore explained to me he got him out and took him over to his office, which is not far away from headquarters. When Witner came into Moore's office he seen a picture he thought was very familiar to him. In fact, he recognized Mr. Paul Martini's picture.

Witner said what is Martini's picture doing in your office. Moore told him the picture was one of Sacco's. Witner insisted it was Martini. Then Moore thought for a minute that maybe Martini is one who committed the crime in Bridgewater and Braintree and they mistook Sacco for Martini. Witner in his heart knew that Martini had nothing to do with it, because Martini was with Witner together in New York at the time these robberies and murders were committed.

Mr. Moore started to questioning Martini about Bridgewater and Braintree, and very soon found out that Martini don't know the first thing about either one of these places, nor neither does Martini know anything about this attempted robbery and murder.

I finally consented to speak to Witner. When Witner came in I asked him what business has he got here, and what did he come for, and he told me that he was working for the Amalgamated Garment Workers' Union of America. He was working as investigator for Mr. Moore on this particular Sacco and Vanzetti case. He was being paid $50.00 a week and all expenses by the Amalgamated Union. He then told me how sorry he was he testified finally against me. He done it because the Pinkerton Agency forced him to testify it, they threatened they would send him to prison for life. He told me that he was willing to confess to the facts that he perjured himself providing I will help him to get Martini to take the blame partly of the Bridgewater attempted robbery.

I asked him then to explain to me fully what he meant. I was talking to Witner while Martini was talking to Mr. Moore. During my conversation with Martini I was interrupted by Moore who said to me "there is no use talking, Martini don't know the first thing about Bridgewater or about Braintree, but is willing to help along and take the blame providing Mr. Moore will keep the promise that he made him." I forgot to state that when Mr. Moore came to

Atlanta he told me he was in Washington, that he seen Mr. William J. Burns and Attorney General Dougherty, and that they told him they would be glad if this case would be disposed of in any way at all, as long as Sacco and Vanzetti go free. He also told me that he had a conversation with Attorney General Allen of Massachusetts, a man I never heard of or never seen in my life before, and that Mr. Allen told him that if he can find a way how to free Sacco and Vanzetti, "we don't care whether legitimate [or] unlegitimate," that he, Mr. Allen, would help him along in any way shape or form.

Q. (Hurwitz). Did he say why the Federal officials and the Attorney General of the Commonwealth of Massachusetts were interested?

A. Yes he says that the Radicals in Italy were throwing bombs at the American Ambassador's building, and they were agitating it over this country on account of that case because Sacco and Vanzetti were considered good union men, and their conviction is a stain on the entire organization and they would stop at nothing to get them free. If necessary there is millions behind it.

Q. You said something about Martini saying he would go through with it if Mr. Moore would keep his promise, what promises did he make?

A. First of all it looked to me very much that Mr. Moore had been to Washington, because he had credentials and permissions to see us private, which I said before is very unusual, and he says Mr. Allen is the one that secured these privileges for him. He also told me that the Governor of Massachusetts offered through Mr. Allen a commutation of sentence to these two men if Mr. Moore will put an application in, but Mr. Moore wanted to get them out free entirely.

Q. You say that Martini said finally that he would agree provided Moore would keep his promise, what were the promises?

A. The promises made to me were these, first that Mr. Moore will use his influence to get Martini and myself out of prison, and second that Witner would go to New York and confess to his part of the perjury which would show my innocence automatically. Third, that we would receive $5000.00 apiece before Martini takes the stand, $5000.00 apiece after he goes off the stand; fourth, that Martini will get a good lawyer who will instruct him while Martini is on the stand testifying, this lawyer will instruct him to refuse to answer questions on the grounds of incriminating and degrading himself, that will create an impression with the judge that he did not want to commit himself, but it is true that he is the one and not Sacco who committed the attempted holdup in Bridgewater, and he believes on these grounds Sacco and Vanzetti will get a new trial. Later on Martini will be able to defend himself by telling the truth and showing that really while this murder and attempted murder was committed Martini was in New York.

Q. What did Moore say he wanted Martini to do?

A. He wanted Martini to confess that he together with another man named Joe Napp and Jas Meade committed the attempted robbery at Bridgewater. He said these two men were willing to take the blame for it, and was also willing to testify that Martini was along with them, providing Martini will consent to it, not otherwise.

Witner suggested to Mr. Moore that Martini send a note to these two men in Charlestown jail telling them that it is perfectly all right to him if they go ahead and admit the Bridgewater robbery and take him on it, that he would be all right. That was the end of that day.

On the next day again Moore, Jocomo and Witner came over to the prison, and we were again called to the warden's office. Martini and I both told Mr. Moore and Witner both that it is not advisable to take Jocomo into confidence. Martini also told Mr. Moore that Jocomo's brother has got part of the money in the bank that was gotten during the Braintree murder. It seems that Moore was kind of surprised, but didn't care to talk about it.

They sent Jocomo out of the office to another room in which the warden's secretary occupies, and the four of us in the presence of Warden Dyche started to talk matters over again. Mr. Moore, as well as Witner, assured us again that Martini will not suffer one bit, and that all the officials concerned will be only too glad to see Sacco and Vanzetti get a new trial and acquitted, in spite of the fact that they may know Martini is lying. He again assured us that Witner would immediately confess to perjury on his part on our case.

Witner then suggested about the Braintree murder case that Martini should admit that he, together with two other men who are both known to be hold-up men and murderers, that they three committed the murder in Braintree.

I then told them I thought they were crazy to expect a man to go forward and lie about himself that he committed a murder of which he don't know the first thing about.

Mr. Moore said I was right, but Witner said he got it planned out this way. These two men who were supposed to be with Martini are both dead. One got shot on Suffolk Street, New York last October 21st, Fat Abie. There was another man the first name I recall was Louis. These two men will not be able to testify of course, but one Fat Abie's wife, Ida, will testify that she was present when the three of them conspired in her house together to go to Braintree and commit that murder. He has also got it arranged with Ida to testify that her husband furnished the car to go to Braintree with.

While Martini is to take the stand and upon the advice of his lawyer which will be furnished him by Mr. Moore he is to refuse to answer on the ground of incriminating and degrading himself, and that would have the proper effect while it would not make Martini exactly guilty of the crime, it will create an impression that he is afraid to deny that he didn't commit the murder, and in the meantime he don't want to admit it. Ida, the man's wife, and the two other witnesses will testify to the rest.

He also stated they had two witnesses, one by the name of Louis Pelser[3] has already been fixed up to change his testimony so it will be in favor of the defendants.

He said they had another witness by the name of Roy Gould[4] who previously did not testify, but will testify now and will identify Martini, but should they want to prosecute Martini for the murder Gould will retract his original testimony against Martini.

One of the man's [sic] witnesses,[5] a certain woman whose name I don't remember, has already changed her testimony. From Mr. Moore's statement to me I first understood she first testified in favor of the prosecution, and now she is ready to testify for the defense, that the prosecuting attorney had coached her and induced her when she identified Sacco, but she will switch over to Martini if necessary, because they look so much alike, and Witner told me in Jewish that it cost a good many thousand dollars to get the woman to change her testimony, and they are ready to spend a good many thousand more. In fact, money is no object at all to get a new trial for Sacco and Vanzetti.

On the third day Mr. Moore wrote out a note addressed to the two men at Charlestown prison, telling them to go ahead and mix Martini into it as much as they wanted, that he will be willing, and that he will have nothing against them for doing so. Martini signed it, I witnessed it, the warden refused to witness it, but made a mark on it so as to identify the paper. I said let Witner witness it, but Moore and Witner said no he didn't want Witner to witness it on account of his bad record of being a perjurer and a framer.

On the 4th day about 4 o'clock we were called to the

---

3 See Chapter 21 ("Louis Pelser").
4 See Chapter 20 ("Roy E. Gould").
5 I suppose this is Mrs. Andrews. See Chapter 23 ("Lola R. Andrews").

Captain's office, and Moore and Witner said they just come in to tell us good bye, assuring us again that the promises made would be absolutely kept, and if I wanted him to he would go to Washington again.

Witner asked me to give him a note, if possible, in Jewish, to that woman Ida, Fat Abie's wife, and tell her she should do what Witner wants her to do, and not to be afraid of Witner, and to accept the money that Witner will offer her.

I refused to talk about any such a thing in the presence of the Captain and the guards. Moore then said well, we will have to stay over another day, and will come in to see you tomorrow.

On the next day which was Saturday Martini and I were called to the deputy warden's office. We found Moore and Witner there. Moore told us he had great difficulty in getting in because the Warden was away and the deputy would not let him in, and they had to call up Washington again and get authority from Washington to instruct the deputy to admit Moore and Witner for the private interview to see us.

Witner again asked me for the Jewish note to the woman Ida, but I told him I would send it by mail, when you get over there you will find it, which I never did.

Moore then wrote out a different note, something to the effect of the first note and had Martini to sign it, and I think he tore up the first one. He asked the deputy warden to witness it, he didn't want to witness it, but just read it. It was a note again to these two men instructing them that Martini had nothing against them if they will go out and say everything they like in favor of Sacco and Vanzetti and against Martini.

Q. Did he say why they changed the note?

A. The first note was addressed to one man, and the second note was addressed to the two men, and that was what he wanted. Witner also gave me a $20.00 bill and Martini $5.00, says that was all he has got. He assured us it was not his money but the money of the organization. Martini passed me the $5.00, and later I was searched and it was found on me, they kept the money and I lost 25 days good time and 4 days in the "hole."

Witner again told me, says, "Jake, as soon as I go to New York I will go to see the U.S. Attorney and confess to having perjured myself if I have to later beat it to Europe," and then Witner says, "if I can't get you out free I am going to put a bullet through my brain," and Moore says to Witner, "what did I tell you last night?" And Moore says tell it to them on the quiet, and Witner told me that he said if he don't get me out free he would put a bullet to himself, and then Moore told it to me out aloud.

Q. Have you heard from Moore since?

A. Not from Moore. He told me not to write to him and he would not write to me, because he said Witner was making an affidavit to the facts that he perjured himself and will confess to a frame-up on me, he would keep Witner in his employ and pay him $50.00 a week and expenses whether he has got anything to do or not. He says I cannot send you any money by mail, I cannot correspond with you until after the case is over. It doesn't make any difference to you boys who is handing you the money when you go to Charlestown, what difference does it make as long as you get it, and if you want me to I will go right now to the Attorney General in your behalf, get Mr. Allen to see the Attorney General in your behalf, if necessary, because Mr. Allen wants to dispose of this case in the worst way, and he don't care how it is disposed of as long as these two men are free, because the Governor and everybody else is sick and tired of it.

Q. Did you hear from Witner?

A. He himself wrote me he was coming back in June or July to see us again, wants to get the pictures, wants to show

Martini the pictures of Fat Abie and the other man. I kept on insisting of Witner that he make affidavits in confession as to frame-up on me.

I later sent my two sisters over to see Witner, Mrs. Bercowitz and Mrs. Goodman, urging Witner to make a confession. Witner told them that he spoke to the U.S. Attorney, and spoke to Judge Groehl, and both of them told him that if he does make such a confession he would be sent away to prison for life, and he is afraid to make such confession yet, but will do so later on.

After Mr. Moore left the prison I immediately got in touch with Mr. Wm. J. Burns, Director of Bureau of Investigation in Department of Justice, and informed him what took place. Some time later Mr. Burns sent down one of his men, and we repeated the whole story of what took place at the Atlanta Penitentiary when Moore and Witner came over to see us.

Q. Did some one come down to see you some months before?

A. Jocomo come. . . . Yes that is right, a man by the name of Anthony Crapraro, General Manager & Secretary of the Amalgamated Garment Workers' Union of America came down to the penitentiary some time in January of 1922. While he said he come over to see a certain man by the name of Angelo it was later proven that he came to see us, as Witner explained to me that his main object in coming over was to take a look at Martini. This was the first time in our life that we ever met the man.

Q. Where did he see you and Martini?

A. In the penitentiary in the regular room in the presence of the guard.

Q. Did he call to see you?

A. Yes he spoke to us, but not about this case at all. At that time I could not understand what his purpose was, because he saw us and gave us some money too.

Q. You are quite certain that Moore came to see you on all these occasions you speak of?

A. Absolutely. There is a record of it at the penitentiary, three of the visits took place in the presence of the warden, one in the presence of the captain and one in the presence of the deputy warden. Martini thinks that interviews in warden's presence was twice and not three times.

When Witner and Moore first saw me they tried to get me to believe that Martini was really the person who committed the murder in Braintree and was really mixed up in the Bridgewater murder, but I said to Witner "you know as well as I do it is not so, and that Martini was in New York living at 250 W. 46th St. at the time these murders occurred." I knew that Witner knew it, because he was to see Martini every day, and was with us quite regular.

Q. Are either of you members of the Amalgamated Union, or any other Union?

A. No.

The following excerpts from Martini's affidavit, which follow a general confirmation of Luban's account, will interest those who like to speculate about where the money stolen at South Braintree went and those who have an interest in the Silva confession sold to *The Outlook and Independent:*

Q. (Hurwitz). How long had you know Jocomo before he came?

A. (Martini-Silva). I had know him a long time, maybe 16 years. . . .

Q. Did Jocomo, as far as you know from anything he told you have anything to [do] with the Bridgewater hold-up?

A. Jocomo told me his brother had come in possession of $12,000 of the money that was stolen at Braintree hold-up, and investigation was started to find from where he got that money.

Q. Did he say whether his brother had any part himself in the hold-up?

A. Nothing except he got the money.

Q. Did he say in what bank his brother had the money?

A. He did, but I don't remember.

Q. What is his brother's first name?

A. Joe, I think it is.

Q. Where did his brother live when you last heard?

A. I think he lived in Matajan [Mattapan?]. Jocomo lived there, I suppose his brother did.

Q. Were you ever in Bridgewater yourself?

A. No sir.

Q. Have you ever been to Braintree?

A. I don't even know where it is.

Q. Did you have any participation at all in either the Bridgewater hold-up or the Braintree hold-up?

A. No sir.

Q. When you had your talk with Moore you told him absolutely you had nothing to do with either, and as a matter of fact you knew nothing about Bridgewater or Braintree?

A. Nothing.

Q. What was it that induced you or prompted you to finally agree with Moore that you would be willing to assume that you had been in Bridgewater and had participated in the hold-up?

A. On the advice of Luban.

Q. Did Moore or Jocomo, or any one else ever show you a picture of Sacco?

A. Witner showed me.

Q. Was it a regular photograph, or Rogues' Gallery photograph?

A. It was a regular photograph, no Rogues' Gallery.

Q. From your examination of the photograph did you think Sacco looked like you?

A. Didn't look like me at all, just a little bit.

Q. Was it a full face picture?

A. Full face.

Q. You say it was a slight resemblance?

A. Yes a little. I don't know whether it was Sacco's picture, he showed me a picture and said it was.

Q. Where were you at the time the Bridgewater hold-up took place and at the time the Braintree murder took place?

A. I was living in New York in one of Mr. Luban's houses at # 250 W. 46 St., in December 1919.

Q. Did Moore suggest to you and Mr. Luban the dates when this hold-up took place?

A. Yes, Witner, Moore and Jocomo.

Q. Did Moore, or either of them prior to leaving you before their final interview undertake to explain to you the locations in Bridgewater?

A. Moore says I will show you the map of Bridgewater and Braintree and started to explain.

Q. Witner showed you the map of both cities?

A. Yes.

Q. Did you make any notes at the time, did they give you any notes so you could get the thing studied out?

A. No sir, he said they would be back in a month, but afterwards he wrote Mr. Luban he would be back in June, and afterwards the 24th of July.

Nothing came of Witner's promises, and Moore never got the confession he had bid for.

THE SILVA CONFESSION

Hurwitz brought the two affidavits back with him to Boston, but they were never used, presumably because Moore's plan to use a confession from Martini (Silva) was not put into effect. Dudley P. Ranney, assistant district attorney, sent for them (Harold P. Williams, also an assistant district attorney, had seen them) on July 10, 1926, but did not use them, presumably because he thought it unnecessary to do so. On January 13, 1929, they were published at length in the *Boston Herald* in an article by Fred R.

Brine. Prior to this, *The Outlook and Independent* had purchased a confession of the Bridgewater crime from Martini (Silva) under the following circumstances.

In January 1928 a freelance writer named Silas Bent and a reformed bank burglar, Jack Callahan, had a discussion about the Sacco-Vanzetti case. As a result, Callahan was employed by the *Outlook* to "dig the story out of the underworld." Callahan met Jimmy Mede, who told him that the Bridgewater job was suggested to him in 1917 by Silva; that he (Mede), Silva, and a man named San Marco went to Bridgewater to plan the crime. Shortly thereafter Mede went to prison; he was there when the holdup occurred. While he was in prison, San Marco arrived with a life sentence and told Mede how he, Silva, and a man named Oates had participated in the Bridgewater holdup. Callahan then succeeded in reaching Silva and induced him to see Silas Bent and the publisher of the *Outlook*. Silva agreed to make an affidavit, with the understanding that, if it were borne out by facts in the possession of the *Outlook,* he would be paid a sum of money.

Silva made an affidavit on August 10, 1928, and thereafter Silva, Mede, Bent, and Callahan drove over the route which Silva said he and his companions had taken. To the holdup party named by Mede, Silva added a man named Doggy Bruno as the man with the shotgun. Doggy had a moustache, but the picture of him in the *Outlook* would not be mistaken for Vanzetti. The discrepancies in detail between the Silva confession and the testimony are several and important, and Silva's ignorance of the locality was apparent. Nevertheless the *Outlook* purchased the confession and published it, with a picture of Silva, in its issue of October 31, 1928. San Marco then wrote to Commissioner Sanford Bates of Massachusetts, saying that he had no part in the holdup and that he had been at work that day. This letter was printed in the *Boston Herald* on November 3, 1928, and, as we have seen, was followed by the publication of the Luban and Martini (Silva) affidavits on January 13, 1929.

This should have closed the matter, but it did not, and some of the mythmakers continued to claim from time to time that the

Silva confession solved the Bridgewater crime and cleared Vanzetti. Silva's confession for cash came after the execution and so could not be used by the defense at any stage.

JIMMIE MEDE

On May 28, 1927, Thompson urged Governor Fuller to see Thomas H. Doyle, who had earlier assisted Moore in investigations. Fuller saw Doyle, who told him about Jimmie Mede. Thompson wrote the Governor, and on July 12 the Governor met with Doyle and Mede. Doyle and Mede then reported to Thompson that Mede had made a full disclosure of his connection with the Bridgewater case; but that before he gave up his information he insisted upon obtaining from the Governor and, as he said, did obtain from him, an assurance that his confession would not be communicated to the State Police in any way that would injure him (Mede); but that, in violation of the assurance, "at the end of the interview the Governor immediately called in Captain Blye of the State Police, told Mede to repeat his confession to him alone, and indicated hostility to Mede by words, tone, and manner." Mede declined to talk with Blye alone and could not be induced to tell his story to the Advisory Committee.

Later, on August 3, 1927, Mede and his counsel went to the State Police Department and told Lieutenant Joseph F. Ferrari that Mede would now tell Captain Blye his story. Ferrari took them to Captain Blye, who said they should go to the Governor. They explained that Mede had already made a confidential statement to the Governor but now was willing to make a statement to Captain Blye, who could then decide what to do about it. Blye nevertheless refused to hear Mede. Mede's story as related to Doyle was this: Mede was one of the planners but did not participate in the Bridgewater crime. San Marco and Silva were planners and participants. The other two he would not name.

Captain Blye's refusal to hear Mede was proper. If Mede had already told his story to the Governor, the latter was obviously not impressed with it, and it would not help Sacco and Vanzetti to have it told to a police officer who could not influence the decision. If Mede had offered to tell it to the Advisory Committee, that committee should and no doubt would have heard him. It is obvious that the defense was here doing a little herring dragging for public effect, with no thought that this incomplete, improbable, and worthless confession had any probative value.

6   THE BRIDGEWATER CASE
BEFORE THE GOVERNOR

IN THE SPRING of 1927, when the defendants had reached the end of their legal resources and a plea for executive clemency was made, the Bridgewater case again assumed importance, because in a plea for clemency the vital question would be guilt or innocence, and Vanzetti's conviction at Plymouth would weigh heavily against him.

Frankfurter, in his book, published in March, 1927, had shrugged the case off in a footnote which, as we have seen, is sadly lacking in the accuracy and completeness we look for in what professes to be an impartial, critical survey by an infallible author.

No eyewitness had been found to deny that Vanzetti was the man with the shotgun, no new witness had come forward to help the alibi, and Moore's attempt in 1922 to buy a confession from prisoners at Atlanta had failed. Vanzetti himself, who could now speak freely, had not offered a fuller account of his activities on December 24, 1919, nor made a credible explanation of his falsehoods or his failure to take the stand. The best that he could do was to launch a succession of vituperations, charging Thayer with prejudice and sadistic fury, Katzmann with professional misconduct, and his own counsel, Vahey, with having sold him for money, as Judas had sold Jesus Christ.[1]

---

[1] The deification of Vanzetti and, to a lesser extent, Sacco is illustrated by the titles of poems and excerpts from them printed in *The Sacco-Vanzetti An-*

Governor Fuller did not ask his Advisory Committee to review the Bridgewater case, and we have no record of the proceedings before the Governor. Thompson, however, in developing his theory of a police conspiracy to frame testimony and substitute false exhibits, thought it necessary to discuss the Bridgewater case with the committee. In a report of that discussion and in two letters of June 15 and June 21, 1927, from Thompson and Ehrmann to the Governor, we find the extent of the argument made by them in criticizing the Bridgewater conviction. That part of their argument which related to the question of guilt has already been discussed in Chapter 3.

The other points were charges of misconduct on the part of Katzmann and prejudice on the part of Thayer.

The first point was an amplification and restatement of Frankfurter's assertion that Vanzetti's prosecution for the Bridgewater job grew out of his arrest for, and was merely a phase of, the Braintree affair.

The assertion was that Vanzetti was first charged with the South Braintree crime and that the Bridgewater prosecution was an afterthought, designed to assist the Commonwealth in the

---

thology of Verse, edited by Henry Harrison (New York, 1927), and elsewhere:
Jeannette Marks, "Two Crucified."
Nicholas Moskowitz, "Jesus Also Sinned."
Henry Reich, Jr., "The New Golgotha," "Pilate," "To Slay These Christs."
Malcolm Cowley, "For St. Bartholomew's Day."
E. Merrill Root, "Eucharist" and "Fiery Cross."
William C. Emory, "Another Pilate."
Clement Wood, "Golgotha in Massachusetts."
Ralph Cheyney, "My Judas Land."
David P. Berenberg, "Once in a while the earth produces a man to die . . . on the cross and to live on forever."
Mary Pate, "Impelled upon a cross of lies, Christ agonizes."
David George Plotkin, "A Young Messiah."
Mary Carolyn Davies, "Unharmed Christ."
In an article, "Massachusetts the Murderer," published in *The Nation* of August 31, 1927, we read of ". . . . men who in the minds of multitudes will take for the moment their places with the Carpenter."
And John Haynes Holmes finds in his review of the Letters that "[This book] is like the 'Apology' and the 'Crito' of Plato, like certain pages of the Gospels . . . [they] speak like Socrates and Jesus."

South Braintree case and to take unfair advantage of Vanzetti in one way or another by trying him first for the lesser crime. This contention was not a criticism of the Plymouth trial itself or of the verdict there. It was rather a charge of misconduct against the District Attorney affecting the fairness of the Dedham trial for the South Braintree murder and was so argued by Thompson and Ehrmann orally and in the brief filed with the Governor's Advisory Committee.

As is so often the case with Frankfurter, Thompson, and Ehrmann, the assertion is not supported by the facts. As we have seen, the arrest was not for the Braintree affair or for any affair but was the result of the springing of a trap set by a Bridgewater policeman investigating a Bridgewater crime to catch a man named Boda. Vanzetti, wholly unknown to Stewart and under no suspicion, happened into the trap and was almost immediately charged with the Bridgewater crime, indicted, brought to trial, and convicted before he was ever charged with the South Braintree murder. Katzmann, testifying before the Advisory Committee, told them that until after John W. Faulkner had gone to the Plymouth jail and identified Vanzetti as the man he saw get off the train at East Braintree on the morning of April 15, 1920, the Commonwealth did not feel that it was justified in prosecuting Vanzetti for the South Braintree murder. This identification by Faulkner was on July 20, 1920, eighteen days after the Plymouth verdict.

And even if we were to assume, contrary to the fact, that Katzmann had in May 1920 a good-enough case against Vanzetti for the South Braintree murder, would that have been a good reason for dropping or postponing as good a case for a holdup in Bridgewater in Plymouth County which could be tried at once? Doesn't Plymouth County have a right to prompt prosecution for crimes committed within its borders? Does a robber by committing a murder in another county get a right to a postponement of his trial for robbery until the murder is tried?

Nor was there anything unusual in the promptness with which

the Bridgewater case came to trial. There was a June session in Plymouth, and it was usual rather than unusual for any Plymouth County case that was ready for trial to be tried at that time.

Judge Musmanno in his discussion of the proceedings in Plymouth adds another point. He criticizes Katzmann because Vanzetti was not given a preliminary hearing in the South Braintree case, asserting that Vanzetti was being held for the South Braintree crime from the time of the arrest but that the prosecution did not dare to give him a preliminary hearing.[2]

The omission of the preliminary hearing was not unusual, unfair, or a confession of weakness. A preliminary hearing before a district court is not a trial in any true sense. The district court has no jurisdiction in capital cases except to find or fail to find probable cause for action by the grand jury. If it finds probable cause, it so declares and remands the defendant to the custody of the sheriff without bail. If it finds no probable cause the defendant is released, but this is not a bar to further prosecution of the case, for in spite of it the district attorney may seek an indictment from the grand jury, and in the trial of that indictment the decision of the lower court is of no consequence. In Vanzetti's case it was not necessary to have a preliminary examination to insure his presence at a trial. He was in State Prison, and for that reason an order holding him for the grand jury and committing him to the custody of the warden or a sheriff without bail was an unnecessary formality. Nor would Vanzetti have profited by a decision that there was no probable cause—if we can imagine such a result. He would still have been in State Prison and Katzmann could still have gone to the grand jury for the indictment. In fact it is probable that Vanzetti profited by the omission, because a public hearing so soon after the Plymouth trial would have hurt him.

[2] Michael Angelo Musmanno, *Twelve Years After*, New York, 1939, p. 85. Musmanno, now a justice of the Supreme Court of Pennsylvania, was of counsel for the defendants in the last stages of the case. He has remained interested in the case and in 1959 appeared before a Committee of the General Court of Massachusetts (our legislature) advocating a posthumous pardon for Sacco and Vanzetti. His approach to the case is highly emotional, and it is often necessary to correct the statements of fact and conclusions of law in his book.

Neither Morgan nor Fraenkel criticizes the omission of the preliminary hearing. The omission was criticized in the circular letter of the New England Civil Liberties Committee quoted in Chapter 7.

The other point made by Thompson was a charge that the trial at Plymouth was only a crude rehearsal of the tragedy later enacted at Dedham. "Whether this is so or not," he said, "it is evident that the Judge who presided at Plymouth brought with him to Dedham a strong prejudice against Vanzetti, which ought to have disqualified him from sitting at the Dedham trial at all."

This contention was not supported by a specification of anything in the record or elsewhere from which prejudice could be inferred. The Plymouth transcript shows that defendants' counsel twice assured the Court of their belief in Thayer's fairness; no exception was taken to the charge to the jury, and the exceptions taken to admission of evidence were, as all now agree, without merit. Thompson's statement, made in the heat of battle, should be contrasted with Morgan's cool appraisal quoted previously that "there is nothing to support a charge of unfairness or prejudice on the part of the trial judge." [3]

The following quotation from Governor Fuller's decision summarizes the proceedings before him and the result he arrived at:

> The next question, and the most vital question of all, is that of the guilt or innocence of the accused. In this connection I reviewed the Bridgewater attempted holdup for which Vanzetti had previously been tried before another jury and found guilty. At this trial Vanzetti did not take the witness stand in his own defense. He waived the privilege of telling his own story to the jury, and did not subject himself to cross-examination. Investigating this case, I talked to the counsel for Vanzetti at the Plymouth trial, the jurymen, the trial witnesses, new witnesses, present counsel and Vanzetti. I have talked with the government witnesses who saw the Bridgewater holdup and who identified Vanzetti, and I be-

[3] Morgan, *op. cit.*, p. 56.

lieve their testimony to be substantially correct. I believe with the jury that Vanzetti was guilty and that his trial was fair. I found nothing unusual about this case except, as noted above, that Vanzetti did not testify.

In the Bridgewater case, practically everyone who witnessed the attempted holdup and who could have identified the bandits identified Vanzetti. (5378f)

THE RADICALS TAKE OVER
THE DEFENSE

IMMEDIATELY after the arrest the Sacco-Vanzetti Defense Committee was organized by Aldino Felicani, himself an anarchist, who became treasurer, and Frank R. Lopez, a Spanish anarchist afterwards deported, who became secretary. Other charter members were found among the anarchist friends of Sacco and Vanzetti living in or near Boston.

In 1925 a ninety-six-page pamphlet was issued by the Sacco-Vanzetti Defense Committee. The title was "Financial Report of The Sacco-Vanzetti Defense Committee From the Date of Organization May 5, 1920, to July 31, 1925." This, as we shall see, is the pamphlet which Celestino F. Madeiros[1] examined on November 16, 1925, a few minutes before he signed the letter addressed to the *Boston American* confessing the South Braintree crime.

The recapitulation at pages 94 and 95 of the Report showed receipts, including loans, up to July 31, 1925, of $287,000 and disbursements of $282,000.

Supplementary information is to be found in the Bulletins of the committee and in newspaper articles. Joughin, at page 237, published the following summary of the Committee's finances:

Receipts, including loans	$360,000
Disbursements:	
Fred H. Moore, personal fees	$ 34,000

[1] See Chapter 27 ("The Madeiros Confession and How It Grew") for an account of the Madeiros confession.

William G. Thompson, fees	25,000	
Other fees	30,000	
		89,000
Moore, expenses	88,000	
Other legal expenses	15,000	
Total legal expenses		103,000
Publicity, printing		52,000
Salaries (for committee employees)		17,000
Return of loans		41,000
Other charges (chiefly unclassified legal and investigative expenses)		58,000
Total disbursements		$360,000

The first entry in the detailed income statement is dated May 5, 1920: Loans, $2,835. The date is puzzling, because the men were not arrested until late in the evening of May 5. The source of the loans is not given. Presumably they were repaid, but if so it was done by instalments.

In mid-August the revolutionary anarchist, Carlo Tresca, moved in and became instrumental in employing Fred H. Moore and putting him in complete command of the legal defense of both defendants. Moore received his first payment, five hundred dollars, on August 19, 1920, and from then on the payments to him were many and, in the aggregate, large.

Up to the time when Tresca and Moore entered the case, the Defense Committee, although composed of radicals, had not used the case itself for propaganda and agitation. Their meetings were primarily to collect money, with propaganda as a by-product, and their collections went for defense and not for agitation.

The expenditures of the committee after Tresca came in included many payments not connected directly with the defense. They were in part the necessary expenses of making the collections and holding the meetings, but they also were for propaganda and agitation. A list of the persons to whom payments were made for travel, "publicity," and other expenses include many figures well known in the radical world: Carlo Tresca, Professor Antonio Dentamore, Felice Guadagni, Frank R. Lopez (who was on salary many months), Elizabeth Gurley Flynn (Tresca's wife), Arturo Giovanitti, John Nicholas Beffel ("publicity"), Fred Biedenkapp, Art Shields ("literary services," "travel," "salary"), and J. J. Ettor.

Morris Gebelow, a young man who had studied at Columbia, now known as Eugene Lyons, took charge of the American and British publicity. His salary was very small (Moore seems to have misrepresented the state of the committee's finances to him), and he had to eke it out by working on the *Boston Telegram,* long since defunct. His releases went to all radical papers in this country and England and to all foreign-language papers here.

Felicani himself looked after the Italian agitation and, indirectly, the French.

John Nicholas Beffel had looked after publicity for Moore in another case, and Moore put him in charge of it here. He wrote magazine articles ("Eels and the Electric Chair" among them) and covered the case for the Federated Press, a radical labor press association serving one hundred papers. Beffel was one of the affiants whose affidavit was presented in 1927 as a proof of Thayer's unfairness.

Lopez sent his appeals to all the radical newspapers in South America, Spain, Mexico, and Cuba. One amusing bit of propaganda which got to South America was that Judge Thayer was the Presidential candidate favored by the Plymouth Cordage Company.

The New England Civil Liberties Committee made its first contribution of five hundred dollars on February 11, 1921, and from then on this Committee and its parent organization, the American Civil Liberties Union, were foremost among the contributors.

John S. Codman, Chairman of the Executive Committee of the New England Civil Liberties Committee, was at first reluctant to intervene. He had sat on a Norfolk County jury and been impressed by the "ability and fairness" of District Attorney Katzmann.

> Under the circumstances [he wrote], every presumption was
> opposed to our concerning ourselves with these cases and
> when they were brought to our attention by the Workers
> Defense Committee of New York we demanded that satis-
> factory evidence should be produced to warrant our taking
> action.[2]

We are not told what evidence was produced, but by February
11, 1921, Codman's Committee had made its first contribution.
On February 19, it sent out the circular letter reproduced on pages
72-74.

Thus it appears that the anarchists were joined by the American Civil Liberties Union before the trial and before there was
any evidence that any civil liberty was in peril. The events upon
which the charge of unfairness in the trial were to be based—
the drawing of the jury, conditions in the courtroom, Ripley's
alleged misconduct, unusual precautions by the sheriff, Thayer's
manner and manners, the resentment against Moore, Katzmann's
cross-examination of Sacco, Captain Proctor's testimony—had not
occurred, and there was no reason to suspect in February 1921
that the trial at Dedham would not follow the course of the Plymouth trial and any other Massachusetts criminal trial with all
civil rights protected. There was in the case no issue of free speech,
free press, religious freedom, unlawful search, police brutality,
wire tapping, or other invasion of constitutional rights.[3] Years
after the trial, charges of fraudulent substitution of exhibits and
of conspiracy between Norfolk County and the Department of
Justice were made, but these inventions of a desperate defense
could not have been foreseen by a Civil Rights organization acting
in good faith in early 1921.

In 1927 the Director of the American Civil Liberties Union
wrote a letter in which the following, as quoted by Joughin, appears (my italics):

---

[2] Mimeographed statement dated March 11, 1921, quoted by Joughin.

[3] The omission of a preliminary examination for Vanzetti is mentioned in the
circular letter shown on pages 72-74, but this was not a denial of any civil
right he had. See Chapter 6 ("The Bridgewater Case Before the Governor").

The Civil Liberties Union has been connected with the Sacco and Vanzetti matter, but has *hidden* its participation under various *false fronts*. We are at present *instigating* a nation-wide movement among lawyers in the various university faculties to join as signatories . . . for a review of the case de novo. This work is being done *behind the name* of a group of lawyers at Columbia: Karl Llewellyn is the chief promotor.[4]

The Sacco-Vanzetti Defense Committee was soon expanded to include Communists, Socialists, and "liberals" as well as anarchists, and by 1927 the original members of the Defense Committee had become a minority group surrounded and outnumbered by a majority, some of whom were primarily devoted to the exploitation of the case for purposes other than the legal defense of Sacco and Vanzetti.

In April 1927 the officers of the Sacco-Vanzetti Defense Committee were

> *John Barry,* Chairman;
> *Mary Donovan,* Recording Secretary;
> *Aldino Felicani,* Treasurer;
> *Joseph Moro,* Secretary.

The following is an incomplete list of other members of the Committee:

John Van Vaerenwyck, who at the time was President of the Massachusetts Federation of Labor and a member of the Workers Educational Bureau of America. Van Vaerenwyck was one of the two men who browbeat and blackmailed Lola R. Andrews into temporary repudiation of her identification of Sacco.[5]

Elizabeth Glendower Evans, widow of a rich Philadelphian and active in many radical organizations. Among other things she was secretary of the League for Democratic Control, which was a part of the American Civil Liberties Union.

---

4 Joughin, *op. cit.,* p. 255.
5 See Chapter 23 ("Lola R. Andrews").

Free Speech   *Free Press*   *Free Assemblage*

New England Civil Liberties Committee

Affiliated with

AMERICAN CIVIL LIBERTIES UNION

138 W. 13th Street, New York City

EXECUTIVE COMMITTEE
of the New England Civil Liberties Committee

John S. Codman, Chairman
Anna N. Davis, Sec.-Treas.
Mrs. Glendower Evans
Cerise C. Jack
Harold L. Rotzel

44 Edgehill Road
Brookline, Mass.
Tel. Brookline 4188

February 19, 1921

To American Friends of Justice:

A fair trial for every man accused of crime: — That has
been an article in the political creed of every English-speaking
freeman since the days of Magna Carta. But today we know that
political maxims do not execute themselves; they must be en-
forced by those who believe in them; and a fair trial is not
secured by merely giving a prisoner his day in court; it in-
volves investigation of evidence, summoning of witnesses, fees
for capable lawyers.

We need your help to secure a fair trial for Nicola Sacco

OFFICERS and NATIONAL COMMITTEE
of the American Civil Liberties Union

Chairman
Harry F. Ward, New York

Vice-Chairmen
Duncan McDonald, Illinois
Jeannette Rankin, Montana

Treasurer
Helen Phelps Stokes, New York

Directors
Albert DeSilver
Roger N. Baldwin

Counsel
Walter Nelles

Field Secretary
Lucille B. Milner

Publicity Director
Louis F. Budenz

Washington Correspondent
Henry R. Mussey

Jane Addams, Chicago, Ill.
Herbert S. Bigelow, Cincinnati, O.
Sophonisha P. Breckenridge, Chicago, Ill.
Robert M. Buck, Chicago, Ill.
Joseph D. Cannon, New York City
Lincoln Colcord, Washington, D. C.
John S. Codman, Boston, Mass.
James H. Dillard, Charlottesville, Va.
James A. Duncan, Seattle, Wash.
Crystal Eastman, New York City
John Lovejoy Elliott, New York City
Edmund C. Evans, Philadelphia, Pa.
Edward W. Evans, Philadelphia, Pa.
William M. Fincke, Katonah, N. Y.
John A. Fitch, New York City
Elizabeth Gurley Flynn, New York City
William Z. Foster, Pittsburgh, Pa.
Felix Frankfurter, Cambridge, Mass.
Ernst Freund, Chicago, Ill.
Paul J. Furnas, New York City
Zona Gale, Portage, Wis.

and Bartolomeo Vanzetti, who are accused of murder in connection with a hold-up at South Braintree last April. Their case has been carefully investigated by our legal advisory committee, which reports that the evidence against them is unsubstantial and that the real reason for the prosecution seems to be that Sacco and Vanzetti are "foreigners" and are active and influential radicals. The same conclusion has been reached by the American Civil Liberties Union, the Workers' Defense Union, the New Republic, the Nation and other organizations; and the Italian Government has made the case the subject of diplomatic inquiry.

Sacco and Vanzetti are Italian workmen of superior intelligence, Vanzetti who has resided for seven years at Plymouth, was there on April 15th, 1920. On that day Sacco, who resides with his wife and two children at South Stoughton, was at his home and later in Boston. That was the day when two gunmen robbed and murdered the paymaster of Slater & Morrill at South Braintree. Vanzetti was held for trial without preliminary examination. Sacco was held on the testimony of a couple of girls, who saw the hold-up from the upper window of a neighboring office building, and one man who saw it from a distance of at least two hundred feet. None of these witnesses had ever seen Sacco or Vanzetti before, and they refused to swear positively to the identification; while another witness who stood within twenty feet of the shooting told the chief of police that Sacco and Vanzetti were not the highwaymen.

A. B. Gilbert, St. Paul, Minn.
Arthur Garfield Hays, New York City
Morris Hillquit, New York City
John Haynes Holmes, New York City
Frederic C. Howe, Washington, D. C.
James Weldon Johnson, New York City
Helen Keller, Forest Hills, L. I.
Harold J. Laski, Cambridge, Mass.
Agnes Brown Leach, New York City
Arthur LeSueur, St. Paul, Minn.
Henry R. Linville, New York City
Robert Morss Lovett, Chicago, Ill.
Allen McCurdy, New York City
Grenville S. MacFarland, Boston, Mass.
Oscar Maddous, Manhassett, L. I.
Judah L. Magnes, New York City
James H. Maurer, Reading, Pa.
A. J. Muste, New York City
George W. Nasmyth, New York City
Scott Nearing, New York City
Julia S. O'Connor, Boston, Mass.
Wm. H. Pickens, Baltimore, Md.
William Marion Reedy, St. Louis, Mo.
John Nevin Sayre, Katonah, N. Y.
Rose Schneiderman, New York City
Vida D. Scudder, Wellesley, Mass.
Seymour Stedman, Chicago, Ill.
Norman M. Thomas, New York City
Edw. D. Tittmann, Hillsboro, N. M.
Wm. S. U'Ren, Portland, Ore.
Oswald Garrison Villard, New York City
B. Charney Vladeck, New York City
L. Hollingsworth Wood, New York City
George P. West, San Francisco, Cal.

That a charge so unfounded should be pressed so earnestly proves the seriousness of the situation to the victims. They must be ready to meet the accusation fully and vigorously, and they need funds for every step. Up to the present time all costs of preparation have been met by contributions from Italian workers. For the many expenses of the trial, such as daily transcript of court proceedings, investigation of evidence and if possible local counsel of distinction, the sum of $10,000 is needed immediately. Already we have received contributions of $1,000 from an "American Friend of Justice" and $365 collected by the League for Democratic Control.

Will you help with a prompt and liberal subscription. Checks may be sent to me at 44 Edgehill Road, Brookline.

(Signed) Anna N. Davis
Secretary-Treasurer

John S. Codman, New England representative of the American Civil Liberties Union.

Luigi Antonini, Secretary of the Italian Dressmakers and Waistmakers Union, an affiliate of the Amalgamated Clothing Workers of America, the latter Sidney Hillman's union.

Roger N. Baldwin, Director of the American Civil Liberties Union, the Garland Fund, and International Labor Defense.

August Bellanca, member of the General Executive Board of the Amalgamated Clothing Workers of America.

Abraham Brownstein, one of the group of the Amalgamated Clothing Workers.

Arturo Giovanitti, a nationally known anarchist, notorious in Massachusetts for his activities in the textile strike in Lawrence.

Bishop Paul Jones, one of the secretaries of the Fellowship of Reconciliation, organized in 1917 to exert all possible pressure against the war, the Espionage and Selective Draft Bills, and loans to the Allies.

Freda Kirchwey, Managing Editor of *The Nation.*

Joseph Schlossberg, Secretary-Treasurer of the Amalgamated Clothing Workers of America.

Helen Phelps Stokes, a famous revolutionary radical.

Norman Thomas, well-known Socialist, one of the leaders in the American Civil Liberties Union and in the League for Industrial Democracy.

Constanzo Pagnani.

Felice Guadagni, one of Sacco's alibi witnesses.

Amleto Fabbri, who went to Dedham to get the Madeiros confession from Sacco.

John F. Moors, a Boston banker.

Felix Frankfurter.

MOORE'S CONDUCT OF THE DEFENSE

Fred H. Moore, a California lawyer, had been defense counsel in several I.W.W. cases, among them the Massachusetts prosecution of Ettor and Giovanitti for a murder occurring during the Lawrence strike of 1912. Moore was interested in money and spent much of his time writing letters soliciting contributions to the defense fund. Payments to him personally were substantial, and his expense accounts were extravagant.

Moore seems to have strung the case out after the verdict more for money than for its propaganda value, but perhaps for both. Sacco resented the long delays and the "speculation" and, on August 18, 1924, wrote from the Dedham jail to Moore:

> . . . And I can see how clever and cynic you are, because after all my protest, after I have been chase you and all your philanthropists friends, you are still continue the infamous speculation on the shoulders of Sacco-Vanzetti case . . . you and your philanthropists has been use it from last three years like a instrument of infamous speculation. . . . I am telling you that you are going to stop this dirty game! You hear me? . . . No, because I know that you are the one that brings in these mud in Sacco-Vanzetti case. . . . (signed) Your implacable enemy, now and forever, Nick Sacco.[6]

Soon after October 1, 1924, when Thayer denied the motions for a new trial and severely criticized Moore for his unprofessional conduct, Moore withdrew from all participation in the case and it was necessary to find new counsel to head the defense.

WILLIAM G. THOMPSON

William G. Thompson, a Boston lawyer who was neither a radical nor associated with radical organizations, had from time to time been consulted by the defense, and he was asked to take full charge of the case. He was reluctant to do this, and as reliable hearsay has it, he hoped that by asking for a retainer of $25,000 he would discourage the committee and thus escape the employment.

At this critical point the American Fund for Public Service,[7] of

---

6 *The Letters of Sacco and Vanzetti*, pp. 21-24.

7 The American Fund for Public Service was popularly known as the "Garland Fund" or the "Free Love Fund," because it was founded by a rich young

which Roger N. Baldwin, Director of the American Civil Liberties Union (A.C.L.U.), was Secretary, made a loan to the Defense Committee. Baldwin describes the loan in a paragraph which was included in the introductory chapter of the Financial Report of the Defense Committee.

The $20,000 loan from the American Fund for Public Service was granted in order to retain Mr. William G. Thompson on the appeal. Mr. Thompson's fee, which covers his expenses as well, was $25,000, and was paid at the time he took the case, November 19, 1924. The loan was made subject to the Committee's ability to repay from receipts. To

---

radical, Charles Garland, of Massachusetts, who later served a prison term for running a Free Love Farm. The Fund was founded in 1922 and by 1930 had given away $1,378,000 and loaned $780,000. During its existence (it ran out of money in the early 1930's) it sustained all the leading Communist, Socialist, and I.W.W. activities.

To list the gifts and loans made by the Fund for radical causes, publications, schools, strikes, Communist-led unions, leagues, defense of criminals, and special projects would be to list all the radical and revolutionary activities of the 1920's. Among its beneficiaries was the Federated Press, which played so large a part in Sacco-Vanzetti propaganda and agitation. The Fund owned the *New Masses* and made loans for special purposes to the *New Republic, The World Tomorrow,* and the *New Leader.*

Activities of the A.C.L.U., which received support from the Fund, are too numerous to list, and only a representative few follow: campaigns against criminal syndicalism laws, the Tennessee Anti-Evolution (Scopes) case, investigation of "reactionary" organizations, "civil liberties" cases, release of Mooney and Billings, Passaic (N.J.) strike, campaign against injunctions in labor disputes, and deportation cases.

One of the loans made by the Fund was for the purpose of investigating "spy activities" in the Department of Justice, an early manifestation of radical hostility to the Bureau now known as the F.B.I. Thompson's attempt to show misconduct and conspiracy on the part of the Department of Justice must have had the full approval of the officers and directors of the Fund.

The officers and directors for the second year of operation were, according to the report of June 30, 1924, as follows:

Scott Nearing, president; Robert Morss Lovett, vice-president; Roger N. Baldwin, secretary; Morris L. Ernst, treasurer; Walter Nelles, counsel, and Elizabeth Gurley Flynn, William Z. Foster, Lewis S. Gannett, Clinton S. Golden, James Weldon Johnson, Freda Kirchwey, Norman M. Thomas, Leo Wolman, fellow directors.

Turning back in this chapter, the reader will find eight of these on the letterhead of the A.C.L.U. in 1921.

date, $12,500 has been repaid, and the American Fund has canceled $2,500 as a contribution, leaving $5,000 still to be repaid. The loans run without interest, and with no security except the good faith of the Committee and the ability of friends of the defense to meet its cost.

I.L.D. ENTERS THE CASE

Thompson was in the midst of his preparation for the argument of the exceptions taken at the trial and to the denials of the motions for a new trial, when another organization entered the case and gave it a new complexion.

On June 28, 1925, the International Labor Defense Committee (I.L.D.), the American section of the Moscow-controlled Communist International Red Aid, was formed in Chicago and from that time cooperated with the A.C.L.U. on the Sacco-Vanzetti case and other cases, including the Mooney and the Scottsboro cases.

The I.L.D. grew out of the Labor Defense Council organized by William Z. Foster in 1922 for the legal defense of the Communists arrested at the Bridgman, Michigan, raid. On the National Committee of that organization we find several of the National Committee of the A.C.L.U., notably Roger N. Baldwin, John Haynes Holmes, and Elizabeth Gurley Flynn.

Among the members of the National Committee of the I.L.D. as organized June 28, 1925, we find many familiar names, of whom the following are representative:

Upton Sinclair, whose services to the Sacco-Vanzetti literature as a "violent literary Socialist" are many.

William Z. Foster, Chairman of the Workers (Communist) Party of America, its 1924 candidate for President, a member of A.C.L.U., and a director of the Garland Fund, for many years the leading American Communist.

Eugene V. Debs.

Scott Nearing, a very prominent Communist, a Garland Fund director from the beginning, and a founder of the A.C.L.U. He had many Communist affiliations and activities.

F. G. Biedenkapp, one of the two men who browbeat and black-mailed Lola R. Andrews. Biedenkapp was later indicted in Massachusetts for strike violence. Governor Frank G. Allen tried to extradite him, but Franklin D. Roosevelt, then Governor of New York, would not permit the extradition.

Every member of the Communist Party was obliged to become a member of the I.L.D.

The I.L.D., from the first, was critical of the Sacco-Vanzetti Defense Committee for abandoning the idea of the class struggle and becoming concerned with the vindication of confidence in Massachusetts institutions and justice. Max Schachtman expressed it thus:

> [The Sacco-Vanzetti Defense Committee] sold the class birthright of the Sacco-Vanzetti case for a mess of liberal milk and pap. . . . This corrupting respectability began to exert a powerful pressure upon the Sacco-Vanzetti Defense Committee in Boston . . . the slow poison of middle-class treachery continued to seep into the ranks of the committee and it began to dominate its words and deeds.[8]

Soon there was a change of policy which introduced into the case new issues and new methods. Under Moore's management of the case, that is, from August 1920 to October 1924, no defense lawyer had accused Thayer of prejudice or unfairness or Katzmann and the Department of Justice of conspiracy, or Captain Proctor of perjury, or anyone of substituting false exhibits for true ones. Under Thompson, these and many similar accusations were freely and recklessly made.

After the decision of April 6, 1927, on the Madeiros motion became known, the militants, represented by the I.L.D., demanded a protest movement.

---

[8] Max Schachtman, *Sacco and Vanzetti, Labor's Martyrs,* published by I.L.D., New York, 1927, pp. 49-50.

The I.L.D. considered Sacco and Vanzetti and their cause the property of the whole working class and that only the working class could transform this cause into a victory.

The struggle raced into the open fields and avenues. One after another of the labor organizations in the United States arrayed themselves with the defense in the demand for a new trial. Unions of the American Federation of Labor, the I.W.W., and other independent unions, the communists, socialists, anarchists, recorded themselves for Sacco and Vanzetti, recording a working-class kinship with the agitators.[9]

The I.L.D. and its associates then began holding scores of protest meetings and staging demonstrations throughout the United States and in conjunction with its parent International Red Aid (Moscow controlled) throughout the world.

The parent organization took the initiative in hundreds of cities in forming committees of action, in organizing protest meetings and demonstrations, and in obtaining the messages of protest and appeal sent to Boston by scores of outstanding scientists, statesmen, men of letters, and prominent men and women of all sections of society.[10]

The issue was not guilt or innocence, fair trial or unfair; that was "liberal milk and pap." The issue was revolution and the destruction of America.

James P. Cannon of the I.L.D., addressing a meeting in Ford Hall, Boston, in January 1927, expressed it thus:

> Our comrades are in prison—our comrades Sacco and Vanzetti, don't forget that. . . . Our time will come. America will topple. Our work will bear fruit. . . . Today belongs to capitalism, tomorrow belongs to us.

From the time that the I.L.D. entered the case, if not long before, Sacco-Vanzetti was exploited for the purpose of toppling

9 Schachtman, *op. cit.*, p. 48.
10 Schachtman, *op. cit.*, p. 61.

America, destroying capitalism, and bringing the world revolution. The case set a pattern of exploitation which has been followed in many other cases where radicals were accused of crime, but no other exploitation has ever had the success of Sacco-Vanzetti.

8   THE DEDHAM JURY

SACCO and Vanzetti were indicted for the South Braintree murder by the Norfolk County grand jury on September 11, 1920. At their urgent request the trial was delayed until May 31, 1921.

On April 20, 1921, the Chief Justice of the Superior Court made an order for a special sitting at Dedham beginning Tuesday, May 31, 1921, and an order for the issue of venires for five hundred jurors drawn from the jury lists of all the cities and towns in Norfolk County in proportion to their respective populations.

The examination of the veniremen took several days, and when the venire had been exhausted only seven jurors had been empaneled. Judge Thayer thereupon, in accordance with practice when a venire is exhausted, ordered the sheriff to summon in two hundred talesmen from the bystanders or from the county at large. The panel was exhausted late in the day, and since there were then no bystanders in the ordinary sense of that word, it was necessary to send the deputy sheriffs into the cities and towns of the county. That evening they went to Norwood, Dedham, Millis, Brookline, Quincy, and Stoughton; to each town or city was assigned a quota of talesmen, apportioned roughly according to population. The sheriff issued no instructions about the method of selection but left the filling of the quotas to the discretion of the deputies.

The talesmen who were summoned appeared the next morning. The defense objected to the method by which the sheriff and his deputies had made their selection and offered to show, and did show, by the testimony of the deputy sheriffs that the deputy sheriffs went into the cities and towns and selected a certain number of men as they saw fit; some used the assessors' lists, some their own knowledge; some went from door to door, and one served the attendants at a Masonic meeting. One deputy selected from his own acquaintances "substantial, intelligent, and eminently qualified men," criteria which drew the scorn of Frankfurter.

After the sheriff and the deputy sheriffs were examined under oath, Judge Thayer ruled that the selections had been made in good faith and in accordance with law. The Supreme Judicial Court later held that this ruling was a discretionary one and that there was no evidence of abuse of discretion. The examination of the jurors then went along and the panel was completed.

In a chapter called "Men of Norfolk," Joughin includes an attack on the jury system as it operated in the Sacco-Vanzetti case. He assumes that the jury at the Dedham trial was drawn from a community and a people whose social mind was unfit to deal with an issue involving its hysterical passions: "A sick society makes sick decisions." Joughin does not suggest any alternative. Since he would have us believe that all Massachusetts judges at this time were as unfit as the jury to deal with the issue and that this unfitness applied to the Governor and his advisers and to the presidents of Harvard and M.I.T., his conclusion must have been that there was no one in Massachusetts fit to try any murderer who was also a radical.

Frankfurter's criticism of the jury was that some members were specially selected by the sheriff's deputies from persons whom they deemed representative citizens, substantial, and intelligent, surely a soft impeachment.

Schachtman says: "The jury was selected. They were all cut out of the same bolt of cloth; staid, torpid, highly patriotic, oblivious to progress or a progressive idea. . . ." [1]

Another criticism was that no Italians were summoned. This clearly was because in 1920 the number of Italians who had been

[1] Schachtman, *op. cit.*, p. 20.

naturalized and were otherwise qualified for jury service was small indeed.

The criticism that the jury was completely middle-class in nature or made up of thick-headed rustics is not borne out by their occupations, even if we adopt radical conceptions of classification, which were hardly understood in the Norfolk County of 1920, when men were, in one lifetime, farmers, mill workers, salesmen, capitalists, proletariat, bourgeois, "exploiter," and "exploited." Vanzetti as fish peddler was a petty bourgeois one week and as cement worker a proletarian the next. Sacco, with $1,500 in the bank, was well on his way to becoming a capitalist. His employer, Kelley, had been farmer, shoe worker, and factory owner. (2297)

Norfolk County could hardly have found twelve men untainted by patriotism and willing to judge a murder case on the principles of a class struggle. By the use of peremptory challenges, Moore was able to exclude a broker and a banker, both of whom Jeremiah J. McAnarney, his associate counsel, knew and wanted to retain, and for this reason the jury had no obvious capitalist. (5052)

The following are the names, occupations, and residences of the jurors:

Wallace R. Hersey, real-estate dealer, Weymouth.

John E. Ganley, grocer, Avon.

Frank R. Waugh, machinist, Quincy.

Frank D. Marden, mason, Weymouth.

Walter R. Ripley, stockkeeper, Quincy.

John F. Dever, salesman, Brookline.

Lewis McHardy, mill operative, Milton.

Harry E. King, shoe worker, Millis.

George A. Gerard, photographer and last maker, Stoughton.

Alfred L. Atwood, real-estate dealer, Norwood.

J. Frank McNamara, farmer, Stoughton.

Seward R. Parker, machinist, Quincy. (2320)

The following excerpt from the Simmons interview[2] with juror Dever is illuminating:

2 In 1950 Edward B. Simmons, staff writer for the New Bedford *Standard-Times,* interviewed Michael E. Stewart, who was Chief of the Bridgewater

The only knowledge the interviewer had of juror Dever before meeting him was based on writer Upton Sinclair's reference to him as a "Beacon Street Blueblood." Sinclair's book in behalf of Sacco and Vanzetti, need it be said, declared the jury was incapable of deciding the guilt of persons of such lowly estate as the defendants.

"Are you a Beacon Street Blueblood? Dever was asked . . ."

"You know, a friend told me about that description. I'm as blue-blooded a Beacon Street resident as anybody can be who was born in the Italian section of Barre, Vermont, grew up in Dorchester, stopped schooling at the 8th grade, lost his father at 11, his mother at 5, and went to work at 15.

"That description of Sinclair's is typical, I suppose. He took one look at my address and decided the whole jury, me especially, was a bunch of stand-pat New Englanders out to convict a couple of foreigners.

"Actually my Beacon Street address [Brookline, not Boston] was a boardinghouse. I was working in Filene's having just come back from Army service.

"I remember in Barre, my birthplace, there was a wonderful statue of Robert Burns of pure marble from the quarries there. It was carved by an Italian. I was brought up near that statue and I acquired a respect for anyone who could create a marvelous work of art like that with his hands. I admired Italians then. . . . I did during the trial and still do. It is nonsense to say we were prejudiced against Sacco and Vanzetti because they were Italian immigrants."

Another reference to Italians came from juror King, who told Simmons this:

"My associations with the jury were very fine. They were a bunch of fine men, none of them vindictive.

Police Department at the time of the trial, and in 1952 interviewed the surviving jurors and other persons connected with the trial. These interviews were printed in the *Standard-Times*. Simmons and the *Standard-Times* have generously given me permission to use and quote this material.

"My conscience never has troubled me. I had to come back to my job, working with other shoemakers in the factory. Most of them were Italians and knew Sacco when he lived in Milford. But my fellow workers never questioned the verdict or insinuated it was anything but justified.

"Sacco and Vanzetti were given every consideration."

CONDITIONS IN THE COURTROOM

The allegation that conditions in the courtroom were prejudicial to the accused was variously phrased. The principal objection was to the unusual guarding of the courtroom and to the searching of spectators for concealed weapons. The guarding of a courtroom and the protection of those in it is the responsibility of the sheriff and not of the judge or the district attorney. Accounts of the precautions taken by the sheriff were much exaggerated. There were no mounted troops outside the courthouse and no deputies with drawn guns within. Spectators were searched for weapons on one occasion at least, probably more, but this was not within sight of a jury. The precautions taken were not designed to inflame or intimidate the jury. Nor can the sheriff be blamed for unusual care. Partisans of the defense included many criminals and many of deranged mentality. Threats to life and property were freely made, and it would have been folly for the sheriff to ignore the possibility of violence in the courtroom.

PATRIOTISM IN THE COURTROOM

To the radical and the international Socialist, patriotism is a poison which must be eliminated from school, church, and court. There were patriots in the Dedham courtroom, the foreman of the jury saluted the flag every morning, Judge Thayer compared the voluntary acceptance of disagreeable jury duty with the sacrifices made by soldiers, but it is nonsense to think that the introduction of what Frankfurter called the "war motif" was an invitation for the jury to convict the defendants because they were slackers and radicals without regard to their guilt. Joughin, following Upton Sinclair, carries his patriotism phobia to the point of absurdity. The setting of the trial, he writes, was most unfortunate:

> On May 29, throughout the Boston area, numerous public squares were dedicated to dead heroes. May 30 was Memorial Day. The trial opened on May 31. The first week of June was the anniversary of Belleau Wood, and Vanzetti first took the witness stand on the day following July 4.[3]

How silly can you get?

[3] Joughin, *op. cit.*, p. 208.

THE EYEWITNESSES

THE Commonwealth's case consisted of direct and circumstantial evidence which we shall consider in the following order: (1) eyewitnesses; (2) Sacco's pistol and the fatal bullet; (3) Sacco's cap; (4) Berardelli's gun, and (5) consciousness of guilt.

The crime was committed in midafternoon, but because of the defendants' claim that they were not in South Braintree at all on April 15, 1920, evidence placing them there at any time during that day was relevant.

Three eyewitnesses of scenes preceding the shooting placed Sacco in South Braintree during the morning or early afternoon of April 15, 1920.

The first of these was Mrs. Lola R. Andrews, who on the stand made a positive, face-to-face identification of Sacco as the man she had seen sometime after 11:00 A.M. near an automobile parked not far from the Slater and Morrill factory.[1]

William S. Tracy also made a face-to-face identification of Sacco. He saw two men in front of a drugstore on Pearl Street between 11:35 and 11:40 A.M. He drove past them three times. He noticed them because they were leaning against a building he owned. One of them was Sacco. "While I wouldn't be positive . . . to the best of my recollection that was the man." (501)

1 After the trial Mrs. Andrews repudiated her testimony under circumstances stated in detail in Chapter 23. Her repudiation was the basis of a motion for a new trial (the Andrews motion), which was denied by Judge Thayer after Mrs. Andrews had repudiated her repudiation.

William J. Heron saw two Italians in the South Braintree rail-road station between 12:30 and 1:00 o'clock. They acted nervous. He was "pretty sure" that Sacco was one of them. (520)

Frankfurter, by limiting his critical survey of the identification testimony to the five witnesses who definitely identified Sacco as in the car or on the spot at the time of the murder, has no space for a man leaning against Tracy's building in the morning or in the railway station at noontime; so he does not mention the unim-peached testimony of Tracy or Heron at all.

Lillian E. Splaine, a bookkeeper employed by Slater & Morrill, on April 15, 1920, watched part of the getaway from a window in a second-floor room in the southeast corner of the Hampton House Building, the windows of which overlooked Pearl Street. From her window, the murder car was in view for a short distance and Miss Splaine saw a man standing between the front seat and the back seat, leaning out of the car with his left hand on the back of the front seat about one third of the way across.

In her testimony at the trial she made a positive face-to-face identification of Sacco as the man she had seen leaning out of the car. Part of her description of the man leaning out of the car was this: "I noticed particularly the left hand was a good-sized hand, a hand that denoted strength." (220-256)

Sacco's hand was shown to the jury at the trial, and if, as the defense afterward claimed, his was a small rather than a good-sized hand, they could take that into account in appraising her testimony. The size of Sacco's hand became an issue when the Madeiros confession was argued.

A Victrola salesman who gave his name as Carlos Edward Good-ridge made a face-to-face identification of Sacco as the man in the murder car who had poked a gun at him during the getaway.[2]

Louis Pelser, a shoecutter in Rice & Hutchins, identified Sacco

[2] Some years after the trial, Moore tried to blackmail Goodridge into a repudiation of his testimony. This attempt failed, but Moore nevertheless filed a motion for a new trial (the Goodridge motion), supporting it with the blackmailing material he had gathered and arguing that Goodridge was not entitled to be believed because of his crimes and bad reputation. See Chapter 22 ("Carlos E. Goodridge").

sitting in the courtroom as the man who was standing over the body of Berardelli with a gun in his hand. He said, "Well, I wouldn't say it was him, but he is a dead image of him." [3]

Frances J. Devlin also saw part of the getaway from a window in the Hampton House Building. She was sure that one of the men in the murder car was Sacco. (464)

Austin C. Cole testified, as he had at Plymouth, that Sacco and Vanzetti boarded a streetcar, on which he was the conductor, on the night of April 14 or 15 at Sunset Avenue near Bridgewater. If it was Wednesday night (April 14), it was about 9:30 or 11:00; if it was Thursday night (April 15), it was about 10:30. (723) Cole was the conductor on the car upon which Sacco and Vanzetti were arrested on May 5, 1920. If believed, and related to April 15, this testimony placed Sacco and Vanzetti near the place where the murder car was abandoned a few hours after the murder; if related to April 14, the night before the murder.

This testimony was not impeached, although it appeared that Cole had at first glance thought Vanzetti was a friend of his called Tony. (737) Tony was in court but gave no testimony. Cole was shown a photograph of a man named Joseph Scavitto; he resembled Vanzetti, and Cole so admitted, but he would not say it was the man who boarded his car. Scavitto, on the stand, denied that he had been at any of the places at which the various witnesses placed Vanzetti. (1533-1534)

John W. Faulkner, a patternmaker of Cohasset, boarded a train at Cohasset for Boston at 9:20 on the morning of April 15.

As the train entered East Weymouth, a man sitting next to him remarked that the man behind him wanted to know if it was East Braintree. Faulkner looked around and saw a man whom he described in court as one who looked like a foreigner, with a black moustache and high cheekbones, with a felt hat and kind of old clothes. (426) The man asked Faulkner at East Weymouth, Wey-

---

[3] Sometime after the trial, Pelser, while on a spree, signed an affidavit repudiating his testimony. When he recovered his sobriety he wrote to Katzmann about this, repudiating his repudiation. Nevertheless Moore filed a motion for a new trial (the Pelser motion) based on the affidavit, which was denied by Judge Thayer. See Chapter 21 ("Louis Pelser").

mouth Heights, and Weymouth whether it was East Braintree. When the train reached East Braintree, Faulkner told him and he got off the train, went to the station platform, and dropped the old black leather bag, sixteen to eighteen inches long, that he was carrying. He walked back and forth on the platform once or twice before the train started. The train was scheduled to leave East Braintree at 9:54. (425)

On July 20, 1920, Faulkner, at the request of someone in Katzmann's office, had gone to the Plymouth jail and from five men lined up for him to look at picked Vanzetti as the man who left the train at East Braintree. In court he made a positive "I couldn't be mistaken" face-to-face identification of Vanzetti as that man. (429)

One of the veniremen summoned for the Dedham trial was Harry E. Dolbeare, a piano-repair man of South Braintree. He was in the courtroom on Thursday, June 2, 1921, sitting on the front bench, about halfway along, and had a profile view of Vanzetti. He recognized him as one of five men he had seen in a large car in South Braintree Square between 10:00 and 12:00 on April 15, 1920. He told the court about this and was excused from jury duty.[4] The man he recognized was sitting in the back of the car, leaning forward and talking to the driver or other person on the front seat. He looked like a foreigner and had a very heavy moustache, quite dark. In the courtroom he had the same view of Vanzetti that he had when he saw him in the automobile, and there was not a particle of doubt in his mind about the identification. (488 *et seq.*)

Michael Levangie, the gatetender at the Pearl Street railway crossing, could describe only one man in the getaway car. That was the driver, whom he described as a "dark complected man with cheekbones sticking out, black hair, heavy brown moustache, slouch hat, and army coat." He was about ten or twelve feet away from him. He saw him again at the Brockton police station, and on the stand he swore that Vanzetti was the fellow. (413-425)

In his argument to the jury, Katzmann had to admit that Le-

---

[4] *Boston Herald*, June 3, 1921.

vangie was mistaken in saying that Vanzetti was driving the car, because of the overwhelming testimony that when the car started it was driven by a light-haired, sickly man. But he asked the jury to consider whether Vanzetti was in the car immediately behind the driver. (2215)

Austin T. Reed, twenty-one years old, was the crossing tender at the Matfield crossing in West Bridgewater. A train was due to pass this crossing about 4:10 on April 15, 1920, but was a little late. Reed saw an automobile up the street and went into the middle of the street with his stop sign. The automobile was coming from West Bridgewater at a pretty fast rate of speed, but it didn't have time to get by ahead of the train. One of the men in the automobile asked Reed: "What to hell I was holding him up for?" and pointed his finger at him. The car had stopped at this time and was about forty feet away from Reed. The man who spoke was on the front seat beside the driver. Reed then stepped back across the track and the train passed. The automobile then came by, and when it was within four feet of Reed the same man pointed his finger again at Reed and said, "What to hell did you hold us up for?" The car then went along but in a few minutes came back and went over the crossing and up toward Bridgewater again. The man who spoke to Reed was a dark-complexioned man, with hollow cheeks, high cheekbones, and stubbed moustache, bushy. His hair was black. He wore a dark slouch hat and a dark suit.

About two or three days after the arrest Reed went on his own motion to the Brockton police station and identified Vanzetti as the man who spoke to him. In the courtroom he swore that he had no doubt that the man in the car who spoke to him was the man in the cage known as Vanzetti.

The defense presented seventeen eyewitnesses. Apart from two of them, who could not tell whether Sacco was at the scene of the murder or not, their testimony was a positive denial that the men in the cage were the men they saw, and the descriptions they gave could not possibly apply to them.

Some of the eyewitnesses, both state and defense, suffered under cross-examination, and some on both sides were contradicted by other witnesses.

METHOD OF IDENTIFICATION

In their brief, filed with the Advisory Committee, Thompson and Ehrmann alleged as misconduct by the district attorney the methods used at the police station "with the assent" of the district attorney to secure identification of Sacco and Vanzetti by exhibiting them to the witnesses alone and not in a police line-up, "as is the approved method," and requiring Sacco and Vanzetti to assume crouching and other significant positions. (5363) And Frankfurter, always suspicious of what goes on at a police station, makes a great deal of this in his book.

The argument was that the method adopted in this case encouraged the witnesses to make a false identification.

Katzmann's answer was that the identification was police work and that the method used by them was a fair one if the witnesses were honest. In addition to this, he could have said that the point had only a limited application in the case.

The most important identification of Vanzetti came from Faulkner, who picked Vanzetti out of a police line-up of five. This line-up has been criticized because it does not appear that the other four had moustaches, a refinement of the method which might well make it unsuited to the ordinary county jail. Nor would the criticism apply to Mrs. Andrews, who was shown all the prisoners in the Dedham jail and without any hint from anyone identified Sacco. And certainly the point would not apply to Goodridge, who recognized Sacco when he saw him in a courtroom as the man who shot at him, or to Dolbeare, who recognized Sacco when, as a prospective juror, he caught a side view of Sacco as he sat in the dock.

The honesty of the witnesses is substantiated by the fact that, although the same methods of identification were used for Orciani, not one of the eyewitnesses identified him as a participant in either crime, just as no one identified Sacco as a participant in the Bridgewater holdup or Vanzetti as one of the men who did the actual shooting at South Braintree.

Carried to its logical extreme, the argument would disqualify any face-to-face identification of the prisoners in the dock unless there were ten docks and ten men sitting in them, five with bushy moustaches.

The lack of a police line-up was a proper subject in the cross-examination of the eyewitnesses and for consideration by the jury in appraising identifications made on the stand, but it was not proof that Katzmann acted in bad faith or was guilty of any misconduct in assenting to it, if indeed he did "assent."

In this connection, it is amusing to compare the methods used to identify Joe Morelli and Steve the Pole which Ehrmann found so convincing.[5]

PRESSURE AND SUPPRESSION

In the last stages of the case, charges were made that Slater & Morrill, by hiring and firing, had brought improper pressure to bear upon identification witnesses in their employ, thereby bringing about great changes in the testimony of the government's identification witnesses. Because of this, misconduct was charged to the district attorney.

The short answer to this charge is that, with the exception of Louis Pelser, no employee of Slater & Morrill changed his testimony to favor the Commonwealth. As for Pelser, he did, to the surprise of the Commonwealth, change his testimony just before he went on the stand, but there is nothing to show that Slater & Morrill had anything to do with that.

The district attorney was also charged with misconduct in that he had suppressed the testimony of Roy E. Gould,[6] Mrs. Minnie Kennedy, Mrs. Louise Kelly, and Mrs. Hewins. Mrs. Kennedy and Mrs. Kelly, who were interviewed by the police shortly after the crime, were not called to the stand. They would have testified

---

5 See Chapter 28 ("The Morelli Hypothesis").

6 The Gould testimony is reviewed in Chapter 20 ("Roy E. Gould").

that just before the crime they saw an empty car in the street in front of the factory attended by a light-complexioned man who was neither Sacco nor Vanzetti. Their testimony would have helped neither side.

During their getaway the murderers stopped at Mrs. Hewins's house in Randolph. Mrs. Hewins would have testified positively that the driver of the car at that time was Sacco. She attended court several days but was not put on the stand, presumably because the district attorney thought that she was mistaken in making Sacco the driver of the car, just as Levangie had been mistaken in making Vanzetti the driver of the car. This "suppression" by Katzmann certainly did the defense no harm.

In summary we must concede with Judge Riddell that the identification evidence at the trial, while sufficient to justify submission of it to a jury, cannot be called strong. Standing alone, it probably would not have convinced the jury that the defendants were guilty beyond a reasonable doubt. But, as Riddell also said, there was other evidence, of the gravest character, against both the accused.[7]

To that other evidence we now turn.

[7] William Renwick Riddell, "The Sacco-Vanzetti Case from a Canadian Viewpoint," *American Bar Association Journal,* December 1927. "In view of the importance of the case and the interest that naturally attaches to the viewpoint of an unbiased and competent critic residing in another country having the same general system of law as our own, the Editor of the Journal requested this article from Mr. Justice Riddell of the Ontario Bench." Judge Riddell disclaimed the omniscience that would enable him to pass positively on the guilt of the defendants, but he had no doubt that the trial was a fair one.

10 SACCO'S PISTOL AND THE FATAL BULLET

WHEN Sacco was arrested on May 5, 1920, he had in the waistband of his trousers a fully loaded .32-caliber Colt automatic nine-shot pistol, and loose in his hip pocket twenty-three steel-jacketed automatic pistol bullets of the same caliber and description as the nine bullets in the pistol.

The thirty-two bullets found in the pistol and in Sacco's pocket were of different makes: sixteen were Peters, three were Remington, six were Winchester, and seven U.S. (783)

On May 6, 1920, Katzmann interrogated Sacco about the pistol and the bullets. Sacco said that he bought the pistol on Hanover Street in Boston, had owned it about two years, paid sixteen or seventeen dollars for it, and gave an assumed name when he made the purchase. He did not remember where he bought the cartridges, but he had bought a brand-new, unopened box of them. This was all false and was so admitted by Sacco on the stand. (1900 et seq.)

His final story was that he bought the pistol in Milford in 1917 or 1918 and bought two boxes of cartridges, one in Milford and one on Hanover Street. The box bought on Hanover Street was not a new box but a mixture of several makes. The thirty-two bullets found on him came from the Hanover Street box. (1858, 1902) Obviously the theory of the defense required a mixed box to explain the different makes of bullets found in Sacco's pocket.

Two .32-caliber, steel-jacketed ordinary automatic-pistol bullets were found in the body of Parmenter and four of the same description in the body of Berardelli.

The four bullets in Berardelli's body were removed after his death by Dr. George Burgess Magrath, medical examiner for Suffolk County, and marked by him with small scratches on the base in the order in which they were taken from the body, with Roman numerals I, II, III, and IIII. (113) At the trial, Magrath identified them and they were admitted in evidence. The bullet which Magrath marked III was the fatal bullet. This was usually called bullet No. 3.

All the bullets were given immediately to the State Police and remained in their custody until turned over to the sheriff at the time of the trial.

James F. Bostock was an eyewitness of the shooting, and after it was over he picked up at the scene of the murder four empty cartridge shells and left them at the office of Slater & Morrill. (195) About an hour and a half after the crime, Thomas F. Fraher, Superintendent of Slater & Morrill, handed the four shells to Captain Proctor, who kept them in his possession until the trial. At the trial, Proctor identified them and they were admitted in evidence. The shells were all .32 caliber, two of them of the Peters make, one a Remington U.M.C., and one a Winchester. These were usually called the Fraher shells. The Winchester one became important at the trial and after.

On Saturday, June 18, 1921 (during the trial), three experts, Captain William H. Proctor and Captain Charles Van Amburgh for the Commonwealth and James E. Burns for the defense, went to Lowell, Massachusetts, and fired Sacco's pistol into a pile of sawdust. The bullets which sprang from the pistol and the discharged shells were received in evidence the following week.

THE OBSOLETE BULLETS

The obsolete-bullet evidence, which appealed so strongly to the jury and the Advisory Committee, came into the case during the cross-examination of the defense expert witness Burns. The Committee expresses it as follows:

Then again, the fatal bullet found in Berardelli's body was of a type no longer manufactured and so obsolete that the defendants' expert witness, Burns, testified that, with the help of two assistants, he was unable to find such bullets for purposes of experiment; yet the same obsolete type of cartridges were found in Sacco's pockets on his arrest. . . . Such a coincidence of the fatal bullet and those found on Sacco would, if accidental, certainly be extraordinary. (5378 w-x)

Years afterward all but one of the surviving jurors were interviewed by Edward B. Simmons of the New Bedford *Standard-Times*, who reported that all of them said that in their minds this was the single most damning piece of evidence.

Juror Dever, who afterwards became a lawyer, had a particularly good memory and gave the reporter an account which checks remarkably well with the transcript:

District Attorney Katzmann asked Burns why he had not used Winchester bullets in his tests with Sacco's gun. Burns replied he had not been able to obtain any bullets like the fatal one because it was of a rare old-fashioned type. . . .

"Did you make a thorough effort to find matching Winchester bullets for your test?"

"I tried all over New England with no success."

"But," Simmons was asked by Dever, "do you know who had some of them? When Sacco was arrested, he was carrying 23, I believe it was, extra bullets, and some were the identical, old-fashioned, unobtainable Winchester .32-caliber bullets, exact duplicates of the one which killed Berardelli."

Recalling the evidence that impressed him most, juror Parker said:

"The bullets, of course. That testimony and evidence on it sticks in your mind. You can't depend on the witnesses. But the bullets, there was no getting around that evidence."

And to cite one more of the concurring opinions, juror Atwood said that the outstanding evidence in his mind was that of the old-fashioned type of Winchester bullets, one of which was found in Berardelli's body and duplicates of which were found on Sacco when he was arrested.

The obsolete-bullet evidence was a separate and distinct piece of evidence dependent upon the facts brought into the case by the defense expert Burns and upon a comparison between the bullets found on Sacco's person and the fatal bullet which could be made by the jurors or any layman without a microscope. At the trial the experts were not asked to make a comparison between the fatal bullet and the six Winchester bullets found in Sacco's pocket, for, as Fraenkel says, it was a fact that all of them showed the same indentations or knurls, and "these would be visible to the naked eye and easily noted by a layman." [1]

THE EXPERTS

We now come to the question of whether the fatal bullet No. 3 was *fired* from Sacco's pistol.

The ballistics experts for the Commonwealth at the trial were Captain William H. Proctor, head of the State Police, and Captain Charles Van Amburgh, an assistant in the ballistics department of the Remington U.M.C. Company of Bridgeport, Connecticut. The defense experts were James E. Burns, ballistics engineer of the United States Cartridge Company, and J. Henry Fitzgerald, who had charge of the testing room at the Colt Patent Firearms Company's factory in Hartford, Connecticut. Fitzgerald did not participate in the testing, and his testimony was limited to an opinion that the No. 3 bullet had not been fired from Sacco's pistol.

Proctor, Van Amburgh, and Burns all agreed that bullet No. 3 (Exhibit 18) was a Winchester (made by the Winchester Repeating Arms Company), identifying it as such by the "W" which that company used as a trade-mark on its bullets. All agreed that the bullet had a left-hand twist. Proctor and Van Amburgh were

[1] Fraenkel, *op. cit.*, p. 375.

of the opinion that bullet No. 3 had been fired from a Colt automatic .32 pistol. Burns thought it had been fired from a Colt or a
Bayard. (893, 916, 1408, 1426, 1430)

As to whether bullet No. 3 was fired from Sacco's pistol, the expert opinions were as follows:

> PROCTOR: My opinion is that it is consistent with being fired
> from that pistol. (896)
> VAN AMBURGH: I am inclined to believe that No. 3 bullet
> was fired from this Colt automatic pistol. (920)
> BURNS: Not in my opinion, no. (1414)
> FITZGERALD: My opinion is that No. III bullet was not fired
> from the pistol given me as Exhibit 28. (1466)

And that is all the opinion evidence given at the trial. It did
not amount to much on either side. Proctor used the word "consistent," Van Amburgh was "inclined to believe." Neither phrasing was a definite opinion upon which a jury could find the fact
beyond a reasonable doubt. Burns and Fitzgerald made definite
denials, but cross-examination discovered weak spots in their reasoning.

In his argument to the jury, Moore contented himself with one
sentence about the experts' testimony:

> "Gentlemen, if the time has come when a microscope must
> be used to determine whether a human life is going to con-
> tinue to function or not and when the users of the micro-
> scope themselves can't agree, when experts called by the
> Commonwealth and experts called by the defense are
> sharply defined in their disagreements, then I take it that
> ordinary men such as you and I should well hesitate to take
> a human life." (2147)

McAnarney attacked the Van Amburgh opinion on several
counts but did not mention the opinions of Proctor, Burns, or
Fitzgerald at all. (2166)

Katzmann asked the jurors to form their own opinion. Enumerating the ballistics exhibits (not including the Fraher shells), he said:

> "Take the glass, gentlemen, and examine them for yourselves. If you choose, take the word of nobody in that regard. Take the exhibits themselves."

He then went on to reply to McAnarney's criticism of the Van Amburgh opinion and paid his respects to the Burns and Fitzgerald opinions. No mention at all was made by him of Proctor's opinion. (2224)

As Morgan phrased it:

> He [Katzmann] emphasized the weak spots in the testimony of defendants' experts, he demolished the arguments of defendants' counsel, he ignored Proctor's testimony, and finally insisted that the jury might and should practically disregard the expert testimony and decide upon the phenomena visible to them. (Morgan, p. 106)

My guess is that the jury paid no attention to the expert opinions as such but did as Katzmann advised them, that is, decided the issue upon what they themselves could see with the glass or the naked eye.

ALBERT H. HAMILTON

On March 30, 1923, Moore asked Albert H. Hamilton, of Auburn, New York, to come to Boston and review the expert testimony. (3564) Thereafter Hamilton by affidavit and oral testimony sponsored several opinions which he called expert supporting the defense, notably the opinion that bullet No. 3 had not been fired from Sacco's pistol.

Hamilton professed to be a micro-chemical investigator and criminologist. His qualifications as an expert were not subject to cross-examination in the Sacco-Vanzetti case until he appeared before the Advisory Committee on July 13, 1927. Then Ranney,

who had been told about Hamilton by New York lawyers,
brought out the shallowness of his pretensions:

Q. [Ranney] For how many years have you testified as an
expert in both criminal and civil cases?
A. [Hamilton] About forty-one years.
Q. And during that time you have testified as an expert in
various different subjects, have you not?
A. I have.
Q. Testified as an expert in chemistry, have you not?
A. Some parts, yes.
Q. And in handwriting?
A. Yes.
Q. And in the general subject of firearms and bullets?
A. Yes.
Q. And you have also testified as concerning gunshot
wounds, have you not, Mr. Hamilton?
A. Yes, external and internal.
Q. And you have also testified in respect to inks, have you
not?
A. Yes . . .
Q. Where did you receive your education in these various
subjects?
A. It began in the Common Union School in a small village
of Sweetsboro where I was born and lived until I was fifteen
years old and it has not yet terminated. I have been studying
ever since.
Q. Are you a graduate of a medical college?
A. I am not, although I am a matriculator.
Q. You have been known as Doctor Hamilton?
A. I am not known by Doctor except the name has been
tacked on to me by a great many lawyers and I cannot suppress it.
Q. And during these numbers of years you have testified at
a number of murder trials, have you not?
A. I have, two hundred twenty-nine. (5018)

AUGUSTUS H. GILL

Professor Gill of M.I.T. was brought into the case as an expert after the trial. His ballistics experience was not great, he had never measured a bullet before, and, as we shall see, although he was a defense witness he was convinced by Colonel Goddard's microscope that the fatal bullet was fired from Sacco's pistol.

THE GOVERNOR AND THE ADVISORY COMMITTEE

The Governor in his decision does not mention Sacco's pistol and the fatal bullet, and I do not find that any of the experts were called before him.

The Advisory Committee heard Hamilton and others and decided that they were more impressed with the witnesses who thought that the fatal bullet was fired from Sacco's pistol.

The defense seems to have been convinced also and in the end was driven to a desperate resort which is described by the committee as follows:

> Before the Committee Mr. Thompson suggested that the fatal bullet shown at the trial as the one taken from Berardelli's body, and which caused his death, was not genuine; that the police had substituted it for another in order by a false exhibit to convict these men, but in this case, again, he offered no credible evidence for the suspicion. Such an accusation, devoid of proof, may be dismissed without further comment, save that the case of the defendants must be rather desperate on its merits when counsel feel it necessary to resort to a charge of this kind. (5378m)

In his offer of proof in the Canter case,[2] Thompson told the Court that in a conversation with Governor Fuller he, Thompson, had told the Governor that Proctor had had bullet No. 3 in his possession for a year and, being the kind of man he was, had made the substitution.

2 See page 16, footnote.

"I said that any man capable of doing that [yielding to pressure] is capable of taking the bullet that Dr. Magrath gave to him a year ago and disposing of it and of firing another Colt cartridge through Sacco's pistol or another Colt pistol of the same caliber so that when Van Amburgh goes out there he will be prepared to say that in his opinion that bullet went through Sacco's gun."

And that suspicion of the ever-suspicious Thompson is all the support the false-exhibit suggestion ever had. Thompson certainly gave the defense its money's worth when desperate accusations were needed. He spared no one. Attorney General Sargent, Governor Fuller, Katzmann, Williams, Proctor, and Stewart were charged with crimes and conspiracy; Vahey and Graham with betraying their clients.

COLONEL CALVIN GODDARD

At the time of the trial, ballistics was in its infancy and its methods inadequate. Honest experts could not be positive; like Proctor, they used the word "consistent" or, like Van Amburgh, the phrase "I am inclined to believe." The charlatan Hamilton was a very positive man but not convincing even to Thompson who, rather than try to support his opinion, resorted to the false-exhibit claim. The fact is that with the microscopes then available no honest expert could be more positive than Van Amburgh. By 1927, however, the comparison microscope had become available and convincing proof could be had by a technique which Colonel Calvin Goddard had developed.

Shortly before June 3, 1927, a newspaper man from New York called on Thompson and, stating that he was familiar with the work of Goddard, suggested that the defense consent to an independent investigation by Goddard of the mortal bullet and the Fraher shell. Thompson refused, but said he would put no obstacle in Goddard's way.

Thereafter, upon application to the Commonwealth, Goddard received permission from Ranney and on the afternoon of June

3, 1927, made tests at Dedham in the presence of Ranney, a stenographer, Ehrmann, Professor Gill, and at least two newspaper men. After the tests, Goddard wrote a letter to Governor Fuller, which was copied in the *Boston Evening Transcript* of August 8, 1927. The letter reads as follows:

> I submit below my report of the tests conducted by me on the afternoon of June 3, 1927, in the courthouse at Dedham, Mass., upon certain bullets and shells which figure as exhibits in the case of the Commonwealth vs. Sacco and Vanzetti. In these tests [Professor Gill], an expert representing the defense, checked on my findings by personal observations through the instruments employed, manipulating the apparatus as he saw fit.
>
> The instrument in question is nothing more than a highly perfected form of comparison microscope, employing optical principles long known. The model used was, however, especially designed for investigations upon bullets and shells and to the best of my knowledge none other equally well adapted to this purpose has been constructed. Its function is to fuse into a single one, the images of two bullets or shells, so that, in case they bear identical markings, the composite picture produced will reveal, after the identical markings have been located and brought into approximation, what appears to be a single object rather than the fusion of two objects. Unless two bullets have passed through the same barrel, they can never be so fused as to present the appearance of a single bullet, the picture always revealing marked differences in its two halves. This holds true also for shells which have or have not been fired in the same arm. (Those from the same arm matching, others failing to match.) The soundness of this statement can be verified by submitting it to any competent board of engineers familiar both with machine-shop practice as employed in the fabrication of small arms, and with the use of the microscope.
>
> Many tests were made, and the findings in substance were:

1.—That "Fraher Shell No. 3" was fired in the Sacco pistol and could have been fired in no other.

2.—That the so-called "fatal" bullet, being one of four from the body of one Berardelli, was fired through the Sacco pistol and could have been fired through no other.

The many points of identity [that] Fraher Shell No. 3 and various test shells fired in the Sacco pistol had in common are readily apparent to any layman who views the shells through the apparatus employed. Points of identity between the fatal bullet and test bullets fired through the Sacco pistol are less numerous, due largely to the fact that the surfaces of fatal and test bullets are overlaid with deposits of dirt which will have to be removed before the individual fine markings on their circumferences will be fully revealed.

While the defense expert is in no way collaborating with me in this report, I am satisfied from his expressions at the time of the test, that he concurs with me in my findings with respect to Fraher Shell No. 3, and also with regard to the fatal bullet, subject in this instance, however, to the qualification that he is unwilling to commit himself to a formal opinion until he has had an opportunity to examine the exhibit bullets once more, after they have been properly and thoroughly cleaned.

I append a record of my training and qualifications. Permit me also to add that I conducted the tests outlined for the simple reason that I knew that the comparison microscope would reveal, with mechanical accuracy, and in a manner which no human opinion could refute, the facts in the case. I felt that the employment of this instrument was essential if the facts were to be arrived at, and so offered to conduct the tests as an impartial observer, not in the employ of the State or the defense, directly or indirectly. I received no compensation of any kind from anyone for what I did, nor do I expect to. I saw to it that both sides were represented, and that the only expert present who represented either side

[Professor Gill for the defense] had ample opportunity to repeat at his own convenience each test which I undertook.

Yours very truly,

Calvin H. Goddard.

A MEMORANDUM FROM THOMAS H. CARENS

On October 23, 1958, Thomas H. Carens, who in 1927 was political editor of the *Boston Herald* and in that capacity covered the major incidents of the Sacco-Vanzetti case from early 1927 until the men were executed, sent me the following memorandum:

In the early summer of 1927, when the case was pending before Governor Fuller, a reporter from the New York *World*, whose name I have forgotten, brought to Boston a man named Calvin Goddard who, he stated, was an expert on ballistics, firearms, etc. The New York *World* was reputed to have hired Goddard to make an independent investigation on the firearms testimony in the Sacco-Vanzetti case.

After negotiations with both the prosecution and the defense, a small group were invited to be present at the Dedham Courthouse on an afternoon in May or June. My recollection is that there were about a dozen of us, but the only names I can now recall are Herbert Ehrmann, counsel for defense, and Dudley Ranney, Assistant District Attorney. The New York *World* reporter was there, and of course, Goddard. I am quite sure there were other reporters, including most of my colleagues from the State House, but I cannot name them now.

Goddard set up an apparatus consisting of double microscopes and explained the method by which he could identify a bullet and prove that it had been fired from a certain gun. Before any of the evidence in the trial was produced, all of us signed an agreement that we would not print anything which developed during the day unless Ehrmann and Ranney were in agreement that it should be printed.

After all these preliminaries, a deputy sheriff brought

from the archives the guns which had been taken from Sacco and Vanzetti on the night of their arrest, the bullets which had been taken from the bodies of Berardelli and Parmenter, the murdered men, and test bullets which had been fired from both guns.

The only vivid recollection I have is in connection with the bullet which had been removed from Berardelli's heart by Medical Examiner George Magrath, and which was identified by a little scratch symbol which Magrath had made with his pincers. By putting the shattered bullet into his apparatus and fusing it with a test bullet fired from the Sacco gun, Goddard put on a pretty convincing show to us laymen that these two bullets had been fired from the same gun.

At the conclusion of the test, it was obvious to us that we were not going to get any mutual agreement to have Goddard's conclusions reported. Some time later I was asked by a newspaperman who had not been present at the test if I had any notes on the test, but I had not taken any notes and so far as I was concerned it was a closed book.

The whole incident, however, did make an impression on me. Up to that time I had half a feeling that there might have been reasonable doubt that the police had caught the right fellows. I had heard Ehrmann's presentation of the Morelli theory before the Supreme Court, and was impressed by it. After the Goddard incident, I became pretty definitely convinced that Sacco at least was guilty. I have never been quite sure about Vanzetti, and in any event I never lost much sleep about it.

THE GUNTHERS

Some years later another study of the ballistics testimony and exhibits, as they appeared in the published records, was made by Jack D. and C. O. Gunther, who arrived at the conclusion that a comparison of the engravings made by the breechblock of Sacco's pistol on the test shell with those made by the breechblock of the pistol that fired the Fraher shell furnished most persuasive evidence that the two shells were fired from the same pistol. This conclusion was communicated by the experts to Morgan and is mentioned by him in a chapter note.[3]

In 1935 the Gunthers published a book, *The Identification of Firearms from Ammunition Fired Therein,* in which they review the expert testimony in the Sacco-Vanzetti case, concluding that the expert evidence at the trial was worthless and misleading and that Hamilton's expert testimony created a suspicion of charlatanism and of trifling with the truth.[4]

DR. MAGRATH

Dr. George Burgess Magrath delivered the Lowell Lectures in 1932 on the subject "Law and Medicine." I am told that he included a discussion of the ballistics evidence in the Sacco-Vanzetti case, but diligent inquiry has revealed no copy of the report of the lectures. The following passage from a letter dated January 9, 1953, from a Worcester doctor to Bill Cunningham of the *Boston Herald* may refer to the same discussion.

> Dr. George Burgess Magrath, Suffolk medical examiner, was my instructor in pathology many years ago. Some time in the '20's he got up a talk for an Annual Meeting of the Mass. Med. Society, entitled "Stiffs I have Met"; after a few years he eliminated some of the more gruesome details and gave it to lay audiences. One slide showed a photomicrograph of the butt ends of two bullets, "one taken from the body of a murdered man, the other fired from a suspect's pistol; they are, very evidently, identical." They were presented thus impersonally; only a few of his professional colleagues knew the truth. But it was Dr. Magrath's opinion that the ballistic testimony at the S-V trial had been bungled. So, when he came here to talk a few weeks after Judge Thayer's

3 Morgan, *op. cit.,* p. 537.
4 Morgan, *op. cit.,* p. 175.

home was bombed, he consented to call names, and pointed them out as having come, one from the body of Berardelli, and the other from Sacco's pistol; the demonstration was very convincing.

AFTER THE MURDER a cap was found near Berardelli's body. The Commonwealth claimed that, if the cap found near the body belonged to Sacco, it could not have been found there unless Sacco lost it at the time of the shooting.

Eyewitnesses for the Commonwealth testified that, when the man they identified as Sacco went away from the scene of the murder car, he was bareheaded; several witnesses for the defendants testified that, although the man whom the Commonwealth's witnesses identified as Sacco was not in their judgment Sacco, yet the same person, whoever he was, was bareheaded; and Mrs. Berardelli testified that the cap did not belong to her husband, who at the time of the murder wore a dark, soft hat. (5555)

Fred L. Loring, a shoe worker employed by Slater & Morrill, heard the shooting and went to the scene of the murder. Parmenter's body had been removed, but the body of Berardelli was lying where he had fallen. Loring picked up a cap, about eighteen inches from Berardelli, which he carried down to the shop, kept for about an hour, and then gave to Fraher, his superintendent. Loring on the stand was shown a cap which he identified as the one he had picked up. He testified that it was in the same condition then as when he found it. (798)

No attempt was made at the trial to trace the Loring cap from Fraher to the courtroom. Fraher, as we have seen, handed the shells which bear his name to Captain Proctor of the State Police, and it would be a fair assumption that he did the same thing with the cap. The defense did not ask Fraher or Proctor about this, and it was not until 1927, when the case was before the Governor and the Advisory Committee, that ex-Chief Jeremiah F. Gallivan of the Braintree police came forward with the story that Fraher had handed the cap to him on Saturday, April 17, 1920, *two* days after the murder, as one picked up the previous night; that he (Gallivan) tore the lining, and that he had carried the cap around in his automobile for one or two weeks before giving it to the State Police. For reasons to be stated later, I find this story unconvincing and am of the opinion that the Loring cap was never in the possession of Chief Gallivan.

On May 6, 1920, Lieutenant Daniel T. Guerin of the Brockton Police Department went to Sacco's house and found in a kitchen a cap which he said, when shown it on the stand, was then in the same condition as when he took it. (2093, 1852) After an initial denial, Sacco testified that he thought this cap was his, and thereafter it seems to have been taken for granted that the Guerin cap had come from Sacco's kitchen and belonged to him.

The cap found at the scene (the Loring cap) was admitted in evidence upon identification by George T. Kelley, Sacco's employer, as a cap in general appearance and color like one he had seen Sacco wearing.

Late in the trial Kelley was recalled as a defense witness and shown the Loring cap and the Guerin cap. He testified that the Guerin cap looked more like the one that Sacco wore than the Loring cap. This weakened Kelley's previous identification of the cap and led to cross-examination by Katzmann in which Kelley admitted that, during a conversation with Stewart and Brouillard about a week before the trial, he had been shown the Loring cap. The police officers had then asked him: "Is that Sacco's cap?" and he had said: "I have my opinion about that cap, but I don't want to get a bomb up my ass." (2009-2010)

Sacco and his wife both denied that the Loring cap belonged to him, and Sacco claimed that it did not fit him. (2065, 5555)

This was the extent of the identification of the cap by witnesses, and on paper Kelley's testimony is not impressive unless we give weight to the fear implied in what he said to the police officers, which apparently caused him to change his positive identification to them before the trial to a reluctant and rather indefinite one on the stand.

THE HOLE IN THE LINING

It was Sacco's habit to hang his cap near his workbench on a nail which he had put there himself, and it appeared that there was a tear or "hole" in both the Loring cap and the Guerin cap which the Commonwealth argued was caused by the nail. No explanation of the tear in the Loring cap was offered by the defense until 1927, when the Gallivan account was introduced before the Advisory Committee. At the close of the examination of Kelley, Jeremiah J. McAnarney asked the jury to consider whether the hole was made by hanging on a nail or otherwise. (2014)

It is impossible to know how much weight if any the jury gave to the hole and the nail. Katzmann, in his argument to the jury, did not mention them, nor did Judge Thayer in his charge. In Thayer's mentions of the cap after the trial he mentions the holes and the nail twice, once in his decision on the motion for a new trial based on the weight of the evidence and once in his review of the conspiracy charge made by Thompson. (5555, 47-65) In both cases he states the evidence as a claim by the Commonwealth and not as anything he himself relied upon.

DID THE CAP FIT?

When Sacco was on the stand he was asked to try the Loring and the Guerin caps on. His first attempts with each cap seem to have caused merriment in the courtroom. The *Boston Post* of July 7 and July 8, 1921, carried cartoons showing how much too small the cap was and how the spectators laughed when Sacco tried it on. A similar cartoon was in the *Boston Herald,* and the newspaper accounts refer at that time to the giggling that took place in the courtroom when Sacco put the Loring cap on.

In the Simmons interview, juror Atwood, after calling the

obsolete-bullet evidence the outstanding evidence in his mind, went on to say that he also recalled Sacco's manner in the cap fitting as important. "He thought Sacco's attitude when asked to try on the cap found at the scene was peculiar, it being the juror's opinion the defendant was determined not to put on the cap in normal fashion because he kept pulling it down virtually over his ears." This was the only mention of the cap in the Simmons interviews.

Katzmann devoted several paragraphs to Sacco's cap, arguing to the jury that if the Loring cap was Sacco's it was

> absolutely condemnatory of this defendant. No, not abso-lutely, but it clinches on the top of all the other circum-stances. Some one of you who wears a 7 1/8 . . . try them both on. There is the acid test for you, gentlemen. Don't take anybody's word. . . . Try the caps on yourself, and if they are not identically of the same size, then so find, so find, gentlemen." (2210-2211)

Neither defense lawyer mentioned Sacco's cap in his argument. This is most significant, for from this failure we may infer that the cap fitted, or at least that the failure to fit was not ludicrous; if the misfit had been a giggling matter the argument would have been made to order.

BEFORE THE GOVERNOR AND THE ADVISORY COMMITTEE

Moore in his posttrial maneuvers made no attempt to break down the evidence about Sacco's cap, nor did Thompson until the case reached the Governor.

By that time George T. Kelley was dead, (5229) and any iden-tification of Sacco's cap he might have made in a private inter-view without fear of a bomb explosion was unavailable. The cap was, however, still a clinching item of evidence which may or may not have been mentioned by the jurors to the Governor or the committee in the interviews.

The Governor does not mention the cap in his decision.

JEREMIAH F. GALLIVAN

On July 15, 1927, Jeremiah F. Gallivan, ex-Chief of Police of Braintree, who had been Chief in 1920, appeared before the Advisory Committee at the request of Thompson. Gallivan had just come from the Governor's office. This is his story about the cap:

On Saturday morning, April 17, 1920, *two* days after the murder, Fraher called him on the telephone and asked him to come to the factory. There Fraher handed him a cap and said:

> "Jerry, here's a cap that was picked up there, last night, last evening, but I don't know whether it amounts to anything or not, but I thought you better keep it here."
>
> "So [said Gallivan], I took the cap and looked at it, and if you were to put the cap before me now I wouldn't know it; I haven't seen that cap for seven years. I took it and looked at it and I took it with me in my automobile. Have in mind we had no police headquarters there at that time; my headquarters then was in my house or in any officer's house.
>
> "I took that cap, not knowing whether it was going to amount to anything or not. I took it and I says, 'I may find a name or something inside this cap. . . .'
>
> "I took that cap and made it as small as I could and pulled the inside out, but I couldn't make much headway with it, so I took and ripped that lining right down myself, but there was nothing inside there.
>
> "No, not the whole lining, but I tore that, and I think you will find a tear in that lining yet. I haven't seen it for seven years. That cap was whole when it was given to me, but I am the fellow that tore it. I took and kept it in my automobile; there was no other place to keep it as we had no headquarters. Finally I turned it over, possibly about ten days or two weeks after. I turned that hat over to John Scott [of the State Police]." (5169-5170)

Gallivan then said that the next time he saw the cap was in Dedham Court, when the cap was handed to Tom Fraher.[1] (5171)

On cross-examination it developed that Gallivan had never told Katzmann or Williams about the cap. He said that he did tell Scott about the lining. (5182)

Ranney, continuing his cross-examination, demolished this preposterous story by one question:

"You knew that the change in the condition of something that had been found as far as you knew near the scene of the murder was a very serious matter?"

"No, sir, I did not." [2] (5182)

Katzmann had agreed to permit Thompson to cross-examine him before the Committee, and on July 14, 1927, he told Thompson that he had never heard that Gallivan had carried the cap around in his automobile for a week or two or that he tore the lining himself. "If I had known that there had been a tear inside of it caused by some police officer, that would have been explained to the jury. Your statement in your question is the first time I ever heard of it." (5077)

FRANKFURTER AND WIGMORE ON SACCO'S CAP

In the March 1927 issue of *The Atlantic Monthly*, Frankfurter published an article about the Sacco-Vanzetti case aimed, he said, "to give in the briefest compass an accurate résumé of the facts of the case," and ending with the allegation that "the reader has now had placed before him fairly, however briefly, the means of forming a judgment." *This article did not say a word about Sacco's cap.*

When Dean John H. Wigmore in his review of the article called attention to this suppression of the evidence, Frankfurter's

---

1 Gallivan or the record is mistaken about this: there is nothing in the latter to show that the cap was shown to Fraher.

2 An affidavit was prepared for Gallivan to execute on August 5, 1927, but for some reason not explained he did not sign or swear to it. It was, however, attached to the Petitioners' substitute bill of exception filed in connection with the writ of error filed August 6, 1927, as "an unsigned document purporting to be an affidavit," and called an offer of proof. (5417; 5379)

retort was that, although he had not mentioned the cap in the article, he did mention it in his book, also published in March 1927, and Wigmore should not have charged him with suppression of evidence in the article when the evidence had been mentioned in the book. It does not appear that Frankfurter corrected the article in the *Atlantic* itself, and readers of the article who did not see the book may never have known about Sacco's cap. Moreover, the only reference to the cap in the book is in a footnote which has a bare mention, without discussion, of "two other items of evidence, relied on by the Commonwealth, which seem too insignificant for detailed attention." The other "insignificant" item is Berardelli's gun.[3]

It is unfortunate that Wigmore did not know enough about the case to mention other significant omissions made in the Frankfurter article *and* book, the most significant being his failure to make any mention of the obsolete-bullet evidence. But the transcript had not then been published, and Wigmore had to rely on incomplete reports.

SACCO'S HAIR

From two sources, Stewart and G. Andrews Moriarty, a friend of Dr. George Burgess Magrath, medical examiner for Suffolk County at the time of the trial, the following off-the-record story has come to me. During the trial, Stewart and Magrath decided to make an experiment. Stewart obtained for Magrath several hairs from Sacco's cap and several hairs from the comb Sacco was using in the jail. Magrath put these hairs on slides and looked at them through a microscope. They were identical, and both Stewart and Magrath suggested to Katzmann that he use the evidence, which certainly would have been conclusive so far as the cap was concerned.

Katzmann was tempted, but he finally decided against it, because he believed that the defense and the newspapers might ridicule an attempt to hang the defendants by a hair or make some other pun on this much-punished word.

[3] Frankfurter, *op. cit.,* p. 32 fn.

BERARDELLI'S GUN

WHEN the arrest was made on the streetcar, police officer Earl J. Vaughn searched Vanzetti and took from his hip pocket a five-shot Harrington & Richardson 38-caliber revolver fully loaded. This was handed to officer Michael J. Connolly and by him marked with a knife cut in the handle. At the trial, Connolly identified it and it was admitted as Exhibit 27. (757) During Captain Proctor's examination the five bullets in the revolver, two Remington and three U.S., became Exhibit 32. (889) This revolver and the five bullets were handed by Connolly to State Police officer John Scott in the presence of Captain Proctor on May 6, 1920, and remained in the custody of the State Police until the trial.

No claim was ever made that any of these exhibits was false. This revolver was not used in the murders, but since it was of the same make and caliber as the revolver customarily carried by Berardelli, and since his revolver was not found on his person or at the murder scene, the Commonwealth asked the jury to infer that it had been taken from his person during the shooting and carried away by some member of the murder party and that it eventually came into the possession of Vanzetti. There was no claim that Vanzetti had himself taken the gun or had done any of the shooting.

In the evening of the day after the arrest, Katzmann showed the revolver to Vanzetti and asked him about it. Vanzetti said that he had bought it four or five years before on Hanover Street for eighteen or nineteen dollars but could not remember the name of the store. He had bought it under a false name because he was scared to use his own, but he did not remember what name he used. At the same time he had bought a full box of cartridges, unopened, and had never bought any more. He had thrown the box away when only *six* cartridges remained, and these he had put in the revolver. (1748-1751)

This was not a very good story and it was abandoned on the witness stand. Eighteen dollars was too much to pay for a five-dollar revolver; six cartridges were too many for a five-shot gun, and the cartridges in the gun did not come out of one box—two were Remington and three were U.S. (889, 1801)

So at the trial Vanzetti said that a few months before the arrest he had paid five dollars for a fully loaded gun at Luigi Falzini's house, (1715) and Falzini testified he, Falzini, had bought it from Orciani in October 1919 and sold it to Vanzetti in January or February 1920. (1630) Vanzetti had never fired the revolver. (1800) He carried it because times were bad and he sometimes had money on his person.

Orciani, who had been in and around the courthouse during the trial and was on the payroll of the Sacco-Vanzetti Defense Committee, was not called as a witness. Obviously, affirmative testimony from him about the sale to Falzini in October 1919 would have been relevant and corroborative. The failure of the defense to call Orciani was commented upon by Katzmann in his argument, who said that the Commonwealth has a right to draw the inference that if Orciani had been produced his testimony would be against the interests of the defendants. (2233)

Miss Margaret Mahoney, paymaster for Slater & Morrill, testified that Berardelli customarily carried a shiny, bright-looking revolver and that she had once seen him take it out of his trousers pocket. On another occasion she had seen him take it from his overcoat and put it in his trousers pocket. (169-170)

James F. Bostock testified that on the Saturday night before the murder he had seen the gun in Berardelli's possession and identified it as similar to the one exhibited to him in court. He had seen Berardelli a number of times with the gun. The gun was a .38-caliber, nickel-plated revolver. (196-200)

Mrs. Berardelli, the widow, testified that Berardelli always carried a gun when on duty as a guard and thought that Exhibit 27 was his gun. She had gone with him about three weeks before the shooting to the Iver-Johnson Company in Boston to have it repaired and thought it was a spring that was broken. He left the gun at the store and later gave the check to Parmenter. While the gun was in Boston, Parmenter let him have another one. (806-809)

Lincoln Wadsworth, an employee of Iver-Johnson, testified that on March 20, 1920, a .38 Harrington & Richardson revolver, property of Alex Berardelli, was brought in for repairs and sent up to the shop on the same day. (814) He testified that Exhibit 27 was of the same description as the gun left for repairs. (816)

It has often been stated that after the trial Wadsworth repudiated his testimony. This is not so. On July 20, 1927, he appeared before the Advisory Committee and told them he was afraid that at the trial he had created the impression that he was identifying the pistol he saw in court as the pistol that came into the shop. He did not want to change his testimony, he said; it was all right as far as it went, but there were thousands of that same, identical revolver, and the possibility that the pistol he saw was the one brought to the shop was very slight. Wadsworth's conscience should not have bothered him: at the trial he had only said that Exhibit 27 was of the same description as the gun left for repairs. (816)

George F. Fitzmeyer, foreman of the repair shop at Iver-Johnson, testified that on a date between March 19 and March 22, 1920, the repair shop had repaired the revolver with the repair number 94765, entering it as a .32 Harrington & Richardson, "new hammer and repairs, half an hour." He was not sure about the caliber; the .38 is a five shot, the .32 is a six shot, and the frames are the same size. Vanzetti's gun (Exhibit 27) was shown to the witness and he testified that it had a new hammer because the firing pin showed no powder mark. (816-823)

James H. Jones, manager of the firearms department of Iver-Johnson, testified that the revolver concerned in repair job No. 94765 had been redelivered. The store kept no records of deliveries of repair jobs, but if they were not called for within a certain time they were sold and a record made of the sale. The revolver was not in the store and it had not been sold. So the witness testified it had been redelivered. (822-835)

From one of the defense witnesses, Peter McCullum, the Commonwealth elicited a description of the shooting which corroborated its theory that a gun had been taken from Berardelli by the man who shot him. McCullum was a shoe cutter in Rice & Hutchins. Looking out from his window on the second story, he saw a man with a bright nickel gun in his left hand putting a box into the automobile with his right hand. Katzmann's argument was that Sacco, after shooting Berardelli, had put his own pistol in his pocket, because he had to use his right hand to put the box into the automobile, and had kept in his left hand the gun he had just taken from the dying Berardelli. (1149, 2184)

The defense offered two witnesses to prove that the gun found on Vanzetti's person at the time of the arrest had belonged to a man named Mogridge, in Dexter, Maine, and had been brought by Mrs. Mogridge several years before to Norwood, Massachusetts, where it was sold by her son-in-law to a fellow employee, Ricardo Orciani, for four dollars. This sale was in the late fall of 1919. Falzini testified that he had bought it from Orciani in October 1919, and sold it to Vanzetti in January or February 1920. (1556-1568; 1629-1634; 1635-1644)

Jeremiah J. McAnarney in his argument asked the jury to believe the two witnesses from Maine and also to consider the improbability of Vanzetti's discarding a powerful Savage revolver "with which they say he was shooting, going in and getting and carrying around this branded gun in his pocket to help identify him. An old obsolete revolver sixteen or eighteen years old, and giving away a good one that was a gun." (1269) To this last-mentioned argument, Katzmann made the obvious reply that the Commonwealth did not claim that Vanzetti did any of the shooting or ever had the Savage revolver from which five of the six bullets found in the bodies were fired. (2184)

After the trial the ever-helpful Hamilton was of the opinion that the hammer was not a new one because the screw holding the hammer in place showed no scratches "such as would ordinarily accompany and be the result of removal"; (3613) but Judge Thayer did not think much of this point; maybe a new screw had been used. (3722)

The Governor did not mention Berardelli's gun in his decision. Newspaper clippings reveal that he interviewed some of the witnesses named above, including the two who told about the Mogridge gun and also Burns, Fitzgerald, and Hamilton.

The Advisory Committee had this to say in its statement of the evidence of Vanzetti's guilt:

> Then there is the fact that a pistol that Berardelli had been in the habit of carrying, and which there is no sufficient reason to suppose was not in his possession at the time of the murder, disappeared and a pistol of the same kind was found in the possession of Vanzetti when he and Sacco were arrested together, and of which no satisfactory explanation is given. It is difficult to suppose that Berardelli was not carrying his pistol at the time he was guarding the paymaster with the payroll, and no pistol was found upon his person after his death. It is natural also, if the bandits saw his pistol they should carry it off for fear of someone shooting at them as they escaped. (5378W)

And again:

> His having a pistol resembling the one formerly possessed by Berardelli has some importance, and the fact that no cartridges for it were found in his possession, except those in it, is significant. (5378Y)

THE Commonwealth claimed that the actions, conduct, and speech of the defendants on the night of May 5, 1920, and at other times indicated that in their minds they were then conscious of having committed the crime of murder. The defendants claimed that they were consciously guilty only of being slackers and radicals liable to be deported, fearing punishment therefor, and were not consciously guilty of murder.

The salient part of the testimony which had a relation to this question was the behavior of the defendants at the Johnson home, their behavior on the streetcar, and the admittedly false statements made to Stewart and Katzmann.

AT THE JOHNSON HOUSE

In the afternoon of May 5, 1920, Boda, Orciani, Sacco, and Vanzetti were at Sacco's house in Stoughton. During the evening they all went from Stoughton to the Johnson house in West Bridgewater, where Boda asked for his car, which had been brought for repairs to the Johnson garage on April 19. Boda and Orciani went by motorcycle, Sacco and Vanzetti by streetcar. They boarded the streetcar at 7:20 P.M. near Sacco's home. They left this car at Main Street, Brockton, and after a delay for coffee they took a streetcar headed for Bridgewater and got off at Elm Square, West Bridgewater. They found no one there and after a few minutes they started walking back toward Brockton. After a little while they saw the light of a motorcycle on the street and found Orciani beside it. They asked him whether Boda had got his car. Boda at this time was talking with Johnson at the door of Johnson's house, which was near the place where Orciani, Sacco, and Vanzetti were standing.

From this point the account given by Sacco and Vanzetti on the stand differs from the testimony of Mrs. Johnson.

Sacco and Vanzetti said that shortly after their arrival at the motorcycle, Boda came back from the door and told them that they could not get the car because it had no 1920 number plates. Thereupon, said they, Boda and Orciani rode away on the motorcycle and Sacco and Vanzetti walked along the street to a car stop, where they took a streetcar going toward Brockton (and Stoughton). Upon this streetcar, they were arrested. While they were standing near the motorcycle, a woman, apparently Mrs. Johnson, had come along the road *from* the direction of Brockton and entered the Johnson house.

Mrs. Johnson testified that about 9:20 she heard a knock at the door. After a conversation with her husband, who had gone to bed, she went to the door. At first she saw no one, then she saw Boda coming toward her. She told Boda that her husband would be right out and said to him, "I will get the baby's milk." At that time she saw two other men (Sacco and Vanzetti) coming over the bridge from the direction of Elm Square. She then left her house and walked along the left-hand side of the car track in the direction of Brockton to the Bartlett home next door. The two men she had seen coming over the bridge walked along with her on her right-hand side in the same direction. She went into the Bartlett house and telephoned to the West Bridgewater police. While in the neighbor's house she saw the motorcycle light flashing back and forth. After her telephone call, which took about ten minutes, she came out, and as she was returning to her home the same two men walked back along the car track. She saw the two men stop at the motorcycle. Sacco (who was shown to her at Brockton, May 6) was one of these men. She went into the house and did not see what occurred outside thereafter. There were telephone wires connected with the Bartlett house which could be seen from the street, but Vanzetti and Sacco swore they did not see them.

Thayer in his charge has this to say:

> The defendants say first, that they did not follow Mrs. Johnson over to the Bartlett house and secondly, that they left without taking the Overland automobile because there were no number plates on it. . . . The Commonwealth claims that they left because of a consciousness of what happened at the Bartlett place.

Here were questions of fact for the jury which we are in no position to decide from the printed record. If we believe Sacco and Vanzetti, they did not follow Mrs. Johnson to the Bartlett house or see her enter it or leave it—all they saw was a woman coming along the road from the direction of Brockton who entered the Johnson house. If we believe Mrs. Johnson, they did show interest in her visit to the Bartlett house and may have guessed that its purpose was to bring the police to the house or to pick them up in the automobile if they took it. Innocent men would have feared neither. The fact that they both denied the visit entirely when they were questioned by Katzmann showed that they were concerned about what happened there.

ON THE STREETCAR

Michael J. Connolly, a Brockton policeman, was stationed at Campello on the evening of May 5, 1920. At 9:57 he received a telephone call from the central station. Thereupon he put on his hat and coat and went out to meet the streetcar from Bridgewater, which he boarded at Keith's Theater in Campello a few minutes later. He entered the car at the front end and, looking down, he saw Sacco and Vanzetti sitting on the end seat, Vanzetti on the inside toward the window. When he got opposite to this seat Connolly stopped and asked them where they came from. They said, "Bridgewater."

Connolly said, "What was you doing in Bridgewater?"

They said, "We went down to see a friend of mine."

I said, "Who is your friend?"

Vanzetti said, "A man by the—they call him 'Poppy.' "

Connolly said, "Well, I want you. You are under arrest."

Vanzetti then put his hand in his hip pocket.

Connolly said, "Keep your hands out on your lap or you will be sorry." (752)

When Connolly testified to this at the Dedham trial, Vanzetti called out in the courtroom: "You are a liar!"

They wanted to know what they were arrested for and Connolly said, "Suspicious characters."

After a ride of about three minutes, the streetcar met an automobile coming from the central station and another Brockton police officer, Earl J. Vaughn, got on the streetcar. Connolly told the two men to stand up. He gave Sacco a slight going over but did not go into his pockets. Vaughn frisked Vanzetti and found a fully loaded revolver in his left hip pocket. The two policemen led Sacco and Vanzetti out the front door of the car. There, Vaughn handed Vanzetti's revolver to Connolly, who "used it on the men to the station."

Connolly put Sacco and Vanzetti in the back seat of the police automobile, a Dodge touring car, and officer Snow got in the back seat with them. Connolly took the front seat with the driver, turned around, and faced Sacco and Vanzetti.

"I told them when we started that the first false move I would put a bullet in them.

"On the way up to the station Sacco reached his hand to put under his overcoat and I told him to keep his hands outside of his clothes and on his lap."

Connolly said, "Have you got a gun there?"

Sacco replied, "I ain't got no gun."

Connolly said, "Well, keep your hands outside of your clothes."

"We went along a little further," Connolly further testified, "and he done the same thing. I gets up on my knees on the front seat and I reaches over and I put my hand under his coat but I did not see any gun. 'Now,' I says, 'Mister, if you put your hand in there again you are going to get into trouble.' "

Sacco said, "I don't want no trouble." (752-753)

Connolly's testimony about the menacing gestures was corroborated in part by another Brockton police officer, Merle A. Spear, who boarded the car en route to the police station, but was denied by Sacco and Vanzetti. (779) This gave to the jury another question of veracity and to us another question we cannot answer from the printed record.

THE FALSEHOODS

Untruths told upon arrest are evidence of consciousness of guilt and can be used against a defendant when such consciousness relates to the crime with which he is charged. This rule, like so many rules of law, is based on common sense and is universally accepted.

It would be tedious to list all the falsehoods which the defendants told Katzmann when he interrogated them on May 6, 1920, and it would be unnecessary, because everyone admits that their answers were a tissue of lies from beginning to end. The only dispute about the lies concerns the reason for them—was it to conceal radical literature and draft dodging, or murder and robbery? A few examples will suffice.

VANZETTI'S FALSEHOODS

Vanzetti's falsehoods about the purchase of the revolver found on his person and the cartridges in it are discussed in Chapter 12. At the trial, Katzmann asked him whether there was any reason "connected with collecting literature that made you say on May 6 to me that the revolver cost you nineteen dollars, when it cost you only five, as you now say." Vanzetti answered, "No, there is no reason."

On May 6, Katzmann asked when Vanzetti left Plymouth (the last time before the arrest), and Vanzetti answered, "Sunday morning."

At the trial, Vanzetti admitted it was Saturday, not Sunday morning, and could give no reason for deceiving Katzmann about this. (1754)

On May 6, Vanzetti told Katzmann that he did not know Boda, did not know that name, never saw Mike Boda in his life. At the trial he acknowledged that these answers were false and could not explain why he pretended not to know Boda. (1764)

On May 6, Vanzetti denied that he had seen or talked with a man sitting on a motorcycle when he walked by to get the street-car, or with any man at all on a motorcycle on May 5, or that he saw a motorcycle in Sacco's yard on Monday, Tuesday, or Wednesday. (1787)

At the trial he acknowledged that all these denials were false.

On May 6, when asked whether he had worked every day in April, the month before, Vanzetti said, "Yes, I think almost every-day I peddle fish." (1791)

But at the trial he testified that he did not peddle any fish after April 15 and was away from Plymouth—in New York, Hyde Park, and Boston—several days. (1791)

SACCO'S FALSEHOODS

Katzmann on May 5 at Brockton asked Sacco, "Do you know Alessandro Berardelli?" and Sacco said, "No, who is this Berardelli?" (1898)

At the trial Katzmann faced him with this denial and asked whether Sacco on April 16 or 17, 1920, had learned from reading the newspapers that a man named Berardelli had been shot at South Braintree. Sacco answered, "Yes, sir." (1894)

To me, this falsehood, which could have no conceivable relation to the radical literature or the draft dodging, is most significant. Sacco testified that he read two papers everyday, the *Boston Globe* and the *Boston American,* that he was living within a few miles of the crime, which must have been the chief subject of conversa-tion for days, and that he had talked with his friends about it the morning after the crime. To deny, three weeks afterwards, any knowledge of Berardelli's name was an obvious falsehood and showed a concern about the murder which cannot be satisfactorily explained by any other concern he might have had.

Sacco's falsehoods about the pistol and the bullets found on his person at the time of the arrest are discussed in Chapter 10. At the trial he acknowledged that all his answers at Brockton were false, and he was not able to tell Katzmann what this effort to deceive had to do with the radical literature or the draft dodging.

At Brockton on May 6 Katzmann asked, "Didn't you see this lady [Mrs. Johnson] and walk along the street and walk back when she walked back last night?", and Sacco answered, "No, sir, we walk about an hour and we didn't see anything." (1908)

Mrs. Johnson on May 6 sat for a while in the same room with Katzmann and Sacco. After she left, this colloquy occurred:

> KATZMANN: This woman that was sitting in here says you followed her across the street last night when she went to a neighbor's house and that you walked up and down and that she knows you. Why don't you tell the truth?
> SACCO: That is not true.
> KATZMANN: This woman never saw you before, why should she lie about you?
> SACCO: Well, maybe somebody else and she wants to blame me.

But at Dedham, Katzmann asked, "Was it somebody else that was there or was it yourself?" and Sacco answered, "That was myself." (1908-1909)

At Brockton, Katzmann asked Sacco if he had ever worked in Braintree and Sacco falsely said No.

Asked by Katzmann at Brockton whether he ever knew Mike Boda, Sacco said: "No, sir, I never heard of him. No. I never heard his name before. I don't even think it is an Italian name. I never heard that name." (1916)

Later he denied that he had ever gone to Ricardo's (Orciani's) house in Hyde Park and also denied that Orciani knew Vanzetti.

These two answers were false, and Sacco had to squirm a good deal to justify them as efforts to protect Orciani and Vanzetti from arrest when, at the very moment, both of them were under arrest in the same building in which he was being interrogated. (1912)

But the most significant falsehood told by Sacco was the one which made his alibi incredible. On May 6, Katzmann asked him whether he was working all day the day before he read about the murder in the *Boston Post,* and he answered, "Sure." At the trial Sacco acknowledged that this was a lie. (1948)

Here we find a lie about April 15, 1920, which could not possibly have anything to do with draft dodging or radicalism but had everything to do with murders that had occurred on a date exactly three weeks before Katzmann asked the question.

14   VANZETTI'S ALIBI AT DEDHAM

Vanzetti's own alibi testimony was substantially as follows. He had bought a pushcart and a knife in the spring of 1919 and had been peddling fish for three or four months in the fall until Christmas, then was otherwise employed in Plymouth at several jobs until about the middle of March 1920. At this time he took up fish peddling again, getting some of his fish by express from Boston and at other times in Plymouth from Antonio Carbone, who brought fish from Boston in his own truck or by express. An express receipt, dated April 8 (Thursday), 1920, showing a shipment of 488 pounds to Vanzetti was produced, and Vanzetti testified that he had bought other fish from Carbone after April 8, he thought on the thirteenth, but no document about this was produced. After April 8 he peddled just one week, ending on Thursday, April 15. It took three days to peddle the 488 pounds. He did not say which days of that week they were, except that April 15 was one of them.

(To corroborate Vanzetti's testimony about the fish, Carbone, the Plymouth fish dealer, testified about sales of fish to Vanzetti at about this time, and Salvatore Bova, a Boston fish dealer, told of sales to Carbone, but neither testified about seeing Vanzetti on April 15, and Bova did not know what Carbone did with the fish he bought.)

On the morning of the fifteenth, Vanzetti had a few, not very many, fish left, and he peddled on Cherry Street, Standish Avenue, and Cherry Court, down Suasso's Lane, where he reached Court Street, from which he turned south toward Plymouth, intending to go onto Castle Street. At the corner of Castle Street he met Joseph Rosen, a Dorchester man who went round the state selling cloths. Rosen stopped him and tried to sell him a piece of cloth. Vanzetti told Rosen that he did not know anything about cloth, and brought him to the Brini house. He knew that Mrs. Brini was in the house and that she worked in the woolen mill and "she knew the cloth."

Mrs. Brini looked at the cloth, and afterward Vanzetti bought it for about $12.75. This was "near one o'clock, about half-past eleven, something like that, half-past twelve, about one o'clock." Later he fixed the time as after twelve but nearer one, because it was the dinner hour and he saw the people going back to work at the Cordage. Still later he said that he was in the Brini home at 12:13 and stayed there ten or fifteen minutes.

Then Vanzetti went to Castle Street and finished selling his fish. He then left his cart in Castle Street and went down to Ocean Street on the shore, where he saw Melvin Corl in his boat, painting it. Here he talked with Corl more than an hour while Corl kept on painting. Two men came along, Frank Jesse, a boatbuilder in Seaside (the name of this part of Plymouth), and Mr. Holmes, who worked in the lumberyard. After he left Corl at the boat, Vanzetti went back and took the cart up the street to the yard of Fortini, with whom he boarded. After changing his clothes, he ate supper about 6:00 o'clock. He stayed in Plymouth that night and went clam digging the next day, April 16 (Friday).

Five witnesses testified that they had seen Vanzetti in Plymouth on April 15. The first of these, Rosen, had testified before Vanzetti took the stand, and this is his story as nearly as I can gather it from his confused and contradictory account:

On April 15, 1920, he rose early, left without his breakfast, and was on the 6:37 train to Plymouth. He told his wife that the poll-tax collector would call (she always had money), and the receipt that he found the next day, dated April 15, made him remember that that was the day he went to Plymouth. (Before the Advisory

Committee, the tax bill had become the gas bill, and he had left her the money.) The train brought him to Plymouth at 7:50, and he went to the Ventura restaurant in the center of town for breakfast.

After breakfast he took a streetcar, at a time he could not remember, to Seaside, where he arrived at 9:30. Then he went to work. He had with him a valise and a handful of men's suitings in his right hand and another valise in his left hand with samples in it. At about 10:15 he sold a Greek in the Greek's ice-cream parlor, a ten-minute sale, and he was out of the store at about 10:25. (The Greek did not testify.) Rosen walked two blocks and then took a rest in the street, sitting on his valise. He did not want to rest in the store because he did not want to be in the way. At about 11:00 he met a milkman and made a five-minute sale. He knew this milkman and had been in his house. (The milkman did not testify.)

At exactly 12:00 noon (11:30 A.M. at the Advisory Committee hearing) he saw Vanzetti at the corner of Castle and Main in the Seaside section. The Cordage whistle was blowing and people were going home to get their dinner. Vanzetti was in the street with a pushcart of fish. Rosen tried to sell him a piece of material, and Vanzetti and he walked two blocks from the corner to a house to show the material to Mrs. Brini who, as an employee of the Puritan Mills, knew about woolens. Vanzetti and Mrs. Brini talked in Italian, which Rosen did not understand, After the talk they came out and Vanzetti and Rosen went back to the pushcart, where a five- or ten-minute sale was made. After this, at about 12:30, Rosen went away from the corner and across a big vacant lot to get his dinner from a friend, a customer whose name he did not know but whom he knew on sight.

In the afternoon Rosen stayed in Plymouth. At 3:00 P.M. he sold a piece of goods to a man in Middle Street whose name he did not know; then he went to the house of the Chief of Police and at 3:30 made a two-minute sale to the wife, who was doing her washing. He then went next door and made a sale to a tall blonde woman who owned a piece of antique furniture. At some point he went back to the Ventura restaurant for a light lunch. He had fifteen minutes to catch the 3:45 train, and it was a three-minute walk, but he did not want to kill himself hurrying with forty pounds of valise. He didn't care whether he missed it, and he did miss it. From 3:45 to 6:10 he hung around town, took a walk, wrote a post card.

At 6:10 he took the train to Whitman, arriving at 6:50, ate in the railroad restaurant, and stayed there three quarters of an hour. He then went to the Littlefield lodging house across the street, got a one-dollar room, was shown to it by a woman, and spent the night there. (The waitress at Littlefield's, Lillian Shuler, testified, with the aid of a daily memorandum she kept, that a room had been rented on April 15, but she did not know to whom. She was not asked to identify Rosen, nor did Rosen identify her. Before the Advisory Committee, Rosen told how he had registered: "I put down my name and my address, according to my best recollection, which I proved to District Attorney Katzmann," but the register was never produced.)

At Whitman the whole town was excited about the South Braintree murder, and Rosen talked about it in the restaurant. That was what reminded him that on April 15 he had been in Plymouth, that and the tax receipt his wife gave him the next day.

Rosen appeared on July 21, 1927, before the Advisory Committee and told them that he thought Katzmann's cross-examination of him had been unfair, "about five or six hours" in the afternoon trying to catch him. He retold his story with variations. The committee was not impressed, and in its report said it seemed to them that the cross-examination at the trial had shown him to be lying.

Rosen's story might have been more convincing if one could find out what it was. Keeping him to the point was, to use a Down East expression, like nailing a jellyfish to the wall. A fatal defect in it is lack of corroboration from anyone except the two Brinis and Vanzetti. The Greek, the milkman, the anonymous friend with whom he dined, the staff in the twice-visited Ventura restaurant, the Middle Street customer, the wife of the Chief of Police, the tall blonde woman, the people he talked with in Whitman about the murder, the woman who showed him his room, his own wife—none of these was called.

The Brinis, mother and daughter, rehearsed their story many times together, and so may be considered together. From them we learn that Mrs. Brini had been ill in the hospital but had come home on April 8. The daughter, LeFavre Brini, fifteen years old at the time of the trial, had quit work to tend her. (Her first testimony was that she was working until noon on April 15, but she later said this was a mistake.) The daughter's testimony showed a visit to the house by a Cordage Company nurse at 9:30 on April 15, 1920. (A Cordage nurse testified that she did make several calls on Mrs. Brini during a period from April 15 to April 25, but she could not recall specific dates.)

At 10:00 or 10:30, Vanzetti brought a fish to the Brini house. The mother was not there, having gone to Mrs. Forni's house. (This was Eva Forni, not the Rose Forni who testified in the Bridgewater case.) Vanzetti put the fish in the sink and then "chased" LeFavre over to Mrs. Forni's, where her mother was. (Mrs. Forni must have seen Vanzetti at this time, but she was not called.)

The Brinis returned to their house, and Mrs. Brini testified that she saw Vanzetti and Rosen then, between 11:30 and 12:00, and talked about cloth. This was the first time she had seen Rosen. She remembered there were holes in the cloth. It was April 15, she said, because on April 14 her sickness was getting worse and her husband had telephoned the doctor the day before from Mr. Brockley's across the way (neither her husband nor Brockley was called). Also on the fourteenth, in the morning, a woman with corsets to sell had called, and on the fifteenth a woman doctor had come to visit her in the morning.

LeFavre Brini was also present at the conference about the cloth, placing the time about 12:00. She saw the cloth and said that it was then (when she testified) at the Fortinis', where Vanzetti boarded. (The cloth was produced at the trial—and it had holes in it.) She knew that it was April 15 because it was just one week after she had left her work to care for her mother; also because her father telephoned that day to call the doctor; also because, the day before, her mother was sick and had called the doctor. She remembered that Dr. Shurtleff called the day before the fifteenth but not on the fifteenth. Vanzetti was a friend of the family and had been at the house the day her mother came home from the hospital—and perhaps other times before April 15.

Angel Guidobone, 10 Suasso's Lane, was coming home from work for his dinner at 12:13 or 12:15. He saw Vanzetti at the corner of the lane. Vanzetti was selling codfish and he gave the witness some in his hand. He fixed the date by the operation he had on April 19 for appendicitis. The pain had begun Saturday, April 17. No, the codfish had nothing to do with it. He had bought fish on Thursday, the fifteenth, to eat on Friday and had done it three weeks before April 15 also. He never paid Vanzetti for it.

The other witness who testified he saw Vanzetti on April 15 was Melvin Corl, who seems to have given his testimony through an interpreter. Corl was a fisherman who had sold fish to Vanzetti. He was painting his boat in the week in which April 15 fell, beginning on Monday and working daily from 7:00 to 5:00. At about 2:00 o'clock on April 15 Vanzetti came to where Corl was working and talked with him for about an hour and a half. Vanzetti had on his working clothes. Corl remembered the date because he put the boat in the water on Saturday, April 17, which was his wife's birthday.

While they were talking, Frank Jesse, the boatbuilder, passed by and also a Mr. Holmes of the lumberyard, and there were men going up and down. (Jesse was called as a witness and remembered seeing Vanzetti talking with Corl but could not place the date. Holmes was not called.) Corl also placed the date because on April 17 he towed a boat from Duxbury to Jesse's boatyard in Plymouth.

Mrs. Corl was also a witness. She recalled that she had seen the newly painted boat two nights before her birthday. The owner of the boat, Joseph Morey, also remembered that he saw that Corl's boat was newly painted, but he revealed on the stand that on the way to court with Mrs. Corl she and he were not sure about the date of the towing, so they talked it over and decided that April 17 was the date.

And that is all for the alibi.

In the Bridgewater case, Vanzetti's neighbors and friends had remembered with particularity exact times on a day over four months in the past at the time the arrest was made. Between the South Braintree murders on April 15 and the arrest on May 5, only twenty days had elapsed and by May 11, if not before, Vanzetti's friends must have known that he was under strong suspicion of that crime and that his whereabouts on April 15 would be important in his defense.

Fortuitously April 15 fell on a Thursday, and since it was the custom of Italians to buy fish on Thursdays to eat on Friday after a day in salt, it would have been natural to connect Thursday, April 15, with the peddling of fish. Guidobone, the chance customer, did as an afterthought relate Thursday, April 15, to his habit of buying fish on Thursday to eat Friday. Unfortunately he had chosen his appendicitis operation on the following Monday as his reason for remembering April 15, and in cross-examination it developed that he did not buy every Thursday.

And there was another apparent advantage in the alibi. The murders occurred at about 3:00 o'clock in the afternoon of Thursday, April 15, 1920, in South Braintree, which is, as the map scales and the crow flies, about twenty-five miles from Plymouth and about twice as far as from Plymouth to Bridgewater. The Commonwealth attempted to place Vanzetti on a train leaving Plymouth at 8:14 A.M., at the East Braintree railway station at 9:45, and in South Braintree from shortly thereafter until after the shooting. Alibi evidence placing Vanzetti in Plymouth at any time after the 8:14 train left would have damaged the Commonwealth's case nearly as much as evidence about the midafternoon when the crime was being committed. Because of the distance from Plymouth to South Braintree, the critical period was much longer than it was in the Bridgewater case, where a man could go and come in an hour or even less. This would mean that approximations would serve as well as the exact times we found in the Bridgewater alibi.

So we would have expected a strong alibi, with witness after witness placing Vanzetti in Plymouth from the time he went to bed on April 14 until he slept again on April 15.

Why was it not forthcoming? Of the alibi witnesses who testified for him in Plymouth, only Mrs. Brini appeared at Dedham. Although Vanzetti was still boarding at the Fortinis', no one of that household (husband, wife, three sons, and Tony Venuste) came to Dedham to remember him fixing fish in the kitchen, coming down in his slippers from his bedroom, putting on his shoes in the kitchen, eating his breakfast, his dinner, his supper. The baker and the shoemaker did not come to testify about seeing him on the street peddling fish. The Brinis bought a fish, so did Guidobone, and they testified, but no other customer. Vanzetti was at the Brini house at the time of the midday meal. Did Mr. Brini come home for it from work, and did the little Brini boy come home to it from school? If Vanzetti was actually in Plymouth all day on April 15, why were the only witnesses who saw him there a woolens peddler from out of town, a fisherman who was painting a boat, the two Brinis, and a customer met by chance?

Vanzetti's defense in the Bridgewater case was an alibi for which the testimony came from his neighbors in Plymouth. It is true that, if any of these had been brought in to testify for an alibi for the South Braintree murder, the Commonwealth could, in cross-examination, ask whether they had testified in another case. This would have brought to the attention of the jury that Vanzetti had been tried for another crime and that he had used the same witnesses for an alibi. This would have weakened the testimony of some of them, because it could be argued (as it was in the case of Mrs. Brini) that the witnesses were always available to help Vanzetti when he needed an alibi. The argument would have been of little force where the events to which the testimony related would naturally occur every day that Vanzetti sold fish. Thus, Vanzetti could go to bed, get up, and eat at the same times on December 24 and on April 15 without exciting suspicion or comment. So it would be natural for a customer to buy fish for Christmas Eve and again for a Friday in April.

Nor was it necessary for him to have the same witnesses. If Vanzetti had his noonday meal in Plymouth at his boardinghouse, others besides Mrs. Fortini could have testified about that—Mr. Fortini, the three sons, Tony Venuste (the Fortinis' nephew, who boarded with the family), no one of whom had testified at Plymouth. No, the answer must be that for some reason Vanzetti's neighbors were unwilling or unable to help him and the defense had to rely on an alibi as weak as could be conceived.

When the radicals took over the case by sending Moore in as chief counsel, the Italians working at the Cordage were cooling off on Vanzetti. He had always been a misfit in the Cordage community, a shiftless unskilled laborer, who had not established a home or found a steady job. In their strike in 1916 they had rejected his leadership, and "more than once he was pushed off the speaker's rostrum by indignant men." [1] They were not in sympathy with his anarchy or his atheism. They, like all immigrants to America from the Pilgrims down, had in their first generation here an arduous life with much toil and some hardship, but they had found that in Plymouth they were living in an atmosphere of freedom, opportunity, and genuine friendliness.[2] They did not hate the Cordage; they were proud of it. They did not hate their adopted country or their church or the American institutions which Vanzetti and the radical propagandists wished to bring into contempt and destroy.

[1] Samuel Eliot Morison, *The Ropemakers of Plymouth, A History of the Plymouth Cordage Company*, 1824-1949, Boston, 1950, p. 114, fn., citing an article in *The Outlook and Independent*.
[2] Morison, *op. cit., passim*.

After the trial, thousands of dollars were spent by the defense to find new witnesses and new evidence, but Vanzetti's alibi was not improved on. If witnesses in the first case had been kept off the stand for fear of the cross-examination, they could be produced after the trial without risk (the fat was in the fire), but no new witness came forward to say that he had seen Vanzetti in Plymouth on April 15 or to corroborate Rosen's story.

The Advisory Committee found that Vanzetti's alibi for the South Braintree crime was decidedly weak. The defense in the closing arguments hardly mentioned it. They had not told in their opening what it was to be, an omission which must have signified that it was not then known what it was to be. Katzmann blew it to pieces. The jury must have disbelieved it. Mrs. Lois B. Rantoul [3] and Frankfurter thought well of it, but they may have liked it because they believed that their own misstatements concerning it were true.

In Mrs. Rantoul's report the following extraordinary comment on the Vanzetti alibi appears: "For Vanzetti, eleven witnesses testified to having seen him in Plymouth that day. Five of them were Americans and six Italians. The corroborating testimony of these witnesses, through means of business books, and outside facts was very strong." (4942)

This is making quite a lot of the five witnesses who were all who testified they saw Vanzetti in Plymouth on April 15 (Rosen, the two Brinis, Guidobone, and Corl) and of business books which did not exist except in her imagination.

Frankfurter found "that the alibi for Vanzetti was overwhelming. . . . Thirteen witnesses either testified directly that Vanzetti was in Plymouth selling fish on the day of the murder, or furnished corroboration of such testimony."

Again Frankfurter has miscounted and is too easily overwhelmed. As we have seen, only four witnesses (Rosen, the two Brinis, and Guidobone) testified directly that Vanzetti was in Plymouth selling fish on the day of the murder. Corroboration, if

[3] For her role in the case, see page 302.

it may be called so, for the fish story came from five: Bova, who sold fish to Carbone; Carbone, who sold fish to Vanzetti; Samuel Hahn, who identified express receipts, and the Cordage nurse who had called on Mrs. Brini. The other four witnesses (Corl, Mrs. Corl, Jesse, and Morey) had to do with the painting of the boat.

Nicola Sacco had learned edge trimming in 1910 at Milford from Michael Kelley and went to work for Kelley in the 3-K Shoe Factory at Stoughton in November 1918, being continuously employed there until May 1920. Kelley's son, George T. Kelley, was the superintendent. Sacco, with his wife and seven-year-old son, occupied a cottage of the bungalow type next door to the George T. Kelleys, and the two families were on terms of friendship, visiting back and forth. Sacco was a devoted home and garden man, a steady worker, thrifty, and well behaved.

In January or February 1920, George Kelley was interviewed by a Federal agent investigating radical activities who inquired about Sacco. Kelley told Sacco about this and had some discussion with him about his radicalism. There is nothing to show that this inquiry had anything to do with Sacco's decision to go to Italy.

In late February or early March 1920 the three Saccos, father, mother, and little son, had a group picture taken by a photographer in Stoughton, who supplied them with twelve prints mounted on 5 by 7 cards.

On March 7, 1920, Sacco's mother died in Italy, and about March 23 or 24 a letter arrived from his brother Sabeno announcing the death. The Saccos who, according to Mrs. Sacco's testimony, had been planning a trip to Italy for a long time, decided to delay no more, and Sacco, some time after March 23 or 24, went to the Italian Consulate at 142 Berkeley Street, Boston, to get information about a passport. According to Sacco's testimony, this trip to the consulate was made late in March or early April. He did not take a photograph with him at this time but was told that he would need one for his passport; he was not told what size would be required. His next trip to the consular office, he testified, was on April 15, when he took one of the big photographs; this was refused as a passport picture because of its size. Thereafter a small photograph was taken and the passport issued on May 4, the day before the arrest.

The "passport" that Sacco applied for and finally received was a *foglio di via,* a paper used in place of a passport by all Italian subjects returning to Italy who did not have regular Italian passports or did not want to go to the expense of procuring a regular passport. (2266b) The two papers are the same size and are both too small for the use of a 5 by 7 cabinet photograph. The *foglio di via* was good only for the trip to Italy. To return, Sacco would have had to get a regular passport in Italy. Katzmann used this as an argument that Sacco did not intend to return and therefore would not fear deportation. (2200-2201)

On May 6, 1920, the day after the arrest and exactly three weeks after the murders, Katzmann interrogated Sacco at the Brockton police station. Sacco told him that the morning after the crime, he, Sacco, had read in the *Boston Post* about the bandits robbing the money over near Rice & Hutchins and had had an argument about it with some of his friends in the shop. He then said to Katzmann that he had been working the day before he read the paper:

> Q. Were you working the day before you read it in the paper?
> A. Sure.
> Q. Worked all day?
> A. Yes, sir.

At the trial, Sacco admitted that the questions and answers had been asked and answered, and he explained his lie this way:

"There was not interest to me very close to find out the date I have been out."

It was soon learned that the working-all-day alibi would not do. George T. Kelley remembered and would afterward testify that Sacco was not at work at any time on April 15. Kelley's story as told on the stand was that on Monday, April 11, or Tuesday, April 12, Sacco asked for one day off that week to go to see the consul in regard to passports. Kelley told him at that time that if he were caught up with his work he might have a day off, and on Wednesday, April 14, Sacco came to Kelley and said he was going "tomorrow" (Thursday, April 15) and if possible would get back to work the same day. He did not get back and did not work at all that day.

On Friday, April 16, Sacco was at work early. Kelley asked him how he had gotten along, and Sacco told him that he had tried to get back Thursday but on account of the crowd waiting for passports it was too late for him to catch the noon train and impossible for him to come out Thursday to work. He testified, "I took the excuse as being all right." (851 *et seq.*, 1684)

So, although Sacco had also told Katzmann on May 6 that the only full day off he had taken on passport matters was April 5 or 8 or 10, "a Tuesday or a Wednesday," the working-all-day alibi had to be abandoned and the passport one relied upon.

Felice Guadagni, a graduate of the Institution of Naples, a professor of Italian and Latin, a philosophical anarchist who had lost his position because of his opinions, and a member of the Defense Committee, had been a friend of Vanzetti for some years before the arrest and an acquaintance of Sacco. Soon after the arrest, Guadagni went to Brockton and talked with Vanzetti. "I was the first man to go to Brockton," he testified. Vanzetti had said to him: "We will go to Italy at Uncle Sam's expense," because he and Sacco thought they had been arrested for radical activities. "I says, 'This is not true, your story; you are in a very serious imputation.'"

After that visit to Vanzetti, Guadagni at once started to work on an alibi for Sacco. Strangely enough, he did not remember at the time he saw Vanzetti that he, Albert Bosco, John D. Williams (an ad collector), and Sacco had met in Boni's restaurant in Boston at lunch time on the day of the murder, an event to which they all were to testify at the trial. The luncheon, although only three weeks in the past, seems to have vanished from the recollection of all of them until long after the arrest.

Mrs. Sacco came to Boston and asked Guadagni whether he remembered that Sacco was with him and at the Italian Consulate. "I don't know," he replied; "wait a minute, we will see." At Mrs. Sacco's suggestion he went to see a man named Baldini, who had known Sacco as a customer for groceries for several years. Baldini remembered that Sacco had bought groceries on an afternoon but could not fix the date; he was a cash customer and no record was made. It does not appear by whom the witness Carlos M. Affe, who testified about groceries, was suggested or by whom he was interviewed. After seeing Baldini, Guadagni went, he said, to the Italian Consulate and found that Giuseppe Andrower (Androa), a consular clerk, would testify that he had seen Sacco on April 15, fixing the date by the fact that the consulate had closed an hour early that day.

A few days after Guadagni's alleged interview with Andrower, on May 18 or 20, the latter left Boston for Italy; his testimony had to be taken nearly a year later by deposition in Rome. We are led to ask why Guadagni failed to call this witness to the attention of Katzmann or the police immediately after he had seen him. Andrower's memory about an event three or four weeks old, with possible corroboration from others in the consulate, might have convinced the authorities that Sacco, like Orciani, had an alibi they could not hope to impeach.

At some point Guadagni, Professor Antonio Dentamore, and Albert Bosco, an editor of the Italian newspaper *La Notizia,* got together and discussed the alibi. As a basis for fixing the date on which they had seen Sacco in Boston, they decided on the banquet given to James T. Williams, Jr., editor of the *Boston Evening Transcript.*

Guadagni spoke to other friends who saw Sacco in Boston,

among them Angelo Monello, the witness who met Sacco in Hanover Street, and probably John D. Williams, the advertising so-
licitor, although he did not mention Williams's name before the
Advisory Committee. He explained to the committee:

> Before I put this alibi of Sacco I do a very careful work, and
> if it happens that I recollect the conversation about the
> banquet and all that, the little things, I had no time in
> court to explain all the work I had done to put Sacco in
> Boston where he was the 15th day of April.

The alibi gathered by Guadagni as presented at the trial may
be summarized as follows:

Sacco obtained permission from Kelley to go to Boston about
his passport and told his wife that he was going there. He left
Stoughton on the 8:56 train to Boston and arrived at the South
Station about 9:35. Dominick Ricci, a carpenter of Needham, living in the Parker house in Stoughton on April 15, who had met
Sacco at a picnic in Milford and known him about two years, testified that he saw Sacco on the station platform at Stoughton between 7:15 and 7:40 the morning of April 15, and had a talk
with him about a passport and the consul's office. Sacco was still
at the station and had not taken the train when the witness
walked away. Ricci established the date because he was fixing
beaverboard on the piazza ceiling of the house he was working
on that day. This did not help much, however, because he was
fixing beaverboard on many other days, including Sundays, in
April and before.

Ricci's testimony could be believed without helping the alibi
materially. In fact, placing Sacco on the station platform at 7:40
or earlier, more than an hour before the 8:56 train was due to
leave Stoughton, disproved rather than proved that Sacco intended
to take that train or indeed to go to Boston on any train.

From the South Station, Sacco walked to the North End and
at about 10:15 bought a newspaper, *La Notizia*, at a newsstand
on Prince Street. He stood there reading for fifteen minutes and
then walked to Hanover Street, reaching it in about a minute,

turned the corner, and started to walk on that street. Here he met his friend Angelo Monello and talked with him at the corner for about half an hour. The two friends then walked to Washington Street, where he left Monello.

Monello, a Roxbury contractor, testified that he had known Sacco a couple of months before he was arrested. He met him at Maverick Square Hall in East Boston: "it was a dramatic people there, and was introduced by the witness's nephew." The next time he saw him was on April 15, when he met him on Hanover Street and talked with him, walking with him about two hundred yards. He fixed the date because on the next Sunday, April 18, Mimi Aguglia of New York, an Italian and one of the greatest artists of the day, was to play Madame X at the Tremont Theater. He and Sacco talked about the play and about Sacco's passport. He did not say how he fixed the time. On cross-examination, Monello, an amateur actor, said that he had talked about the play on several days in April but could remember no one with whom he had talked about it except Sacco.

After Monello left Sacco, the latter went back along Hanover Street, looking at straw hats and "some suits," pricing the hats but seeing and talking with no one produced at the trial. At some point he decided to get the passport in the afternoon. He testified: "I say [to myself] probably I go to get my dinner first, so I have a little time and I go then, so I went over to Boni's restaurant."

At Boni's restaurant, near the place where he bought the paper, he met Guadagni, Williams (the ad collector), and Bosco. He stayed there one hour and fifteen minutes.

Sacco's attendance at Boni's was corroborated by those three witnesses. Guadagni testified that he had met Sacco at some hall in Boston where he, Guadagni, was speaking and had seen him ten or twelve times before April 15. He ate frequently at Boni's and at 11:30 (later changed to 12:30) on April 15 he saw him in the step door. They ate together and the witness stayed with Sacco about an hour. There were some friends of the witness's in Boni's but he remembered only Williams and Bosco. Guadagni had a conversation with Sacco about the latter's going to Italy as soon as possible. There was talk about the passport. While they were eating, Williams and Bosco came in and talked to them. Sacco and Guadagni left together and parted in the Square.

John D. Williams testified that he met Sacco only once, on April 15 at Boni's restaurant between 1:15 and 1:30. Guadagni and a stranger were eating together when Williams came in. Guadagni introduced him to Sacco, saying he was leaving for Italy and was going after his passport that afternoon. There was more conversation about passports. He never saw Sacco again until "just now" —in the courtroom. Guadagni and Sacco had practically finished eating when Williams came over and ordered his dinner. In ten or fifteen minutes from the time he came, Guadagni and Sacco were ready to go. The witness fixed the date because he remembered that he had solicited a help-wanted ad from the Washington Knitting Mills that day (Thursday, April 15) for *La Notizia,* to run April 17, 18, and 19. He usually solicited in the North End on Thursdays. A help-wanted ad for April 17, 18, and 19 would not be placed on April 8. He also fixed the date because he remembered that after dinner he had had a treatment from his physician, Dr. Howard A. Gibbs. Dr. Gibbs, using his card records, testified that he had treated Williams on April 15, but Williams's equally definite testimony about other treatments in April was not confirmed by Dr. Gibbs. It appeared that Williams, prior to the trial, had asked Dr. Gibbs whether he had had a treatment on April 15.

Albert Bosco, of *La Notizia,* testified that he was sitting in Boni's with Mr. Reffi when Guadagni and Sacco came into the restaurant. Guadagni introduced Sacco to Bosco as the man who was going to Italy, and there was talk about passports and going to the consul's office. Bosco and Guadagni talked about a banquet to be given to James T. Williams, Jr., editor of the *Boston Transcript* on the evening of April 15, and Bosco had fixed the date by looking up the paper and discovering that the banquet did occur on April 15. Sacco did not attend the banquet. Neither did Bosco, who was not invited. Neither did Guadagni, although he was invited.

During this conversation, in which he discussed passports with three intelligent Italians, Sacco did not show them the big photograph which he had with him and which he intended to offer to the consul as a passport picture. This would have been a telling bit of corroboration but it could not be used, because they would probably have laughed at him and told him that the consul would not accept it as a passport picture. This would have made Sacco's story of his visit to the consul's office after luncheon more incredible than it was anyway.

Returning to Sacco's testimony: he tells us that he left Boni's about 1:20 and walked to the Italian Consulate on Berkeley Street, arriving about 2:00. He stayed ten minutes and passed in a group picture of himself, his wife, and his son for the passport. It was too big and was refused. Sacco took his picture and walked back to the North End.

The corroborating evidence about Sacco's visit to that office came by deposition of Giuseppe Andrower.[1] Andrower was in the employ of the Royal Italian Consulate in Boston on April 15, 1920. The office had regular hours, 10:00 A.M. to 3:00 P.M., except on Saturdays, when the hours were 10:00 A.M. to noon. Andrower was charged with answering questions and giving information to the public and with receiving passports for visas. On Thursday, April 15, at about 2:00 or 2:15, Sacco showed Andrower the group photograph,[2] which was too large for a passport.

Previously, early in April, Sacco had come to the consulate for information on how to get a passport to Italy. Andrower testified:

> I gave him the information and told him that he should bring two photographs, one to be attached to the passport and the other for the records of the office.

1 Taken before a vice-consul of the United States in Rome on May 11, 1921, by order of the Superior Court of Norfolk County issued April 13, 1921.
2 Attached to the deposition as Exhibit B.

Sacco then left, and on April 15 he returned with the group photograph. When this was refused he left, saying he would be back later, but Andrower never saw him again. Andrower fixed the date as follows:

> April 15, 1920 was a very quiet day and since such a large photograph had never been presented for use on a passport I took it in and showed it to the Secretary of the Consulate. We laughed and talked over the incident. I remember observing the date on a large pad calendar while we were discussing the photograph.

Sacco was with the witness personally about six or seven minutes. Andrower fixed the time because the office closed at 3:00 and it was about half an hour before that when Sacco left. The secretary did not testify, nor was his absence from the stand explained.

We return to Sacco's testimony. When he left the consul's office, he walked back to the North End to get groceries and some coffee in a coffee shop or café near Boni's restaurant. He went to the café first and stayed there from about 3:00 to 3:20. In the café he saw Guadagni again and also met Professor Dentamore, who testified in substance as follows:

Dentamore at the time was a foreign-exchange man in the nearby Haymarket National Bank and a former editor of *La Notizia*. When Sacco entered the café, Dentamore was arguing with Guadagni. Sacco, whom Dentamore had never seen before, was introduced by Guadagni, and there was conversation about passports and the consul's office. Dentamore fixed the date as April 15 because there was also talk about *a banquet from which he had just come*. This banquet was held on April 15, about noon, at the Italian Friars Priory. It was in honor of Williams, editor of the *Boston Evening Transcript,* because of the attitude of his newspaper during the war in favor of Italy. Dentamore remembered that he had had an argument in the café with Guadagni at about 2:45. This, he said, was before Sacco came, but he seems to have forgotten his earlier testimony to the effect that Sacco entered the café *during* the argument. Sacco came, according to Dentamore's later testimony, a very few minutes after the argument, about 2:50—before 3:00, in any event. Dentamore was in Sacco's company about twenty minutes.

Guadagni, who had discussed the Williams banquet with Bosco at Boni's, had a further discussion about it with Dentamore in the café. He was invited to that banquet, which was to be *on the night of April 15*. At the time Sacco came into the café Guadagni and Dentamore were discussing that banquet. This was the only banquet Guadagni had ever been invited to; the invitation came a week before.

From the café, Sacco walked fifty or one hundred steps and spent twenty or twenty-five minutes on something vaguely concerned with groceries. Here he met Carlos M. Affe, whose testimony in substance was this:

Sometime between 3:00 and 4:00 on April 15, Affe saw Sacco at 180 North Street, in the North End of Boston, and received from Sacco $15.50 for a bill of $15.67 for groceries bought by Sacco on March 20. The sale had been made in a cigar store, or maybe in Boni's. Affe, who had no place of business, went from the cigar store or from Boni's, bought the groceries, and brought them back to Sacco. He thought he had bought some from Majoli and Salini, on Fulton Street. About the macaroni, he was not sure, giving a choice of 141 Richmond Street, Maravigna, and other persons and places. Affe sold on cash and credit and had about one hundred customers. He kept no set of books. When the sale was on credit, he sometimes marked it in a book: "Sometimes I do not put any date, because I remember in my head."

About two or three weeks before he testified, Affe had found a little book in which he had entered the date of the sale to Sacco —because this was the first sale to him. He put down the date, April 15, "to see how good customer he was, and the length of time that took him to pay."

During a long cross-examination the book was produced and shown to the jury. Also, Affe was asked to write some words and figures for the jury. It is impossible to tell from the transcript how effective this examination was, but it may be significant that the defense did not rely on the Affe encounter in its arguments, and that Katzmann asserted in his argument that the important entries in the book were not written by Affe. (2231-2232)

After the Affe transaction, Sacco walked to the South Station and took a train for Stoughton. Upon arrival he walked home, buying some elixir for physic on his way. He got home about six.

During the trial, Sacco noticed a man named Hayes sitting as a spectator and told his counsel that this man had been on the same train with him the afternoon of April 15, 1920. Hayes took the stand, and it was established with some difficulty that he had been on that train, but he did not remember seeing Sacco on it.

The alibi would have been strengthened if the defense could have proved that the little photograph actually used on Sacco's passport, which was issued May 4, 1920 (the day before the arrest), was taken after April 15. In an effort to fix the date that the photograph was taken, a Stoughton photographer, Edward Maertens, was called. He produced the photographic plate and a print of it, but because it was a passport photograph Maertens had kept no record of when the photograph was taken but thought it was "between April and the first of May." He fixed that indefinite date by the fact that the plate was stored with the plate of a certain soldier who he remembered had come in during the month of April.

The difficulties inherent in the Boston alibi were many. Sacco, if at work all day in Stoughton, would have been seen by family, friends, and fellow employees, and every minute of his day accounted for. Sacco could get corroboration of being in Boston only from strangers, all of whom, except the consular clerk and Affe, he met by chance on the street or at Boni's restaurant or in a café. His own story was improbable. We have to believe that he made three and not two trips to the consular office about his passport, and that on the second trip, that of April 15, he offered a large photograph as a passport picture, although he had made one trip to the consul in late March or early April to get information about passports and had himself had a passport in 1908 and knew its size.

We also have to believe that Sacco, who had come to Boston on business which, as it turned out, took him only ten minutes, did not go directly from the train to the consulate and then back to Stoughton on the noon train but postponed his business to the afternoon to wander aimlessly around the streets of Boston all morning.

THE GUADAGNI-BOSCO AFFAIR

During the proceedings before the Advisory Committee, President Lowell caused a search to be made of the *Boston Evening Transcript* and of an Italian newspaper, *Gazetta del Massachusetts;* from this it appeared that there had been a dinner for James T. Williams, Jr., editor of the *Transcript,* on *May 13, 1920.* Inquiry was made of Williams, who told President Stratton over the telephone that a dinner, and only one dinner, had been given for him. The *Gazetta* of May 14 and the *Transcript* of that date stated that the banquet was held the night before, on May 13.

Guadagni and Bosco, who had testified that they fixed the date of their encounter with Sacco on April 15 by the banquet to be given Williams that *evening,* were confronted by President Lowell with the newspaper accounts showing May 13 as the date and with Williams's statement over the telephone that only one dinner had been given for him. This threw everyone into confusion, and then William G. Thompson, chief counsel for the defense, said he was ready to withdraw from the case because of the possibility that the alibi had been based on feigned testimony. The next day, however, Bosco brought in the April 16, 1920, issue of *La Notizia,* and from then on the committee in its deliberations assumed it to be a fact that, besides the larger public *dinner* given to Williams on May 13, a *luncheon* was also given to him at the Italian Friars Priory in the North End on April 15.

After Bosco's production of *La Notizia,* there was a colloquy

among the committee, the counsel, and the witnesses. This was
not recorded by the stenographer, who had previously been in-
structed not to record colloquies. President Lowell also refused
permission to have the matter reported in *La Notizia*.

When the Holt Transcript of the trial was in preparation, the
editing committee found a note about Bosco's having produced
the copy of *La Notizia* and wrote to President Lowell and to
Thompson and Ehrmann for an explanation. The committee's
letter, signed by Bernard Flexner and Charles C. Burlingham, is
dated November 27, 1928. President Lowell answered this on
December 8, 1928, with a short note:

> On the day following the testimony of Guadagni, Bosco pro-
> duced before the committee the files of the NOTIZIA, by
> which it appeared that there was a luncheon given for Mr.
> Williams on April 15 (the date of the murder) at an Italian
> priory in the North End. The committee, in their subse-
> quent deliberations, assumed it to be a fact that besides the
> larger public dinner, given to Mr. Williams on May 13, this
> luncheon also took place on April 15. (5256b)

Thompson and Ehrmann answered at greater length, claiming
in their letter of December 26, 1928, that Lowell had acknowledged that he had made a mistake and had apologized for it.

But Lowell had not made a mistake.

The facts are clear. There was a *noonday* luncheon for Williams on April 15, and Dentamore fixed the date on which he saw
Sacco by that luncheon, which he had just left. This luncheon
was reported in *La Notizia* as *un banchetto,* without the hour being named. Bosco and Guadagni, in fixing the date of their
meeting with Sacco, saw in *La Notizia* that there had been *un
banchetto* for Williams on April 15, and supposed it had been
held in the *evening*.

When it was found that the *banchetto* of April 15 was held at
noon, the fixing of the date by the *evening banchetto* held May 13
was still unconvincing and they were just back where they were
before.

Lowell has been criticized for his refusal to let the stenographer record the colloquy in which the mix-up was explained; but I cannot see how the explanation helped Bosco and Guadagni, who had fixed the date by a *banchetto* to be held in the *evening* of April 15 and not by a *banchetto* which had been held at *noon*.

RADICALISM was introduced into the trial by the defendants. It could not have been introduced by the Commonwealth. The political and social opinions of the defendants could under no theory be regarded as part of the proof of participation in armed robbery and murder, and if the Commonwealth had attempted to introduce evidence of radical opinions or activities, such evidence would have been excluded and any attempt to influence the jury by asking questions loaded with improper insinuations might well have made the trial a mistrial requiring a new start before another jury. The same would be true of draft-dodging evidence.

Nor could radicalism be used by the Commonwealth in cross-examination[1] unless the defense had brought the subject into the case.

Judge Thayer in his decision of October 22, 1926, denying the Madeiros motion for a new trial, states that before the trial

[1] *Jones v. Commonwealth*, 327 Mass. 491. In that case the question asked in cross-examination was "Are you a Communist or a member of the Communist Party?" The Supreme Judicial Court held that where the issue was whether the defendant was guilty of a certain crime, proof that he was a Communist or a member of the Communist Party was not admissible to establish guilt. The Court also considered whether the question was competent for purposes of impeachment, and held that it was not, saying: "Whatever the rule may be elsewhere, it is settled in the Commonwealth that a 'witness cannot be asked on cross-examination, in order to affect his credibility, about his part in transactions irrelevant to the issue on trial. . . .' The defendants' political beliefs were not the proper subject of inquiry for purposes of impeachment."

opened he called all counsel into conference and informed them that he could see no reason why radicalism should enter into the trial, (4767) and when the Commonwealth completed the presentation of its case on Wednesday, June 22, 1920, the nineteenth day of the trial, there had been no mention in the presence of the jury of radicalism or draft dodging.

It was not until the twenty-ninth day of the trial (Tuesday, July 5, 1921) that radicalism was introduced, when, under direct examination by his own attorney, Vanzetti himself introduced it. (1720)

In the meantime, counsel for the defendants had on several different occasions inadvertently opened up the question. Katzmann would have had the right to cross-examine about this subject but upon the suggestion of Judge Thayer, counsel on both sides came to the bench and were informed of what the effect of this would be; thereupon the questions and answers were by agreement stricken from the record. (4767)

On one occasion Katzmann himself was the moving party in excluding the subject. During the examination in chief by Jeremiah J. McAnarney before radicalism had come into the case, Vanzetti was asked why he had gone to New York on Sunday, April 25, 1920. Since Vanzetti had gone there as the member of a committee to find out about the radical Andrea Salsedo, an answer to this question would have opened up the radical issue, but upon objection of Katzmann to its competency, McAnarney withdrew the question. (1710)

These occasions, as it seems to me and as it seemed to Judge Thayer, should for all time dispose of the contention that he or Katzmann wanted to bring radicalism into the trial.

Judge Thayer then went on to say that, shortly before adjournment one afternoon, counsel for the defendants told the Court in the absence of the jury that they all were agreed that it was necessary to go into the subject of radicalism in order to meet the Commonwealth's claim of consciousness of guilt. Judge Thayer suggested that, before a decision was made, counsel should consult with John W. McAnarney, eldest of the three McAnarney brothers and one of the leading lawyers of the State. Counsel seemed grateful for the suggestion and adopted it. The next morning they informed the court that a conference had been held and that all counsel, together with the brother and another distinguished lawyer [perhaps Thompson] had decided that it would be fatal if the evidence of radicalism was *not* introduced. (4768-4769)

When John W. McAnarney appeared before the Advisory Committee he confirmed Judge Thayer's account and said that he had advised his brothers:

> I saw no way that those men could avoid going on the stand and telling fully and frankly their connection with the Communistic movement or the radical movement they had been allied with. The only thing to do was to take the full responsibility of that and, if they did that much, their conduct which otherwise would be very suspicious and the crushing force that would come back on them would be truthfully taken away; their being up trying to get the car at the Johnson house, their being on the electric car with revolvers on them, lying to the officers and the district attorney before they knew they were charged with murder . . . (4993)

And on July 11, 1927, when Thomas F. McAnarney appeared before the Advisory Committee, President Lowell asked him this question:

> Do you mean by this, that if the radical purposes of the prisoners doesn't account for their conduct, there would be no question of their being innocent?

To which Judge McAnarney replied:

> There wouldn't be any defense in my mind. No explanation . . . There would be no explanation by which to justify the lies they gave to the district attorney. (5057)

Jeremiah J. McAnarney, who conducted the direct examination of Vanzetti, first had him supply biographical items carrying Vanzetti from his birth through his education, his arrival in New York, his various employments and habitations there and elsewhere, his arrival in Plymouth in 1913, his employments there, and his fish peddling. No mention of his draft-dodging trip to Mexico was made during this preliminary examination.

The next subject was the alibi for April 15, and from that McAnarney took him day by day from April 16 to May 5, 1920, including his trip to New York, with no mention of radicalism until the events of the evening of May 5 were related. Then McAnarney asked:

Q. What were you going to get the automobile for?
A. We were going to take the automobile for to carry books and newspapers.[2] (1721)

After this mention of the radical literature, Vanzetti was asked by McAnarney whether he had told the police officers or the District Attorney that he was going to get literature and he said, No.

Q. Why not?
A. Because in that time there, there was the deportation and the reaction was more vivid than now and more mad than now. . . . It mean the authority of this country and every country in the world was more against the Socialist element in that time than before the war and after the war. These were exceptional times. (1726)

At this point McAnarney had Vanzetti testify to his draft dodging. (1726-1727)

[2] The story about the radical literature as told by Sacco and Vanzetti was vague and varied. At one time they were going to gather the literature that night; at another, they were going to Plymouth that night to find a place to dispose of the literature. At one time the literature was located in five or six different towns, about 400 to 500 pounds of it in Plymouth. At another it was in Brockton, Bridgewater, "all the towns around there," and Salem and Everett. Again, there was some in Bridgewater, some in Brockton, some in Sacco's house in Stoughton, some in Orciani's house, some in Haverhill, some in Salem, and "many other places that I don't know." In cross-examination the story suffered a great deal. Why did they need an automobile to find a safe place for the literature? Why couldn't Orciani and Vanzetti have done this on a motorcycle? Why were Sacco and Vanzetti needed on the night of May 5? Why did they leave the books and papers in Sacco's house?

Now let us pause for a moment and consider what these explanations by Vanzetti opened up for Katzmann's cross-examination. Under Massachusetts law, Katzmann could not have examined Vanzetti about the draft dodging, the meeting to be held in Brockton, the radical literature, Vanzetti's opinions, the deportation of alien radicals, the "reaction" against the radicals, the trip to New York, or Salsedo, unless and until Vanzetti opened up these subjects himself. Katzmann then was entitled to ask him about every one of them "to test his accuracy, veracity or credibility or to shake his credit by injuring his character." [3]

Under this rule, which is general and not confined to Massachusetts, Katzmann could, to the extent that Judge Thayer would permit, have brought in the bombing outrages of 1919 and 1920 and other facts which might indeed have prejudiced the jury and created emotional issues. If Katzmann had done this and Thayer had permitted it, there would have been some justification for Frankfurter's assertion that there was in this case a "deliberate effort to excite the emotions of jurors still in the grip of war fever . . ." [4]

But Katzmann did not ask Vanzetti a single question about his political or social views or about his radical opinions and activities. He did ask eleven questions about his draft dodging, and he did refer to the radical literature to test Vanzetti's story and to show how inadequate that story was as an explanation of Vanzetti's conduct and admitted falsehoods. The jury could have inferred that Vanzetti was a poor liar, but there was nothing brought out by Katzmann to show that his *opinions* were dangerous or offensive enough to arouse hatred or abhorrence or, indeed, what those opinions were. Nothing the jury heard about Vanzetti's radicalism came from Katzmann's cross-examination. It was all volunteered by Vanzetti himself on direct examination. Katzmann knew what his rights were—he was an excellent lawyer—but he

---

[3] *Commonwealth* v. *Sacco,* 255 Mass. 369, 439 (4339). The extent of the cross-examination could be limited in the discretion of the trial court as to the length of time or the nature of the questions, but unless there was an abuse of that discretion the trial judge's decisions as to any question would be final.
[4] Frankfurter, *op. cit.,* p. 63.

also knew that he was trying a murder case and that it would be unfair and confusing to introduce extraneous subjects in the trial, even for the legitimate purposes of impeachment of credibility. In his argument he expressed his opinion thus:

> The defendant Vanzetti says that on April 25th, Sunday night, he took a train from Boston to New York, that he went over there in the interests of some people in whom his organization had an interest, with whom we have no concern, gentlemen of the jury. That issue is not being tried here. Neither is Radicalism being tried here. This is a charge of murder and it is nothing else. . . . (2198)

Katzmann's failure to cross-examine Vanzetti about his radical opinions and his failure to cross-examine Sacco or Vanzetti at all about their radical *activities* disposes of the contention that one of the purposes of the murder trial was to get evidence of radical actions which could be used by the federal authorities to deport or punish Sacco and Vanzetti, and that Katzmann was a party to this plot. He had permitted the Department of Justice to put a stool pigeon in the Dedham jail to see if he could elicit any information from Sacco about the bombing outrages, but in the trial he did not ask a single question which would have helped the department to solve those outrages or to give a reason for deportation or other punishment of the defendants as radicals.

Now we come to Sacco, the cross-examination of whom has been so widely criticized. Here again we should distinguish between what Sacco volunteered in direct examination and what came out in cross-examination.

DIRECT EXAMINATION OF SACCO

In his direct examination Sacco told of his trip to Mexico to evade the draft and that he had used an assumed name, Nicola Mosmacotelli, from May 1917 until he went to work for the Kelleys in Stoughton in November 1918. (1820-1822)

He then told of meetings in Naturalization Hall in East Boston, at the first of which it was decided to send Vanzetti to New York to find out what was happening to the money that Sacco, Vanzetti, and their associates were sending to New York for the defense of Andrea Salsedo and Roberto Elia, who were under arrest there; was the money going to a friend or to a spy? (1827) The date of this meeting was April 25, 1920. In the transcript, Sacco seems to have erroneously dated it May 2.

The next meeting, dated May 4 by Sacco, heard the report of Vanzetti. He brought back word from New York that somebody had told him that "they were trying to arrest all the Socialists and Radicals" and had advised Vanzetti to collect and conceal the "Socialist literature." Vanzetti also said: "New York says it is pretty kind of dangerous for Radical." (1848)

Sacco testified that at this meeting the decision to collect the literature was made. Orciani suggested that they have Boda, an active Socialist, furnish a car. Sacco had known Boda for three years, having met him at a Socialist hall in Boston. (1850)

Sacco also told, still in direct examination, of the streetcar trip on May 5 from Stoughton to Brockton. During the trip Vanzetti wrote out a handbill advertising a meeting to be held in Brockton; Sacco took it and put it in his pocket, with the intention of having it printed.[5]

Against the objection of Katzmann, Sacco in answer to Moore's question "Did you know of various men who had been held and deported by reason of their ideas or opinions?" named Fruzetti, from Bridgewater, (1849) Papette from Brockton, and Mondanari —"I forget the first name"—and said there were others whose names he had forgotten. (1848)

Sacco then testified about the lies he had told Stewart on the night of the arrest and explained them by saying that he thought he had been arrested on a Radical charge and so did not tell the truth. (1865-1866)

CROSS-EXAMINATION OF SACCO

We thus find that in his direct examination Sacco had told of his draft dodging, his association with men who had been deported,

[5] For a translation of the handbill, see page 8.

his interest in Salsedo and Elia, and his desire to hide dangerous books and literature. Here, as in the case of Vanzetti, Katzmann could have gone into several subjects which might have made the jury think him a dangerous radical. That he failed to do this shows again that he had no interest in the defendant's radical activities or opinions except as they were related to issues of fact in the trial or to the credibility of the defendant as a witness.

The first part of Katzmann's cross-examination of Sacco was addressed to the impeachment of Sacco's credibility. In his direct examination Sacco had testified that he loved this country. Katzmann asked him whether he loved this country in May 1917, when he had gone to Mexico under an assumed name to avoid being a soldier. Sacco replied that he had and that he did not believe in war and thought it a brave thing to avoid the draft. After several other questions about his love of country and his reasons for it, Katzmann asked him: "What did you mean when you said yesterday [in direct examination] you loved a free country?"

In reply, Sacco made a long, uninterrupted speech, from which we can gather what his political and social opinions were. The following is a fair summary of his answer:

As a boy in Italy he was a Republican because he thought a Republican had more chance for education and development, a better opportunity "to build some day his family, to raise the child and education."

He did not have to work so hard in Italy—only about seven or eight hours a day—and the food was better. Here, the food was good but not for the laboring class. In Italy there was more opportunity for the laborer to eat fresh vegetables.

After he came here, he worked hard for thirteen years but could not put money in the bank.

The idea of freedom, he said, gives any man a chance to profess his own ideas, to enjoy free speech—unlike Spain of twenty centuries ago. As for his idea that there was free speech in this country, "I see it was all wrong." The best men—intelligent and educated men like Eugene Debs—were sent to prison, because they were Socialists. Debs wanted the laboring class to have better conditions, but he was put in prison.

The capitalist class, he said, don't want the laborer's child to go to high school or college. They want the laboring class under foot, not in the lead. The Rockefellers and Morgans give money to Harvard, but the poor get no chance to go there.

Sacco said he loved people who work and seek better conditions and do not try to make war. He did not want to fight with a gun or destroy young men. War, he said, is for the millionaires and for business.

He had worked with the Irish, the Germans, the French, and many other people, and he loved them. Why should he kill them?

The government, he said, should publish literature and educate the people and give Socialist literature a chance to be read. He loved Socialists. (1875-1877)

Katzmann now turned from questions testing the credibility of the witness to questions about Sacco's explanation of the reasons for his falsehoods at the time of the arrest. Inquiries about the nature of the literature which was to be distributed revealed that Sacco used to get *Le Martello,* an Italian weekly published in New York, and before the war he got *Cronaca Sovversiva;* both papers were stopped during the war. On May 5, 1920, he had in the house the *Boston Globe,* the *Boston American,* some Socialist papers from Italy, *Le Martello, Cronaca Sovversiva,* some anarchistic papers, more than a dozen books. The books they intended to collect related to socialism, democracy, syndicalism, anarchism, communism.

Katzmann also inquired about Sacco's fear of deportation, which Sacco had given as one reason for the falsehoods. On this subject Sacco testified that he knew Fruzetti of Bridgewater who had been deported. He had talked with him about anarchy, was aware of his anarchism, agreed with him in some respects and not in others. Fruzetti was deported for having anarchistic views and for writing in the newspapers, "and I am not sure why the reason he been deported."

He himself on May 5 was afraid of deportation.

He did not know what the words Bolshevism and Soviet meant. Anarchy, he said, is not criminal.

Telling Katzmann a lie about buying the box of cartridges had nothing to do with the names and addresses of Socialists or Anarchists.

He knew that Vanzetti was going to talk at a radical meeting in a public hall about the political prisoners Salsedo and Elia and the Radical movements. Sacco was willing to take a chance on going there, although he said he had lied to Katzmann to conceal his radicalism. (1867 *et seq.*)

And that is all that came out in the cross-examination about Sacco's radical opinions and activities.

ON REDIRECT

It was on redirect examination by the defense that Sacco denied the opinion which might have made him subject to deportation.

Moore asked, "Mr. Sacco, do you believe in the use of force and violence in connection with any of your social opinions?"

Sacco replied, "Absolutely not." (1962)

After Sacco left the stand, the defense produced several witnesses to corroborate the radical-literature story. Katzmann did not take advantage of their testimony on direct examination, however, to bring radical opinions and activities into his cross-examination of them.

Walter Nelles, a New York lawyer who was counsel in 1921 for the American Civil Liberties Union, testified that he had been retained to represent Salsedo but had never seen his client, and that he had advised Luigi Quintiliano who had retained him about disposing of literature shortly before the death of Salsedo. Katzmann's cross-examination of him was confined to the fixing of the date of the advice and the fact that he, Nelles, had never talked with Vanzetti. (1981-1983)

Rocco Dalesandro of Brockton testified that on May 3, 1920, Sacco had advised him to gather all his books, papers, and pamphlets and that on the next night he, Dalesandro, had had conversations on this subject with Michael Colombo and Padro Montagano. Katzmann's only question to him was this: "Was Mr. Vanzetti there Monday night [May 3]?"

The answer was "Monday night, no, sir." (1984-1987)

Colombo and Montagano, both of Brockton, testified that they had had a conversation with Dalesandro about disposing of the literature, and each had gone home and bundled up his. Katzmann asked no questions. (1989-1991)

Louis (Luigi) Quintiliano of New York testified he had had a conversation with attorney Nelles about disposing of literature and had told Vanzetti about that conversation on April 27 or 28 in New York. There were no questions from Katzmann. (2047-2049)

Frank R. Lopez, a Spanish anarchist who was the original secretary of the Sacco-Vanzetti Defense Committee, remembered the meeting in East Boston at which it was decided to send Vanzetti to New York. Also he recalled conversations about the disposing of literature. Katzmann asked him if he was a member of the Defense Committee and if he was affirming rather than taking an oath. Both questions he answered in the affirmative. There were no other questions. (2049-2050)

Mrs. Sacco testified that she heard a conversation at supper on Wednesday, May 5, between Orciani, Boda, Sacco, and Vanzetti about picking up the literature. (2059) She had burned some of the literature in her house on May 6, and some had been brought into court. (2062) Katzmann asked no questions about the literature.

Later the books and papers which were not burned were introduced in evidence by the defense, but there was no discussion of their nature.

Frankfurter's discussion of this subject inflamed the world against Massachusetts justice and against two honorable men, Judge Thayer and District Attorney Katzmann, and is inexcusable. He admits that, up to the time that Sacco and Vanzetti testified to their radical activities, their pacifism, and their flight to Mexico to escape the draft, the trial was for murder and banditry, but he asserts that "with the cross-examination of Sacco and Vanzetti, patriotism and radicalism became the dominant emotional issues."

A reader confident of Frankfurter's good faith would gather from this that radicalism had come into the case with the cross-examination. But, as we have seen, this was not so. Nor is there any support in or out of the record of the assertion that patriotism and radicalism became dominant emotional issues in the closing days of the trial. Frankfurter's assertions should be compared with what the jurors told Simmons in his interview with them about the role of radicalism during the trial, particularly the juror who said that anyone who thought that radicalism influenced the verdict was "all wet."

THE DEATH OF SALSEDO

On May 3, 1920, two days before the arrest, Andrea Salsedo, an anarchist friend of Sacco and Vanzetti, committed suicide in New York or, as the radicals have it, was murdered. Salsedo and his death came into the trial during Vanzetti's testimony about his radicalism. After the trial Thompson filed affidavits about the death in purported support of the contention that there was a conspiracy between the Department of Justice and Katzmann to secure the conviction of Sacco and Vanzetti. The true circumstances were the following.

During the week preceding May 1, 1919, more than two dozen explosive packages were gathered from street mail boxes into the General Post Office of New York in the regular course of mail collection. Sixteen of these were stopped by a postal clerk because of insufficient postage and sent to the Short Payment Division in the Post Office Building, where they remained until their destructive possibilities were discovered. On April 29, near midnight, this postal clerk left his desk for home. On his way he read in an early-morning paper of the thirtieth that a bomb, delivered by mail to ex-Senator Hardwick's Georgia home, had been opened by a colored maid and had exploded and blown off her hands and severely injured Mrs. Hardwick, who was standing near. The postal clerk returned at once to the Post Office and segregated the sixteen packages. The next day these were minutely inspected by the Chief Inspector of the Bureau of Combustibles of the city fire department. They were found to contain bombs, which were destroyed without causing damage.

May 1, 1919, was marked by rioting and violence in many parts of the United States. In the Roxbury district of Boston a policeman was killed and many people hurt. More than ninety-four were arrested. Their cases came before Judge Hayden of the Roxbury District Court.

On June 2, 1919, there was a series of bomb explosions throughout the country. Judge Hayden's house was bombed, and also the house of my law partner, Leland Powers, a representative in the General Court who had been active in the passage of an anti-anarchy bill.

The most sensational explosion occurred in Washington, D.C. It damaged the front of the residence of Attorney General A. Mitchell Palmer and killed the man who was placing the bomb. Except for his ineptitude, the house and all its inmates would have been destroyed.

Shortly after this, Palmer appointed William J. Flynn, a private detective, to take charge of the investigation of criminal activities of which radicals were suspected. Under Flynn's direction, agents of the Department of Justice made the investigations which led to the arrest of Salsedo and Roberto Elia.

Flynn had very little evidence to go on. The man who had placed the bomb had been blown to pieces, and the only belongings that could be found were fragments of his clothing, the heel of a shoe, a portion of an overcoat collar, a sandal, a laundry tag, and a polka-dot tie.

The polka-dot tie seemed to be the best clue, and the manufacturer was soon found in New York. He said that he had made up an even dozen of the ties in a unique design as a test of their selling value. One dealer had purchased the whole dozen, and when the agents visited that dealer's shop they found that he had disposed of only one. He gave a rather vague description of the purchaser.

In the meantime, other agents, working on the heel, had discovered the cobbler who had made repairs on it. He gave a fair description of the man whose shoe had been repaired. A comparison of the two descriptions revealed some points of similarity.

Other agents sought the maker of the overcoat, basing their inquiries on the small portion they had found. Eventually, an East Side tailor was found who remembered making an overcoat of material something like that in the hands of the agent. A good description of the overcoat buyer was supplied by the tailor, who remembered his customer well.

The three descriptions were pieced together and the composite fitted a well-known Italian radical who had disappeared after telling a friend, about a week before the Palmer bomb was exploded, that he planned a trip to Washington.

Then, in a manner which the agents refused on May 3, 1920, to divulge to the press, the dead man's connection with the Galleani group[1] was determined. But efforts to identify which of the group had been associated with the man in the outrages led nowhere until Salsedo and Elia were apprehended.

A circular printed on pink paper was found at the scene of the Palmer explosion, and similar circulars were found at other places where bombs had been placed. The caption read "Plain Talk" and the printed signature, "The Fighting Anarchists." One of the paragraphs read:

> There will have to be bloodshed; we will not dodge. There will have to be murder. We will kill because it is necessary. There will have to be destruction. We will destroy to rid the world of tyrannical institutions.

While efforts to identify the man who was killed went on, agents were gathering clues to the origin of the circular. After months of careful investigation they discovered that it had been

[1] Luigi Galleani, a well-known Italian-born anarchist, published the paper *Cronaca Sovversiva* ("Chronicle of Subversion") in Lynn, Mass. His paper was denied the mails and subsequently was distributed privately by Boda and others. Galleani was deported in 1919, arriving in Genoa, Italy, on August 10. For a time he had lived on a farm in Wrentham, Norfolk County, Mass. He was reputed to be the leader of a group of anarchists known as the Galleani group. He emphatically denied that there was such a group but admitted that he was acquainted with Sacco and Vanzetti and knew them as anarchists.

printed at Canzani's printing shop in Brooklyn, New York, by two of Canzani's employees, Salsedo and Roberto Elia.

Salsedo was born in Sicily and came to New York in 1902, when he was twenty-five. Until June 1914 he was closely connected with the Italian anarchist group in this country and participated in the printing of the Italian anarchist paper *Cronaca Sovversiva.* In June 1914 he returned to Italy and served nine months in the army. He came back in October 1916 and joined the Galleani group at Lynn, Massachusetts, where he issued several newspapers of the Italian terrorist type.

Elia was born in Italy and came to America in 1906. He was for many years connected with the anarchist group at Paterson, New Jersey, and printed the anarchist newspaper *Quistione Sociale.* He also was with Galleani in the printing of *Cronaca Sovversiva.*

Salsedo admitted that he had printed "Plain Talk," and the Department of Justice learned that in May 1919 he had turned out seven hundred copies of the circular. He told the Department that the work was done under the direction of Nicholas Recchi, who furnished the manuscript. Recchi, a notorious anarchist, was one of the principals in the June 1919 plot and had later escaped to Italy.

After their arrest both men agreed to aid the government, but requested that they be protected against vengeance from their former confederates. At their request they were lodged in the Department of Justice offices at 21 Park Row, New York, and an office was fitted up for them to use as a bedroom. No attempt was made to put any restraint on them, and far from being held incommunicado they were visited twice daily by their attorney, Marcus C. Donato.

Acting on information furnished by Salsedo and Elia, the Department vainly sought the suspected principals. The police in the big cities of England, France, Italy, Portugal, and Spain were asked to cooperate. Reports from them indicated that some of the men sought were in hiding in Italy but that most of them had managed to get into Russia.

About two months after his arrest, at about 4:00 o'clock in the morning of May 3, 1920, Salsedo jumped through a window on the fourteenth story of 21 Park Row and killed himself. The crash of a shattered pane of glass awakened Elia, who was asleep in the same room, and he ran into the corridor, shouting for help. Federal agents rushed to the room and guessed what had happened from the shattered pane.

At first the Department tried to conceal the identity of Salsedo, but newspaper men somehow got a hint of it and of his connection with the June bombing. The agents then acknowledged Salsedo's identity but declined to discuss the matter further, lest full publicity should hamper their search for the suspects.

Their hand was forced, however, and they dropped the secrecy when Marcus C. Donato, counsel for Salsedo and Elia, charged publicly that his clients had been held for alleged connection with the bomb plots without his consent; that they knew nothing of the plots; and that Salsedo had been driven insane "by two months' confinement."

"I am confident that Salsedo was driven to a state of insanity by his confinement," Donato told the reporters. "He said to me the other day, 'I have told them all I know, but they keep me here, and it is dreadful. While I am here someone else may be guilty.'"

Donato admitted that he had been shown Salsedo's "alleged confession" but made light of it and according to the newspaper account was disinclined to talk about it. He admitted that neither Salsedo nor Elia had been subjected to the third degree and that the two times Chief Flynn had questioned them, he, Donato, had been present. Pressed by the reporters, he said that he had visited the men twice a day and had frequently conferred with Chief Flynn and with Charles T. Sculley, head of the Red Squad, about releasing them on bail. He admitted that, when he asked that they be discharged, Chief Flynn had pointed out that they would immediately be arrested on a charge of violating the New York State Anarchy Act; he, Donato, had decided not to apply for a writ of habeas corpus in their behalf.

When Flynn was shown Donato's statement, he told the reporters the whole story substantially as I have stated it, my authority
being the account which appeared in the *New York Times* of
May 4, 1920. Accounts of the death were also in the Boston morning papers of May 4, and Sacco testified that he first learned of it
on that morning. (1974) At that time there was no hint in the
papers that it might have been murder by the Department of Justice rather than suicide.

The death of Salsedo and the publicity materially hampered the
Government's effort to identify the perpetrators of the bomb
outrages, and soon thereafter Elia was permitted to leave the
country. On June 2, 1920, before he left, he executed an affidavit
in New York. This affidavit, said to have been found in Moore's
papers, was presented on July 12, 1927, to the Governor's Committee by Thompson, who stated that he did not know its origin
except that it was taken by a notary public.[2] (4983)

Elia's affidavit, obviously, as it seems to me, drawn for propaganda purposes, contradicts his counsel and the Department and
furnishes the following account:

[2] Thompson told the Governor's Committee that when Moore left Boston he
left an enormous pile of papers in charge of one Carpenter and it was a long
time before Carpenter would let Thompson see them. Carpenter told him, "I
will examine these papers and I will hand over to you those I think you
ought to have." Carpenter claimed a lien on the papers to secure a debt of
$300, and finally the Defense Committee paid this and he turned over the
papers. Some were handed to Thompson, but he had to rely on the Defense
Committee to sort them out. "They have been laboring day and night and
have produced from time to time different papers, most of them of no value.
This [the Elia affidavit] was handed to me last night and I thought it was of
value. They also fished out a copy of an editorial in the *New York American*
about this Salsedo case. I don't know whether Sacco and Vanzetti read that
particular editorial or not, but they must have read something like that because they [*sic*] went down and tried to defend the people arrested in New
York like the people arrested here." (4987-4988)

This does not ring true. It is hard to believe that Thompson would let
Carpenter retain control of Moore's papers or that the Defense Committee
would not have raised $300 to obtain them forthwith. Nor would Thompson,
a thorough man, permit the Defense Committee to decide what papers were
of value. I suggest that the Elia affidavit came from the files of the A.C.L.U.
or the I.L.D. Albert DeSilver, the Notary Public before whom it was sworn,
was a director of the A.C.L.U. and had acted as Treasurer of an I.W.W. Defense Committee.

I am in fear of the agents of the Department of Justice, and I want to go where I can be in peace. It is my desire that the matters in this affidavit be not made public while I remain in the United States. . . .

I was arrested on February 25, 1920 . . . and kept overnight at Police Headquarters. There they took my finger prints and photograph, and had me pass to be inspected before a hundred masked men . . .

. . . Lesley [a Department of Justice agent] was present at the beating of Salsedo, and directed the cessation of the beating "because there is danger," he said this after he had looked at Salsedo's eyes and fingernails. So Salsedo told me; he was on the point of fainting; he felt that his life had been saved by the intervention of Mr. Lesley.

. . . When they were conducting me to the interrogation room . . . through a dimly lighted corridor, Salsedo was standing there, surrounded by four agents with their coats off and their backs toward me . . . I heard from within the screams of Salsedo.

. . . Salsedo's face and forehead were bruised from the beating he had received. He had red spots and scratches on his cheeks and temples and his eyes were vacant. He was depressed. I never saw him normal [again]. (4983-5)

Elia did not complain of being beaten himself but only of long and tiring questionings and promises that were not kept. He admitted that he and Salsedo had preferred to stay at Park Row rather than go to prison and speaks of many conferences with his counsel, Mr. Donato. He does not suggest that anyone pushed Salsedo out the window. (4985)

The news of the arrest and detention of Salsedo seems to have come to Vanzetti by means of a letter from Salsedo's lawyer; he did not remember exactly when. (1812)

This news must have been disturbing to Vanzetti and other members of the Galleani group of anarchists in Massachusetts, for both Salsedo and Elia had been associated with that group and with Galleani. These questions must have occurred to them: What had they been arrested for? Was it something that suggested that other members of the group were in peril? Sacco had learned from Kelley in January or February that Federal agents were investigating him. (2004-2006) Was there a connection between this investigation and the arrest of Salsedo?

In any case, Vanzetti, Boda, and others (Sacco probably not included) formed a committee to raise money for the defense of Salsedo and for propaganda.

Toward the end of April 1920, that committee thought it necessary to send Vanzetti to New York to get information about Salsedo. From Sacco's testimony we gather that the committee wanted to know why Salsedo, Elia, and others had been arrested, whether there was a spy, and who the man was who was receiving all the money sent from Massachusetts and elsewhere in New England for the defense. (1848-1849)

So, on April 25, 1920, Vanzetti went to New York and on May 2 reported to the committee at a meeting held in East Boston at which Sacco was present. In New York, Vanzetti seems to have learned nothing about Salsedo. He had not seen him or Salsedo's counsel. Twice he did see Luigi Quintiliano, who told him that Walter Nelles had given advice about disposal of radical literature in anticipation of May Day raids by the Department of Justice.

In their arguments to the jury, Moore and Jeremiah J. McAnarney hinted rather vaguely that the death of Salsedo may have been in the minds of their clients when they were arrested and when they were telling falsehoods, but did not suggest that he had been murdered or that Sacco and Vanzetti feared murder for themselves. Katzmann in his argument did not name Salsedo, and he used the following language about Vanzetti's trip to New York:

> The defendant Vanzetti says that on April 25th, Sunday night, he took a train from Boston to New York, that he

went over there in the interests of some people in whom his organization had an interest, with whom we have no concern. . . . (2198)

Judge Thayer in his charge did not mention Salsedo.

By 1925 the death of Salsedo had been incorporated into the pronouncements of the Sacco-Vanzetti Defense Committee, in whose account of the arrest of Sacco and Vanzetti the following appears:

> Nicola Sacco and Bartolomeo Vanzetti were arrested May 5, 1920, on a streetcar in Brockton while on their way to arrange a meeting of radicals to protest the tragic death of their friend, Andrea Salsedo, at the hands, directly or indirectly, of Department of Justice agents. Salsedo had been seized two months before *on a deportation warrant* and was confined *illegally incommunicado* in the department chambers on Park Row, New York. His fellow prisoner, Roberto Elia, says Salsedo was *tortured* in the effort to get a confession of radical activities. On May 3, he pitched fourteen stories to his death, *whether murdered or a suicide is unknown.* Vanzetti had been active in the movement for Salsedo's release before his death and he and Sacco immediately became active in the movement of protest after the event. A handbill advertising the meeting at which Vanzetti was to speak was in their possession when they were arrested. (My italics.)[3]

The *death* of Salsedo is an event of no consequence in determining any issue in the Sacco-Vanzetti case. Sacco and Vanzetti learned about it on May 4, 1920, from newspaper accounts which do not suggest that it was anything but a suicide. It is impossible to believe that before the evening of the next day they had decided that Salsedo had been murdered and that they too were in danger of being murdered by the Department of

[3] Financial Report of the Sacco-Vanzetti Defense Committee, 1925, p. 4.

Justice and for that reason armed themselves, menaced a policeman, and told lies to Stewart and Katzmann.

There is a hypothesis upon which the Salsedo *arrest, detention, and confession* could have been used by the defendants. By the morning of May 4, 1920, if not several days before, Sacco and Vanzetti knew that two members of the Galleani group, Salsedo and Elia, had been aiding the Department of Justice in its efforts to find the perpetrators of the bomb outrages of June 2, 1919, and that the man who had been killed at the Palmer house had been identified as a member of that group. Sacco knew as early as January or February 1920 that federal agents were investigating him for something. If Sacco and Vanzetti, as members of the Galleani group or closely associated with it, had participated, directly or indirectly, in the bomb outrages or knew about them, they might well have feared that they were in danger of prosecution for their participation as conspirators or accessories. If that was in their minds, the consciousness of guilt to be inferred from their armed condition and their menacing of the policeman could be interpreted as consciousness of guilt of (or fear of prosecution for) bomb outrages rather than of murder, and *some* of their falsehoods might well have related to the bomb plots and a desire not to be associated with other members of the Galleani group or to implicate them.

But to use this explanation it would have been necessary to implicate themselves in charges nearly, if not quite, as serious as a murder charge. And it would not have helped them in the murder case, for there was still Sacco's pistol, the obsolete bullets, Berardelli's gun, identification witnesses, and the falsehoods about April 15 to explain. So Vanzetti had to testify that he had not learned anything about the Salsedo case in New York but had returned with advice to hide literature because of threatened raids on May 1, which was the day *before* his report to the committee and four days *before* Boda's car was sought.

Still following the hypothesis, the fear that through Salsedo or otherwise the Department of Justice had solved the bomb plots and implicated the Galleani group would explain Vanzetti's trip to New York and his desire to hide evidence (euphoniously called literature) and might even provide a motive for a robbery to obtain funds for defense of someone. It might also explain Sacco's plan to leave the country on a one-way passport to Italy. This trip seems to have come into his mind in March shortly after Salsedo and Elia were arrested and not long after Kelley told Sacco that the latter was under federal investigation. Surely it was not fear of deportation that led Sacco to deport himself. That the Department of Justice supposed that it had reason to believe that Sacco had some knowledge of the bomb plots is shown by its placing a man named Carbone[4] in the Dedham jail to spy on Sacco.

But this is all hypothesis and speculation and, so far as the merits of the Sacco-Vanzetti case are concerned, irrelevant. Certainly there was never any evidence that Sacco and Vanzetti did participate in the bombings, and as we have seen, Katzmann in his cross-examination of them did not mention Salsedo or the Galleani group or the bombings.

[4] Not Antonio Carbone, the fish peddler.

18 WHAT THE JURY THOUGHT ABOUT THE TRIAL

THE MOST SWEEPING CRITICISM of the fairness of the trial was that in Massachusetts in the year 1921 two Italian philosophical anarchists could not, because of race prejudice and hysterical fear of Reds, get a fair trial for murder.

This criticism rests on the assertion that prejudice and fear did exist and did operate on judge, jury, and prosecutors to such an extent that they all abandoned truth, honor, decency, and humanity in a frenzy of sadistic rage.[1]

No evidence of this sadistic rage is found in the recorded utterances of court or counsel during the trial or of seven of the surviving jurors. These jurors were interviewed in 1950 by Edward B. Simmons, staff writer of the New Bedford *Standard-Times,* who sums up their views in these words:

> The verdict of guilty was in accordance with the evidence, was a just verdict, and they would vote the same way today.

[1] Morgan in his discussion of the unfairness of the trial suggests that a defendant should be allowed to waive trial by jury and be tried by a judge or body of judges in cases where local feeling and prejudice make it difficult to secure a jury free from conscious or unconscious bias. The suggestion is worthy of consideration, but it should be pointed out that in the Sacco-Vanzetti case the defendants had even more than Morgan would have given them. Their case was "tried" three times, first by the jury, then by the Governor and Joseph Wiggin, and finally by a committee consisting of the President of Harvard, the President of the Massachusetts Institute of Technology, and a Judge of the Probate Court. "Without asserting that any human device is infallible, one may agree with Professor Samuel Williston that rarely, if ever, have accused men been so repeatedly and unanimously convicted by such competent tribunals." Henry Aaron Yeomans, *op. cit.,* p. 491.

The trial judge was eminently fair, indicated no inkling of prejudice, if he had any, to the jury, and his memory has been inexcusably sullied by defenders of Sacco and Vanzetti.

The so-called radicalism of the defendants played absolutely no part in the verdict. In fact, the jury is astounded still at the charge to the contrary, and amazed the trial ever became a worldwide *cause célèbre* on that basis.

From children of the four jurors known to be dead, it was learned that their juror-parents shared the sentiments of the survivors.

Juror Dever was interviewed by Simmons:

"How about the enduring charge that the defendants' radicalism was the basis for the finding of guilt by the jury?"

"That had nothing whatsoever to do with it," Mr. Dever replied. "Absolutely nothing. The question never came up. I think every juror will tell you that.

"The only thing we considered in the jury room was whether the defendants were guilty as charged by the prosecution in the indictments, or, as I would have expressed it before becoming a lawyer, whether Sacco and Vanzetti did what they were accused of or whether they did not.

"I can repeat it over and over again. That talk of radicalism is absurd. Radicalism had nothing whatsoever to do with it."

"And what about Judge Thayer, Mr. Dever? His conduct of the case has been the bullseye for every piece of literature ever printed condemning the trial."

"The judge was A-1. He never in any way, shape or manner let us know what his views were. Thayer may have had an opinion. He may have expressed it outside of court. But he didn't indicate his preference to the jury, I say that quite frankly."

Juror Ganley recalled:

"I was impressed by one aspect of the trial especially. That was that Judge Thayer was absolutely fearless and absolutely on the level. He was trying to do his job, thoroughly and not leaning either way.

"At the final showdown, when the jury was reaching its verdict, there were no objectors. It was 'Guilty.' Nobody had to put up an argument at all. Every member of the jury thought they were guilty.

"The more I've seen and heard, even after the trial, the more I am convinced they were guilty."

Testimony on the bullets stands out in juror King's recollection of the evidence. He remembers also his impression that Judge Thayer was "very fair":

"Every day he cautioned us to remember these men are innocent until proved guilty. He told us to keep our minds open. Repeatedly, repeatedly, he emphasized fairness.

"Anybody who says Sacco and Vanzetti were convicted because they were radicals and not on the evidence is all wet. Propaganda about their being radicals and being framed on the charges did not reach me before the trial. I was just a man in the street, minding my own business."

More reticent about commenting on the trial than any of the other jurors, George A. Gerard of Stoughton said his memory was none too good. He thought the verdict was entirely fair but that the case is best forgotten. He said:

"The outstanding thing about that trial was the judge. You can quote me on that. The fairest judge I ever saw or heard of.

"Who are these people who keep bringing up the case and complaining about the verdict? If they say the country was witch-hunting those days it must have escaped me. I don't remember all the radical talk. I always thought it was propaganda only.

"Am I bitter about it? Oh, no, not a bit of it. Such things

happen every day, trials like that. Heavens, no, I am not bitter, I just think the trial is best forgotten. Being on that jury did not affect my life, though it was a new experience for me. I suppose a murder trial is an everyday affair over the nation, though. That's the way I look at it."

Juror Marden's clearest impression from the trial was "the outstanding fairness of Judge Thayer. He was fair to the other side too, fair all around." Marden also recalls "the fairness of Mr. Katzmann. He didn't seem to be trying to put anything over on the defense."

Considering the evidence, Mr. Marden was impressed by identification witnesses, particularly Pelser, and the bullet testimony. He made the observation that all trial witnesses were not in agreement, but added;

> "In the case of life and death of a man I think people will testify as best they can.
>
> "I never have had a bit of reason to think the trial was anything but fair. I don't think we jurors thought of the defendants in any way except as two persons accused of murder.
>
> "The jury got along fine. I remember that when we went out we had a smoke, talked about something else for a few minutes and gradually brought up the subject. Everyone was of the same mind, the same opinion, that Sacco and Vanzetti were guilty."

At seventy-three, juror Seaward Parker of Quincy was still "rarin' to go" and, in a good-natured way, somewhat miffed that his machine-tool company thought his thirty-eight years with the firm merited him a pension.

"I'm tired and too old to work, retired at last," laughed Mr. Parker, who, with his wife, had just returned from an active summer of outdoor work in Maine.

The last juror chosen, he thought it a

"very fair trial by a good judge and heard by a good bunch of fellows. There never was a nicer crowd of men than that jury.

"I can't understand why the trial went around the world. They talked of Reds being involved in it, somehow. There never was a mention of Red in the courtroom or among the jury. I've been in hopes lots of times they would forget that trial, but it looks as if those so-called sympathizers will forever be bringing it up. I never could see where the idea of prejudice was picked up.

"Why should we want to pick up two Reds and try to convict them of murder? We did not know if they were Reds and we did not care.

"To my mind, and I really think this, the judge tried to help the defendants. He was square with us too."

"I am absolutely satisfied no jury ever would find Sacco and Vanzetti innocent. They might get a disagreement, but little possibility of that.

"I always thought it might have been a good idea to give them another trial in the years before sentence was carried out. The verdict of two juries would be more convincing, I believed. There was no doubt in my mind a second jury would have found them guilty like the first.

"I had no difficulty in my own mind arriving at a verdict."

The outstanding evidence to juror Atwood was that of the old-fashioned type of Winchester bullets, one of which was found in Berardelli's body and duplicates of which were found on Sacco when he was arrested. Sacco's manner also was recalled by Mr. Atwood, who at sixty-four was physically vigorous. He thought Sacco's attitude when asked to try on the cap found at the scene was peculiar. It was this juror's opinion that the defendant was determined not to put on the cap in a normal fashion, because he kept pulling it down virtually over his ears. He continued:

"Of course, both sides made a mess of some witnesses. To my mind it shows what was going on, the pressure I mean, for winning the case. But this we learned later. Never did there come to the knowledge or eyes of the jury any of the out-of-court pressure about the defendants being radicals.

"I never saw things so well balanced as they were by that judge. If Katzmann made a point, Thayer would lean over backward to find something to balance it for the defense. If there was anything against those two fellows, he would do all in his power to compensate for their side.

"He never showed any bias to us. We never knew he had been the presiding judge at Bridgewater. He never showed any favoritism. If I remember anything with absolute clarity, it was the judge's fairness."

Undoubtedly the heaviest burden of taking on that jury service fell to the lot of Lewis McHardy of East Milton. McHardy died May 1, 1947, aged eighty-three, almost exactly twenty years after his home was demolished by a bomb, presumably placed by radical Sacco and Vanzetti sympathizers, none of whom was apprehended.

His son, John McHardy, who lived in the new house built on the site by popular subscription of Milton residents, said his father never had any regrets about the verdict.

"My father was a straight-shooter. He never liked to talk about the trial and avoided mentioning it. He had taken a juror's oath and felt it binding until his death. He was as honest as any man could be, and as good.

"He discussed few details with his children. He greatly admired Judge Thayer, though, and stood up for him whenever the occasion demanded. He always was fond of the other jurors and said he had had a happy time with them despite being locked up so long.

"I never heard him express an opinion about any influence radicalism had in connection with the trial. There wasn't much talk about on that subject during the period. That came afterward. We didn't hear about radicals until those who wanted Sacco and Vanzetti to be martyrs went to work.

"It was always kind of hard for our family, that trial. We received notes and crank letters, and finally our house was blown up. After that trouble at home, father was even more determined to forget the trial.

"I don't know why they picked out our house. I suppose it was at that time there was no other building within 200 yards and many trees and bushes afforded the perpetrators adequate concealment."

Wallace Hersey was eighty-one when he died August 13, 1942. As with other Sacco-Vanzetti jurors who have passed on, the family was pleased that no connection with the trial was mentioned in his obituary. The jury has been so neglected in discussion of the Sacco-Vanzetti verdict that most community records on its members have been lost, but the Hersey children made no reference to their father's trial connection at his death.

"He thought they had a square deal," said Miss Mary E. Hersey, a daughter, who added:

"He thought it was a civic duty to accept jury service, but he was glad to forget that case the last few years. Their sympathizers made it so hard for everybody."

After the Simmons interviews were published, the eighth surviving juror, R. Frank Waugh, who had been "missing" but who had seen the Associated Press condensed account, wrote to the New Bedford *Standard-Times*[2] that he shared the view of the other jurors, as published, that Sacco and Vanzetti were convicted on the evidence, that radicalism played no part in the verdict and that the presiding judge, Webster Thayer, was eminently fair.

Elwin H. Hauver, one of two official court stenographers at the Dedham trial, told Simmons in November 1950:

"You can't put it too strongly, my belief in the justice of the verdict and guilt of the men and the fairness of the trial.

[2] November 15, 1950.

"Of course, I've seen a lot of murder trials, and other trials in 40-odd years and I think I'm in a position to be a pretty good judge. At the time of the Sacco-Vanzetti trial there was not a single person I ran across in the courtroom who thought they were innocent. With one exception, a newspaperman."

Of Judge Webster Thayer, who has been accused of prejudice by Sacco-Vanzetti sympathizers, Mr. Hauver declared:

"There was no question about his fairness. There was no question about his courage, either. He was not afraid of man or the devil."

In his opinion the so-called radicalism of the defendants played no part in influencing the verdict of guilty. Most of the sensational emphasis on this came after the trial, he believes.

"We, the other stenographer and I, heard every word said, we heard every consultation between judge and counsel and prosecution. There was not a single word relating to that trial involving the court we did not hear. And in my mind there was no question that Sacco and Vanzetti were guilty as charged."

ALLEGED MISCONDUCT OF THE JURY: THE RIPLEY MOTION

WE NOW COME to the consideration of the posttrial motions and maneuvers which kept the case alive for six years after the verdict. The first of these was the Ripley motion.

Walter H. Ripley, a stockkeeper in Quincy, was the foreman of the jury. The McAnarneys were Quincy lawyers and knew Ripley. In his *voir dire* of June 2, 1920, Ripley answered all questions satisfactorily, but Katzmann rose to inform the court and defense counsel that Deputy District Attorney Adams had acted as counsel for Ripley at one time. Judge Thayer asked if that would influence his judgment, and Ripley replied it would not. Thayer said he would excuse him if counsel desired. The district attorney said he would acquiesce if the defendants wished to challenge him for cause. The defendants' lawyers said they were satisfied with the juror and he was accepted by both sides.[1]

Ripley, described by Simmons as a big, solid man with drooping handlebar moustaches like those of William Howard Taft, was nearly seventy years old at the time of the trial and died suddenly at his workbench on October 10, 1921. Because of the turbulence of the Sacco-Vanzetti case, his death led to suspicion, unusual police activity, and public concern, but the final decision was that his death was from natural causes.

On November 8, 1921, less than a month after his death, the First Supplementary Motion for a New Trial, which was based on

[1] *Boston Herald,* June 3, 1921.

Ripley's conduct as a juror and is known as the Ripley motion, was filed.

This motion was based on the affidavit of Jeremiah J. McAnarney, one of the defense counsel, who recalled a conversation in Quincy with Ripley shortly after the conclusion of the trial. In this conversation Ripley had told him this story:

Ripley, at the time of the trial, owned a .38-caliber Harrington & Richardson revolver of the same make, caliber, and model as the revolver found in Vanzetti's pocket at the time of the arrest. The latter was the revolver which, as the Commonwealth claimed, belonged to the dead guard, Berardelli. Ripley expected to be an official at a fireman's muster on May 30, 1921, and to prepare for that had taken three shells loaded with powder from his revolver and substituted blank shells, to be used at the muster to give signals in various competitions. He put the three loaded shells in his vest pocket and carried them with him into the courtroom when he was summoned as a juror. He did not remember that he had them until the revolver and the five unexploded cartridges found in Vanzetti's pocket were introduced in evidence. (3550-3551)

On Friday, October 7, 1921, three days before Ripley's death, McAnarney had another conversation with Ripley. At that time Ripley showed him the three shells and McAnarney called his attention to the fact that two of the shells were marked with a straight scratch across the percussion cap and one with a cross. Ripley refused to tell when the marks had been made.

Ripley then said that, when he placed his shells side by side with the Vanzetti shells, his appeared to be slightly longer. He had made the comparison before the verdict was rendered. There had been a discussion about this with Ripley's fellow jurors, but Ripley refused to tell McAnarney who participated in it or what was said.

"Ripley died suddenly on the 10th day of October 1921 before his affidavit could be taken." (3550)

Affidavits of the surviving jurors were filed, indicating the following: Hersey and Dever had seen the Ripley bullets during the trial. Ganley, Gerard, McHardy, McNamara, Atwood, King, Marden, and Parker had never seen them. Waugh did not expressly deny seeing them or say he had. Ganley swore that "after the jury retired to deliberate upon its verdict no bullets or objects other than the exhibits in said case were produced, examined, or discussed by said Ripley or by any of the jurors, so far as I know." The affidavits of the other ten jurors contained the same or similar language. (3558 *et seq.*)

This was the state of the Ripley record in November 1921 (the last of the jurors' affidavits was dated November 22), and it obviously was not much to go on as evidence of misconduct by the jury.

On March 20, 1923, Moore asked the firearms expert Albert H. Hamilton to come to Boston and examine the exhibits and review the expert testimony. Among other things, Hamilton was asked to look at the Ripley shells and the Vanzetti shells. His findings as to these were incorporated in an affidavit dated April 14, 1923. In this affidavit Hamilton had the effrontery to say, as an expert, that the ink marks on the Vanzetti cartridge bullets (i.e., the cartridges taken from the pistol found in Vanzetti's pocket at the time of the arrest) were placed there at a time after the cartridges were taken into the juryroom and before the return of the verdict. This meant that the expert claimed he could tell nearly two years later the very day and hour when ink marks had been put on cartridges. (3577)

With nothing more than this to go on, and in the teeth of the jurors' affidavits, the defense contended that the jury had used the Ripley cartridges in the jury room to determine the comparative age of the Vanzetti cartridges and Ripley shells, and for that purpose had marked the Ripley shells with scratches and the Vanzetti shells with ink marks.

A second contention was that the microscope showed that the Ripley bullets had been pressed into the Vanzetti revolver during the deliberations of the jury. This contention was based on Hamilton's measurements which were disputed by Captain Charles Van Amburgh, the Commonwealth ballistics expert. (3569)

Judge Thayer overruled the Ripley motion on October 1, 1924, and filed a long decision reviewing the facts and passing on fifty-four requests for rulings filed by the defense. The motion was elaborately argued by the defendants in their briefs before the Supreme Judicial Court, which had all the affidavits and Thayer's decision before it. It is quite possible that Thayer could have disposed of the motion on the technical ground that a juror cannot impeach a verdict by testifying to his own misconduct, but he preferred to consider the merits and did so. The Supreme Judicial Court sustained the denial in an opinion which reviewed the facts rather elaborately before determining that there was no abuse of discretion shown and no error of law.[2]

Frankfurter does not make much of the Ripley motion and does not mention the affidavits of the jurors or of Hamilton. "Presumably," he says, "comparisons were made . . ."

Fraenkel states the evidence but makes no comment. Morgan admits that the Ripley motion could not seriously be considered as a ground for a new trial but criticizes Judge Thayer for laboring unnecessarily to make this plain and spending pages in an elucidation of the obvious.[3]

THE DALY AFFIDAVIT

In support of the Ripley motion, the affidavit of William H. Daly was also filed. Daly remembered a conversation he had with Ripley a few days previous to May 31, 1921, at the Quincy-Adams railway station at or about 4:15 P.M., which ran something like this:

> RIPLEY: I will be leaving you for a couple of weeks.
> DALY: Where are you going?
> RIPLEY: I am going to Dedham to serve on the jury.
> DALY: Are you going to be a juror in the case of the two "ginneys" charged with the murder at South Braintree?
> RIPLEY: Yes, I am going to sit on the petit jury.

2 *Commonwealth v. Sacco*, 255 Mass. 369, 445-450. (4345-4350)
3 Morgan, *op. cit.*, pp. 116-117.

DALY: I do not believe that they are guilty. It is not reasonable to suppose that a man would go and rob a factory where he had worked, was well-known, and in broad daylight.

RIPLEY: Damn them, they ought to hang them anyway. (3579-3580)

Judge Thayer in his decision on the Ripley motion did not mention the Daly affidavit, and this omission was the ground of an exception which went to the Supreme Judicial Court and of a criticism by Morgan. That court, in the opinion cited above, held that the affidavit was filed as a supplement of the Ripley motion, and that Judge Thayer's order denying that motion carried with it the denial of the supplement thereto. Further:

> Even though the Daly affidavit was undisputed, the judge was not bound to believe him, nor was he required to give the reasons for his action. . . . Furthermore, before being sworn as a juror, it must be assumed that Ripley had answered in the negative . . . whether he had expressed or formed an opinion or was sensible of any bias or prejudice. (4350)

If Ripley did enter the jury with the feeling that "they ought to hang them anyway," he should not have served. That is obvious, and the question is whether Daly quoted him correctly. It is significant that Daly did not tell the defense about this conversation much earlier, preferably during Ripley's lifetime. And how did Daly know that one or both the defendants had worked at the factory that was robbed? No one else ever knew that.

The Governor does not mention the Daly affidavit. The Advisory Committee reviewed it and came to the conclusion that Daly must have misunderstood Ripley or that his recollection was at fault. (5378q)

SOME TIME before the trial, Frank J. Burke, who became a defense witness, told Moore and Moore's investigator, Robert Reid, that he, Burke, had seen an itinerant salesman named Roy E. Gould in the streets of South Braintree immediately after the commission of the crime.[1] Burke knew Gould but did not know his address, except that he knew that it was customary for Gould to travel with shows and carnivals during the summer months, and during the winter to go from factory to factory demonstrating and selling merchandise. The efforts of Moore and Reid to locate Gould failed. (3506-3509)

Burke also endeavored to find Gould.[2] At the State House in Boston he made inquiry and found that a peddler's license for 1920 had been issued to Gould and that his address on April 17, 1920, was 137 Columbus Avenue, Boston. Inquiry by Burke at that address did not reveal the whereabouts of Gould at that time, nor did other inquiries in Massachusetts. For some reason not divulged, Burke did not tell Moore and Reid that he had Gould's

---

1 When Burke came to make his affidavit of April 6, 1923, he had forgotten that he had told Moore and Reid that he himself had *seen* Gould in the streets of South Braintree on April 15, 1920, but remembered that, while living at the Norris Hotel in Brockton, *he had been told* by a man named Wolf that he understood that one Roy E. Gould was a witness to the crime. (3509)

2 When Burke was on the stand, Katzmann inquired about several visits Burke had made to Moore's office and asked: "Now, I do not want anything of a confidential nature, but weren't you really assisting in the preparation of this case?" A. "No, absolutely not." (998) This answer seems inconsistent with what Burke did in the Gould matter.

permanent address. With it, and with Burke's knowledge of Gould's habits, it should have been possible for Reid to locate him before the trial.

Some time during the early spring of 1921 and previous to May 31, 1921, when the trial began, Burke wrote a letter to his brother, Edward P. Burke, of Hartford, Connecticut. This letter was lost, but Edward P. Burke remembered that it was on the letterhead of the Sacco-Vanzetti Defense Committee, 68 Pemberton Square, Boston. In this letter, Frank told Edward that he had *heard* that Gould was a witness to the shooting and that Moore wanted to locate him. Edward then devoted half a day and a number of nights to visiting half a dozen carnivals and shows at irregular intervals but did not locate Gould. Edward's affidavit is dated September 24, 1923. (3511-3512)

And so Roy E. Gould did not testify at the trial.

On the evening of Wednesday, November 2, 1921, Burke was at the Hotel Windsor in Portland, Maine, and, happening to look at the register, saw the name of Roy E. Gould. Some time after this, Gould came in to the hotel and Burke engaged him in conversation and in a casual way asked him about things. The following morning, at 10:00 A.M., Burke wrote to Moore a letter from which the following is quoted:

> He [Gould] tells this story in substance. Came to Braintree from Brockton on 2:30 train, got off train and talked with taxi driver for a few minutes, asked driver what time they paid off as he wanted to open up and sell some paste, the driver said "right away now and there goes the paymaster." *I followed them down the street and when they got in front of the shop the things happened. I was right behind them and one of them aimed and shot at me, the bullet going through the lapel of my coat.* . . . He describes the man who did the work and says he will never forget his looks. (My italics.)

Gould in his affidavit, which is dated March 17, 1922, told a very different story. In the affidavit he walked from the station only to a point on Pearl Street, where he was standing when the murder car approached and passed him. He saw a man jump into the car, and shortly before it passed him he saw a man climb from the back of the car over the back of the front seat and settle down in the front seat on the right-hand side of the driver. This man had a revolver in his hand which he pointed and fired at Gould when he was within five or ten feet of him. The bullet passed through Gould's overcoat. The man who shot at him was wearing a cap. Gould's description of the man who shot at him is detailed and would not have fitted Sacco. (3504)

This revised version of Gould's story is, except for the bullet hole, very like the story which Burke himself told on the stand. He, too, was in South Braintree by chance, he too was standing in the street when the murder car went by, he too saw a man climb from the back of the car to the front, he too was shot at, he too described the man who shot at him in a way which did not fit Sacco, and he too put a cap on the man in the car.

On Sunday, November 6, 1921, Moore saw Gould in Portland. On the tenth, Gould came to Moore's office in Boston and was shown pictures of Vanzetti and Sacco. He was sure that neither was the man who shot at him. Moore told him that he wanted Gould to see the two men personally, and on the same day Gould was shown Sacco at the Dedham jail. For some reason, he was never shown Vanzetti, but from the three photographs he saw he was sure that Vanzetti was not the man he saw in South Braintree and in no sense resembled him. He was equally sure about Sacco. (3505)

Although this visit to Sacco occurred on November 10, 1921, and although Moore knew from Burke's letter that Gould intended to go south for the winter, Moore did not get an affidavit from Gould until March 17, 1922, and it was not until May 4, 1922, that the Gould motion for a new trial on this "newly discovered evidence" was filed. This delay has never been explained.

In his affidavit of March 17, 1922, which gave his second story of the shooting, Gould went on to say that after the shooting he went down to the immediate scene of the shooting and saw the dead man and shortly thereafter was spoken to by Mr. Jeremiah F. Gallivan, Chief of Police of South Braintree, who asked him what he was doing in South Braintree. Gould explained to Gallivan what his business was and opened up his case and showed him the shaving paste he had to sell, and then Gallivan took his name and address. (3504)

But Gallivan did not remember it that way. On January 25, 1923, he made affidavit that on April 15, 1920, after the shooting of Parmenter and Berardelli, he went to the scene of the shooting; that at that time or any time thereafter, no one by the name of Gould approached him or said anything to him; that he talked with no one who had with him a case with any articles used in connection with razors or safety razors or with anyone who had a bag or travelling case with him; and that he never heard of Roy E. Gould until his name was brought to his attention by the District Attorney after the filing of the Gould affidavit in 1922. (3507)

The Gallivan affidavit did not stop Moore. On March 15, 1923, Gould "corrected" his original affidavit by substituting officer John J. Heaney of the Braintree Police for Chief Gallivan as "the officer who interviewed him." (3508)

Heaney, in an affidavit of the same day, swore that on April 15, 1920, he had in the absence of Gallivan taken charge of the investigation and

> within a very short time of the shooting he interviewed a man who was *near the gatetender's shanty* at the railroad crossing near the shooting and took his name, address, and what he saw of the shooting and the occupants of the so-called bandit car, and this information was given to the police department of Braintree and the State Police; that the man's name was Roy Emerson Gould. (3508-9; my italics.)

When Chief Gallivan appeared before the Advisory Committee on July 18, 1927, he had forgotten that he had never heard the name of Gould until after the Gould affidavit of March 17, 1922, was filed, but he remembered the following conversation on April 15, 1920, in the Rice & Hutchins factory:

> HEANEY: Jerry, there's a fellow outside here that I am holding and he's willing to stay but he wants to get away as soon as he can; I have kept him for two hours; his name is Gould and he was shot through the coat.
>
> GALLIVAN: Well, John, we are kind of busy in here now but I will take it up with the State Police.

Then Gallivan called officer Scott of the State Police over and told him about Gould, and Scott said, "We'll be out in a few minutes." The few minutes drifted into half an hour, and when they went out Gould had gone. Gallivan never had Gould's name and address and guessed that Heaney had kept it. (5169)

The actions of Gallivan and Heaney are inexplicable. Gould, if either of his stories was true, was an eyewitness of the greatest value. He had been fired at by one of the murderers at a distance of five or ten feet and had a bullet hole in his overcoat. A little curiosity about the bullet hole and a little search for the spent bullet would seem to have been in order. The overcoat itself might be a valuable exhibit. Gould should have been interviewed at length and taken with other eyewitnesses to the State House the next day to look at pictures from the Rogues' Gallery and brought to Brockton after the arrest.

Gould appeared before the Governor but did not appear before the Advisory Committee. (We are not told why.) The Governor did not mention him, but the committee considered the affidavits and Thompson's argument and said in their report: "Two questions arise in his case: first, whether his evidence discovered by the defendants since the trial is sufficient to demand a new trial; and second, whether it shows a suppression of evidence by the Commonwealth." (5378-5380)

The committee dismissed the first question because the new evidence was merely cumulative and was balanced by the evidence of two witnesses who had not testified at the trial but would have identified Sacco (Mrs. Hewins[3] and Lottie Packard[4]); and the committee did not find suppression.

Thompson's argument that Gould had been suppressed by the Commonwealth was a curious one. The affidavits show that Moore and Reid knew of Gould before the trial, that Burke knew his permanent address, and that his name had appeared in the *Boston Post*. There is nothing to show that Katzmann ever heard the name or that the Commonwealth ever had the address, but even if they had, what harm was done to the defendants in "suppressing" something which they knew themselves and was public knowledge? (5289)

But, be that as it may, it is obvious that Gould's two stories were fabrications, either one of which would have been shattered in cross-examination.

3 See Chapter 9 ("The Eyewitnesses").
4 See Chapter 24 ("Lottie Packard").

Louis Pelser, a young man in his twenties, was a shoecutter in the Rice & Hutchins shoe factory, working in the first floor above the basement. He identified Sacco sitting in the courtroom as the man who was standing over the body of Berardelli with a gun in his hand, and he used this language: "Well, I wouldn't say it was him, but he is a dead image of him." He also gave the number of the bandit car as 49783.[1]

Pelser had talked with State Police officer Albert L. Brouillard shortly after the murder, saying he had the number of the car, but that was all he could testify about. Later, on March 26, 1921, Robert Reid, an investigator for the defense, had talked with Pelser, and Pelser had told him about what he told Brouillard but in more detail. (5578-5587) Pelser was summoned as a witness by the Commonwealth and came to court on the morning of June 10, 1921.

At the noon recess on the day Pelser testified, Assistant District Attorney Harold P. Williams talked with Pelser for the first time. He had expected to get nothing from him except the num-

---

[1] The number plate bearing the number 49783 belonged to Warren H. Ellis, a witness who testified that he lost it in Needham, January 6, 1920. (667) This number was seen on the murder car by Pelser at the time of the shooting, (296) four digits of it (83 at the end and a 9 and a 7) by Julia Kelliher in Brockton during the getaway, (591) and two digits of it (a 4 and a 9) by Francis Charles Clark in North Stoughton, also during the getaway. (575)

ber of the car, but in the course of the interview he learned where Pelser had been standing at the time of the shooting.

"Well," said Williams, "if you were standing there, you must have been in a position to see who was doing the shooting."

"Yes."

Williams then showed him a picture of Sacco, and Pelser said, "That looks like the man."

Williams then asked Pelser to go to the rear entrance of the courthouse a few minutes before 2:00 o'clock to see the prisoners brought back from the jail at the end of the noon recess. Pelser did this and came back to Williams's office, where Williams said, "Is Sacco the man?" With the sweat pouring off his forehead, Pelser said, "By George! If Sacco isn't the man, he is a dead ringer for him."

Williams then said, "It is your duty to go into court and testify to the truth."

A few minutes later Pelser was put on the stand and gave his testimony, identifying Sacco in the words he had used to Williams.

Moore in his cross-examination used the transcript of the Reid interview, and Pelser admitted that he had lied to Reid and to the police, giving as his reason that he did not want to go to court.

The defendants introduced two fellow employees of Pelser to impeach his testimony by evidence that Pelser, at the time of the murder, did not have the opportunity to observe what he had claimed in his direct testimony but had ducked under a bench when the shooting started. Another fellow employee testified to hearing Pelser say the same day that he did not see anybody. (1161-1164; 1122 *et seq.*; 1168 *et seq.*)

Katzmann in argument had this to say of Pelser:

> He was frank enough here, gentlemen, to own that he had twice falsified before to both sides, treating them equally and alike, and he gave his reason. I think he added that he had never been in court before. . . . He is big enough and manly enough now to tell you of his prior falsehoods and

his reasons for them. If you accept them, gentlemen, give such weight to his testimony as you say should be given.

On Saturday afternoon, February 4, 1922, Pelser, who had been out of work for four weeks and on the bum, was brought by Thomas Doyle, an employee of the Sacco-Vanzetti Defense Committee, to Moore's office at 68 Pemberton Square, Boston, and there, behind a locked door and in the presence of three other men and a stenographer, was interrogated by Moore. Questions and answers were recorded by the stenographer and signed and sworn to by Pelser that afternoon. (5565-5577) In this statement Pelser repudiated his identification and swore that he had been "forced" by Williams to testify as he did.

In the course of the afternoon Pelser was promised a job by Moore and was also invited to a party at the Westminster Hotel that evening.

Pelser sobered up by Monday, February 6, and wrote the following letter to Katzmann that day:

> 287 Centre St.
> Jamaica Plaine
> Feb. 6, 1922

Mr. Katzmann,

Dear Sir: Saturday afternoon a man called for me in regards the Sacco Case. He did not say which side he represented.

He asked me if I could give a little information on the case.

I was drinking pretty heavy that day. He said I want to show a couple of pictures and got me on the way in town gave me some money bought a dinner cigars & cigaretts we went into some office in Pemberton Sq. he introduced me to Mr. Moore then he sat me down & locked the door Moore said to me you look like a white man.

He patted me on the back & gave me a Cigar & said give me a little dope on the Sacco Case he handed me a couple of pictures & asked me if I ever saw them. I said "no," he showed me some more. One word led to another, he got around me some way & I didn't know what I was up against. He had 3 or 4 men in his office & a girl stenographer. He asked me one question & other and finally had my whole story contradicted what I had said at the Dedham Court. I am worried at the way they have framed me up & got me in to trouble. When it was over one of the men asked me if I would not have a drink & invited me to a big dinner & dance at the West Minister Hotel. Some how I refused to go because I felt it was another trap to get me to say more.

When I came to my Senses the next day & had a little talk with my folks they told me to get in touch with you as soon as I could I tried to get you on the phone and then decided I had better write you.

Hoping you will give this your immediate attention and favor me with an early reply.

Respectfully
Louis Pelser

P.S.   I forgot to mention that I also signed two papers of some kind.

L.P. (5584)

Afterwards, on February 12, 1922, Williams took his statement; in it the circumstances of Pelser's testimony and the circumstances of the statement taken by Mr. Moore were related. (5587-5595)

The allegation in the Pelser motion was that his testimony given at the trial was false and that it was made at the time in response to some sort of force, either physical or psychological, tantamount to fear or intimidation. Judge Thayer in his decision on this motion quoted the letter of February 6, 1922, referred to the affidavit of Pelser taken February 12, 1922, and two counter affidavits of Messrs. Katzmann and Williams in which they denied that there was any influence whatever exercised upon Pelser as to what his testimony on the witness stand should be. Judge Thayer found that these affidavits were true and that Pelser's statement to Moore was not at all satisfactory or trustworthy. (5596-5597) The defendants did not take the Pelser matter to the Supreme Judicial Court for review. (5564)

Pelser was only five or six feet away from the shooting and so, perhaps, in the best position of anyone to identify the man who killed Berardelli. The fact that he got the car number is proof that he was not under the bench all the time, and his falsehoods before the trial may be explained by the natural desire of a nervous and unstable young man to avoid trouble. It is difficult to find in him a motive for perjury on the stand. Williams would not and could not have "forced" his testimony except by urging him to tell the truth. Pelser's letter of February 6, 1922, is proof that he was not without conscience and wanted his identification to stand as the truth.

In the Simmons interview, the Pelser testimony was mentioned by jurors Marden and Dever. Both were impressed by it and thought that Pelser on the stand was telling the truth, although he had lied before.

A Victrola salesman who gave his name as Carlos Edward Good-ridge was playing pool in Magazu's poolroom near the railroad on Pearl Street at the time of the murder. He testified that he heard several shots, went to the door, and stepped out. As he did so, he saw an automobile coming toward him. A man in the automobile poked a gun at him when he was about twenty-five feet away, and he went back into the poolroom.

After the car went by, the witness ran out into the middle of the road to see if he could get the number. "I took it to be a Buick car from the back end of it." The car was dusty and the window torn out in the back, and something was sticking through the hole in the back curtains. The side curtains on his side were flapping. Because of the dust, Goodridge did not get the number.

Shortly after the murder, Goodridge got himself into trouble with the law by committing larceny from his employer. For this he was indicted by the same grand jury that indicted Sacco and Vanzetti, and on the same day. On September 28, 1920, at a session of the Superior Court in Dedham, Goodridge pleaded guilty. Upon his promise to make restitution (a promise he kept), his case was "filed," and he was placed on probation. While Goodridge was waiting in the courtroom for his case to be reached, Sacco and Vanzetti were arraigned and pleaded not guilty. Goodridge at this time recognized Sacco as the man who had pointed the gun at him. On the stand he made a positive face-to-face identification of Sacco as that man.

Goodridge's real name was Erastus Corning Whitney. He was born in Greene County, New York, and brought up in Cohocton, Steuben County. In 1892, when seventeen or eighteen years old, he stole two gold watches worth twenty dollars each from his aunt and on a plea of guilty was sent in 1893 to the New York State Reformatory. In 1908 he stole $62.50, and again after a plea of guilty he served part of a sentence of not less than one year, six months nor more than two years at the Auburn State Prison.

On November 24, 1911, he was indicted in Livingston County, New York, for second-degree grand larceny, the amount of the theft being forty-two dollars. This indictment was never served on Whitney, who had escaped from New York and was never sought outside the state by the authorities.

Whitney adopted the name of Carlos E. Goodridge in 1914 without order of court.

After the Sacco-Vanzetti trial, Moore gathered proof of Goodridge's criminal record and supplemented the court records and prison photographs with affidavits about other alleged crimes of Goodridge, his marital and extramarital adventures, divorces, changes of name, and religious experiences. These affidavits are detailed and contain copious quotations from letters written by, to, or about this weak and wayward petty criminal and bigamist. Quite naturally, his reputation for truth and veracity in the various communities in which he had lived was bad, and Moore gathered a sheaf of affidavits to that effect from several towns.

In the evening of July 12, 1922, Moore, accompanied by Mrs. Ethel W. Lee, a deputy sheriff of Kennebec County, Maine, and her sister-in-law, Marjorie L. Lee, a stenographer, drove to Vassalboro, Maine, where Goodridge was then living, and found Goodridge and his wife at a friend's house attending a religious service described by Moore as "singing hallelujahs in divine worship." Goodridge was called from the house and came out alone, leaving his wife with their friends. Moore and Goodridge sat on the front seat of the car, the two women in the back. The stenographer took notes of the conversation, at first without Goodridge's knowledge, later with his knowledge.

Mrs. Lee's notes (3873-3886) and Goodridge's affidavit (3850-3855) give a consistent account of what happened at this time. Moore showed Goodridge the prison pictures and several affidavits. Goodridge admitted that his real name was Erastus Corning Whitney and that he was under indictment in New York for grand larceny, and he said, "Well, the game is up, and I suppose I will have to go back to New York."

Moore then told Goodridge that he was not interested in the New York matter but that he was working for the interests of Sacco, and through a long series of questions tried to get Goodridge to repudiate his identification of Sacco and to state that pressures had been brought upon him by the police and by the District Attorney. Goodridge resisted this, and Moore asked for and was given a few minutes of private conversation with Mrs. Goodridge in the house. This had no result except to reduce her to tears. At this point, Moore returned to the car and told Goodridge that he would have to go back to New York. Turning to Mrs. Lee, the deputy sheriff, he said, "I think it is your duty to take him back to Augusta and notify the authorities."

She said, "Are you sure that he is wanted in this indictment?"

Moore said, "Yes, I had a talk with the District Attorney and also with the Sheriff of Livingston County and they want him."

Goodridge, although he knew that he could not be arrested without a warrant, consented to go to Augusta and did so. He was taken to the county jail, but the man in charge refused to take him in because there was no warrant for his arrest. Then the party went to police headquarters and Moore said to the officer in charge, a man named Corbett, that Goodridge was a fugitive from justice in New York State. Corbett asked him if he had a warrant for his arrest and Moore said he had not. Moore then said, "I am the lawyer representing Sacco and this man was popped on us, so I had no chance to look him up until after the trial, and in tracing his history I find he is wanted in New York State under an indictment for grand larceny."

Corbett then called up Judge Robert A. Cony of the Municipal Court of Augusta on the phone. It was about 1:30 A.M. and the judge told him the way in which Goodridge could be held until the next morning. The next morning Moore came to Goodridge and brought him a box of cigarettes and some cigars. Goodridge asked Moore if they had heard from New York, and Moore said Mrs. Lee had telegraphed to New York and that he would probably have a reply before noon.

At 9:00 A.M. Mrs. Lee and Moore came and took Goodridge before Judge Cony, who held Goodridge until they should hear from New York.

That night, when Judge Cony came to Goodridge, the latter asked him if he had heard from New York yet. Cony said that Moore had telegraphed to his man in New York and expected a reply at any time. Goodridge asked Judge Cony why he had not telegraphed himself instead of leaving it up to Moore; Moore, he said, was trying to put him in the wrong. Judge Cony asked him when the crime was committed and Goodridge told him in 1911. Judge Cony then said, "They will never bother you on it, and unless I hear from them tonight I will let you go in the morning, and I do not intend to have this office used by any lawyers to build up any cases for the State of Massachusetts or any other state, and the best thing you can do is not to see Mr. Moore again."

Moore came to Goodridge's cell that same evening and said he wanted to talk about the case, but Goodridge said he had nothing more to say. Moore then left and Goodridge never saw him again. Soon thereafter Goodridge was released.

Although he had not been able by blackmail or arrest to get a repudiation from Goodridge, Moore used the affidavits and records he had gathered as the basis for the Third Supplementary Motion for a New Trial (Goodridge), alleging that, since the witness had used a false name and had a bad record, he was not entitled to due faith and credit nor was his testimony worthy of being submitted to any jury.

Judge Thayer, in denying the motion, reviewed the manner and method adopted by Moore in seeking to obtain from Goodridge the evidence and characterized Moore's conduct as cruel and unjustifiable and a most atrocious invasion of the rights of

Goodridge. "To the credit of Goodridge, this scheme did not succeed." (3887-3891)

Thayer's decision, filed October 1, 1924, was not taken to the Supreme Judicial Court.

On April 15, 1920, Mrs. Lola R. Andrews, a divorced woman living in Quincy, went by train with an elderly woman, Mrs. Julia A. Campbell, from Quincy to South Braintree in search of work, arriving at the South Braintree station sometime after 11:00 A.M. The two women walked from the station to the Slater & Morrill factory on Pearl Street, passing Rice & Hutchins as they went. In the Slater & Morrill factory they inquired for work but were refused. They then retraced their steps as far as the Rice & Hutchins factory, went in, and again inquired for work. This time they were successful and were told to report the following Tuesday, April 20, 1920, the day after the holiday (Patriots Day). After the hiring they left the factory, walked to the station, and returned by train to Quincy, arriving there about 1:00 P.M.

Mrs. Andrews testified that, as she went into Slater & Morrill's, she saw a car standing by the roadside of the Slater factory on Pearl Street and that a man was working on the car, at the front part of it, and another man was sitting in the back of the car. The first man, who was bending over the hood as she went into the Slater & Morrill factory, was dark-complexioned, of medium height, smooth-faced, and dressed in dark clothing; the second was very light and emaciated, looked sickly, and had on a cap and long coat. She had no talk with either when she went in.

When the two women came out of Slater & Morrill's, the car was in the same position. The light man was standing behind the car and the other man was down under the car, back of the forward wheels, as if he was fixing something. Mrs. Andrews spoke to the dark man and he got up. She asked him to show her how to get to the factory office. He asked her, "Which factory office, the Slater?" and she said, "No, sir, the Rice & Hutchins." He then told her how to get into the factory.

At the trial Mrs. Andrews made a face-to-face identification of Sacco as the man who directed her. (337)

Mrs. Andrews was first interviewed by the defense, but not until January 1921. The original investigations had overlooked her, presumably because she was not an eyewitness of the shooting, had been in South Braintree only a few hours on April 15, and although hired that day was not at work until the following Tuesday. At the trial she testified that in January 1921 an Italian called on her at her room in the Alhambra Building and talked about the shooting. This, she said, was two or three days before Moore came to see her. (458-459) She could not name and was not asked to identify the Italian, but she said that he made her nervous.

On January 14, 1921, Moore went to Mrs. Andrews's room in the Alhambra Building, accompanied by two other men and his stenographer, Miss Wilhelmina Preed. (458) During the cross-examination at the trial Mrs. Andrews testified that Moore offered her a vacation if she would leave the state so that she would not have to testify. Also he offered her as good a job as she then had if her absence from the state resulted in her losing it. Moore did not deny this and did not put Miss Preed or the two men on the stand. Before the Advisory Committee in 1927 Miss Preed testified that she had not heard Moore make the offer. (5201)

On February 14, 1921, Michael E. Stewart, Chief of Police of Bridgewater, and State Police officer Albert L. Brouillard took Mrs. Andrews to the Dedham jail, where she was shown all the prisoners, including Sacco.

Soon after the trip to Dedham, Mrs. Andrews was assaulted at 1:00 A.M., on a day in February 1921. She had been out, and when she came home, she went into the toilet on the street floor before going up to her apartment. As she stepped into the toilet, she was grabbed by a man and forced down onto her knees. Her clothing was torn. The man was a tall, heavy, dark-complexioned man who wore a sailor's short winter coat. During her cross-examination Mrs. Andrews saw or thought she saw in the courtroom the face of the man who had assaulted her. She fainted, and her testimony had to be interrupted for a day or so.

After the trial, Moore made an elaborate effort to overcome the force of the Andrews testimony. Investigators in Quincy failed to find any evidence against her past life, and two men and a woman were sent to Maine, where they gathered several affidavits. Mrs. Andrews had been married to a man named Hassam and had by him a son, John Andrew Hassam. She divorced Hassam on the ground of drunkenness, but at the time of the divorce or later the custody of the son was taken from her because of her unfitness and awarded to another. An affidavit was obtained from the judge, Stephen S. Lancaster, who had made this order.

With these affidavits in hand, *Mrs.* Moore went to Maine and persuaded the son, then nineteen years old, to come to Boston on the representation that his own future depended upon his mother's recantation of her testimony. In September 1922 the boy came to Boston and registered at the Hotel Essex. Shortly after his arrival, Mrs. Andrews, still living in the Alhambra in Quincy, received a telegram from her son to the effect that he wanted her to come right away to Boston to see him at the Hotel Essex. He could not come to see her, the telegram said, because he was on business. "Well, of course, I could not understand what business my boy could be up to in Boston and I got excited," she testified. After sending a telegram and having an unsatisfactory telephone call with her son, Mrs. Andrews came to the Hotel Essex in the evening of September 9, 1922, and went with her son to his room.

> He said he had been brought up here on very urgent business and that his whole future was at stake and that I was the cause of it. I asked him what he meant and he referred to the Sacco and Vanzetti trial. He said that he had been told,

and was ready to believe, that the men were innocent, and he had been brought up here to get me to give my evidence to clear those men as it meant a whole lot in his life. We talked a few moments about it, and I think that perhaps I was angry and excited at him for coming, and he said "I have a couple of friends I want you to meet," and as he spoke those words he crossed the room and knocked on a door that was in the same room, as we went in. And these two men came out of the room to me. (3912-3913)

The two men were Fred G. Biedenkapp and John Van Vaerenwyck. Biedenkapp was a prominent Communist leader and a committeeman of the International Labor Defense after its organization in 1925, when it came into the Sacco-Vanzetti case. Sometime after the trial he was indicted in Massachusetts for violence in a New Bedford strike. Governor Allen tried to have him extradited from New York, but Governor Franklin D. Roosevelt denied the jurisdiction of Massachusetts, and Biedenkapp stayed in New York. Van Vaerenwyck was a member of the Sacco-Vanzetti Defense Committee and vice-president of the Massachusetts State Branch of the American Federation of Labor.

The two men started in on Mrs. Andrews at once about Sacco and Vanzetti, telling her what a wrong she had done.

Mrs. Andrews replied: "If I did that, I would be willing to undo it, but I thought I was right."

Then both men jumped to their feet and told her they were going to clear those men and that the witnesses that had testified against them, like herself, would be punished. (3913)

Fred [Biedenkapp] then saw that I would not have anything more to say about it, and in a few moments he told me that they had been to Maine a number of weeks for the purpose of gathering damaging evidence that could be used against me. He said he had the affidavits of twelve or thirteen different people, and that they were so black that I would never want to see them published. . . . He said this evidence that he said he had against me would not be used if I would be sure that I did not recognize Sacco as the man that I saw at South Braintree. (3914)

But Mrs. Andrews still refused to agree to change her testimony, and at 11:30 P.M., after more than three hours of pleading and threats, they all went out to supper at a nearby restaurant and from there drove to Moore's house at 5 Rollins Place, Boston, where they arrived about midnight. There they found Moore with two stenographers, one in the room in which they talked and one outside. Both were at work, one as a stenographer, one typing. The threats, blandishments, and appeals for the boy's future continued for hours.

> I told them that if I put my name to the paper that they had already drawn up for me that I was ruining all my future and that I could see that it meant a terrible disgrace to me.
>
> They told me no, that I was doing the grandest thing a woman could do, and that by doing what they wanted me to do I would gain the respect and friendship of everyone, and that my boy would not be ashamed to look upon me as his mother, and the evidence that they had brought with them from Maine would not be submitted to the court or to the eyes of anyone, not even to my son. On the other hand, if I refused they would use the evidence against me and that things would be made very disagreeable for both me and the son.
>
> I broke down and started crying. I asked them again if I could go home. I did not want to sign no papers, that I was in no condition to. They did not seem to take any notice of what I was saying, and my son offered no aid whatsoever. They let me rest from talking for a few moments, and left the room, returning with a colored man who they said was a Justice of the Peace. They then told me to sign my name to the paper and they started reading. I remember hearing the name of Sacco and Vanzetti being called, and I heard them saying something about that I had lied. . . .

Mr. Moore took me over to a small desk and laid the paper in front of me and told me to sign it.

I told him I would not do it, for I did not realize what I was doing.

Mr. Van Vorbrick [sic] and Fred both came over to me and patted me on the shoulder and told me to brace up and come through clean, that they knew that I was intending to do right, and that I was a good woman down at heart but that I had been misled. They dipped the pen in the ink and tried to pass it into my hand.

I refused again and said, "No, I can't sign it." All the time I was crying and asking them not to force me to sign it.

My son then said, "Mother, I want you to sign that paper, for it means a whole lot to me."

I do not seem to remember much what happened after that, only that some one of the three men—I do not remember which one did it—put the pen in my hand and told me to sign it, and asked my boy to come over to me and help me. My boy came over and put his arm around me and said, "Mother, sign this paper and have an end to all this trouble, for you did not recognize these men,"—meaning Sacco and Vanzetti—"and you will be only doing a terrible wrong if you send those men to the chair."

They made me believe that my evidence would be the sole means of electrocuting those men, if they were, and under that impression that perhaps I could have made a mistake in the identity of Sacco, and not having the affidavit showed, to protect the boy I signed my name to the paper. I was completely exhausted afterwards.

They told my boy that "Now, your mother needs you, we will leave you alone." They left me alone with my son. I cried and told the boy that I felt as though I never could look anyone in the face again, whereupon he told me that he knew that I had done the right thing and that he was proud of me, and that he would stand by me, and Mr.

Moore, Van Vorbrick [*sic*], and Fred would be my fast friends; that they would be the ones that would care for me, you know, meaning if anything happened, I suppose, that they would aid me.

Then Mrs. Moore came in with a tray of hot tea. She gave me tea and took me down to her room to rest a few moments before we started home. When I got home to Quincy it was four o'clock in the morning. (3917-8)

Mr. and Mrs. Moore, her son, and one of the others took her home to Quincy and stayed about half an hour. She wanted the boy to stay all night, but he left with the Moores and did not see her again except when he was sent out by the Moores.

Two days later, during the forenoon of September 11, 1922, Moore, Biedenkapp, and Robert Reid (the defense investigator) came out to Quincy and induced Mrs. Andrews to sign a short affidavit attesting the correctness of a purported statement made by her to Moore on January 14, 1921. (3903-3910)

About a week later Biedenkapp and Mrs. Andrews's son called for her and took her to Moore's house on the pretext that he wanted to see her about her affidavit, but it turned out that he wanted to question her about witnesses who had testified at the trial, Miss Devlin, Miss Splaine, and the one "that turned yellow, whoever he was."

Then and there I made up my mind to say no more about the trial. I said, "Mr. Moore, will you tell me how my boy came to be up here?" He said, "Yes, my wife went down and got him." (3920)

The Andrews motion for a new trial, filed September 11, 1922, was based on Mrs. Andrews's affidavits and on affidavits of Biedenkapp and Moore.

In the motion it was alleged that Moore and Jeremiah J. McAnarney had both interviewed Mrs. Andrews before the trial and had been led to believe that she would not identify Sacco; that, subsequent to the trial, having been taken by surprise by her testimony, they caused an inquiry to be made about her private life and had in their possession affidavits which included one by her son; that on September 7, 1922, he (the son) met Mrs. Andrews at the Hotel Essex and thereafter they called on Moore; that Mrs. Andrews then asked Moore whether he had caused inquiry into her private life and wanted to know the details; that Moore refused to divulge the details but did read to her an affidavit of Stephen S. Lancaster (the judge who had ordered the custody of her son taken from her); that Mrs. Andrews then signed the affidavit of September 9, 1922, admitting perjury at the trial, and that

> she now makes a repudiation of her testimony . . . either in response to an appeal directed to her sense of justice and a square deal and to her conscience, or in response to the appeals of her son . . . that she tell the truth and nothing but the truth, *or under the duress of revealing her private life . . . and her reputation for truth, integrity and veracity in the various communities where she has resided.* (3892-3895; my italics.)

This unblushing admission of duress by blackmail was signed by Moore and Jeremiah J. McAnarney, but it is noteworthy that McAnarney did not execute any affidavit in support of the motion. In the argument on the motion, Moore told Thayer, "There can be no coercion when the truth is spoken," (3950) but I am sure that none of the McAnarney brothers would have subscribed to that cynical justification of brutality and blackmail.

The affidavit signed by Mrs. Andrews on September 9, 1922, besides confessing perjury and repudiating her testimony, charged Stewart, Brouillard, the officers at the jail, Katzmann, and Williams with coercion and subornation of perjury. The depths to which the defenders of civil liberties sank in phrasing this document may be gathered from a clause relating a supposed interview between Williams and Mrs. Andrews the day before she testified: "That said conversation was not had in the District Attorney's office . . . but was had in a private room in which there were two small beds, with the door closed." (The interview was held in a small conference room adjoining the district attorney's office which did have a little bed in it.) But Moore, when he was dictating the affidavit, turned to Van Vaerenwyck and said, "It is a private room with beds in it," and the latter said, "There is more dirt for you." (3929)

On January 9, 1923, Mrs. Andrews was interrogated by Katzmann and signed and swore to a transcript of his questions and her answers from which I have quoted above. This was filed on March 7, 1923, and on that day and the next, affidavits by Katzmann, Williams, Stewart, Brouillard, and two Dedham jail officials were also filed. On October 23, 1923, Reid and Moore filed counter-affidavits. The motion was argued before Thayer in October-November 1923 with the other supplementary motions, the entire argument occupying six different days.

On October 1, 1924, Thayer denied the motions and filed a separate decision with respect to the Andrews motion in which, after an elaborate finding of facts, he found that Moore had been guilty of duress and intimidation and of unprofessional conduct deserving the most severe condemnation.

Thayer's denial of this motion was not taken to the Supreme Judicial Court, and shortly after this Moore retired from the case.

Mrs. Andrews was shamefully treated by Moore and the Defense Committee. It took courage for her to repudiate her forced repudiation: she knew that other witnesses were carrying revolvers for protection against partisans of the defense, and she herself had been assaulted by an unknown person before the trial. Yet she did repudiate it, and it seems to me that this would be a consideration of great weight if we were to appraise her testimony. The mythmakers have given her a bad character without proof. She may have been an erring woman but she was a brave one.

CARLOTTA PACKARD, known as Lottie, was a shoe worker at Rice & Hutchins for several years. She had been a pretty girl, but her morals were not above reproach. She was eccentric and was regarded by many as half crazy, a kind of "nut," but not stupid.

She was not a witness at the trial but was interviewed by the Governor and at his suggestion testified before the Advisory Committee on July 15, 1927. At that time her name was Carlotta P. Tattilo. After her testimony a paper headed "Statement of Carlotta K. Packard, Nov. 10, 1920" was handed to the committee. (5145) This was a statement taken stenographically and transcribed by Wilhelmina Preed, Moore's stenographer, in the evening of November 10, 1920, and was in question and answer form. Miss Preed appeared before the Advisory Committee and identified the statement as her work and told of the circumstances under which it was taken. (5197 *et seq.*)

From this statement and from Miss Packard's testimony before the Advisory Committee, the following account is gathered.

Sometime during the fall of 1920, a man who gave his name as Joseph Meyers but who also used the name Mirra came to work at Rice & Hutchins and was soon asking questions of Miss Packard about what had happened on the day of the murder.

As the acquaintance ripened, Mirra made a date with Miss Packard to come into Boston and go to the theater. They went to Gordon's Olympia on a Monday night. The following Saturday they went to Revere Beach and then he began to make dates with her. She was "single and had a right to make appointments." He kept asking her questions about Sacco and Vanzetti.

One night Mirra asked her to his home in East Boston for supper. At the supper table he asked her, "Would you please come up and talk to Mr. Moore?"

"Why, yes," she said, "I am only too glad to talk to Mr. Moore, but you understand, Mr. Mirra, I don't want to be implicated in this murder because Mr. Sacco belongs to the Black Hand Gang and when the Black Hand Gang gets lined up. . . ."

Mirra then took her on the East Boston Tunnel through Boston, and they came to a room in which there were Moore, a stenographer, and three other men.

Miss Packard then and there told the following story:

She had worked in the Rice & Hutchins factory for nineteen years. In 1915 (*sic*) Sacco was working there in the Finishing Room and she knew him. One morning he had an argument with a boy and threw a last at him which missed him but hit Miss Packard on the foot. About two days after this she asked somebody, "Who is that fellow over there, he threw a lace [last] the other morning?" She was told that his name was Nick Sacco and that he was quick-tempered and was a devil in the factory. Later he was fired.

On April 15, 1920, at about 11:30 A.M., a car was stationed on Pearl Street, opposite the stable on the right-hand side of the street.

> Sacco was standing on the right-hand side of the street going up and Vanzetti was standing on the opposite side and they both looked very much as if they were in a hurry and as if something very important was on their minds and I heard Vanzetti talking of selling clams that he had an appointment at 3:30 that afternoon. Sacco was looking in all directions and the chauffeur, the young man who I cannot identify, was down in front of the car, I judged between the two front wheels. . . . I know Sacco, I remember him when he

worked at Rice & Hutchins five years ago, at that time he
weighed about 145 lbs. dark complected and wore his hair
straight back. I have identified pictures of him. I identified
his picture on August 31. (5145-5146)

I was looking more at Sacco [not Vanzetti]. I got to this
post [indicating on photograph] and then I turned and
looked at him. I don't know whether it was that he remembered the time he struck my foot or not but anyway he
bit his lip and then I wondered where I had seen him before and it came to me the day in the factory and I said to
myself that is Sacco. Then when the pictures came out in the
paper and I didn't even look at the name when I saw Sacco's
pictures and I remarked to one of the girls, "Why what has
Sacco done?" and she said, "He is held for the murder."
(5149)

Moore showed her a picture of Vanzetti, and she thought it
was the man she saw talking to Sacco. (5153)

After Miss Packard had told her story, Moore said to her: "Your
statements and your story sound pretty good. You identify the
pictures all right."

"Yes."

He said, "If you were called into court to testify, would you
identify the same picture?"

"Yes."

"Very well then, would you accept $500 to leave the state?"

"What, sir?"

"Would you accept $500 to leave the state?"

"No sir. Why should I accept $500 to leave the state that I was
born and brought up in? . . . Mr. Moore, I absolutely see now
that I have been tricked. Mr. Mirra, you came into Rice & Hutchins to find out what I had to say and to find out what I saw that
morning, and you found that out and you brought it to Mr.
Moore, and you brought me in here to Mr. Moore to take $500
to leave my state. No, no, never. If you want to take that $500
you take it, and don't call me in here again. Don't do it because if

you do I will open up the case to the Judge and we will find out." (5143)

During the taking of the statement, the following remark by Joseph Mirra was recorded by Miss Preed:

"If she is here in the state she will have to testify. They will make her speak whether she wants to or not, she can't refuse to talk. If she is out of the state, if the case is on trial they cannot make her come to testify, can they, and after it is over they cannot harm her?" (5155)

Miss Packard's statement as it appears in print is consistent and does not reveal a confused or disorderly mind, although Miss Preed thought she was rather excitable and a nervous type of person.

When she came before the Advisory Committee she was excited, abusive, and obviously somewhat deranged, and her story differed in many respects from the statement. Most significant, she placed Sacco's employment in 1908,[1] not 1915, and remembered him by his activities in a strike and not by the throwing of the last. At one moment she said that she did not know Sacco, and at another she stuck to her original story with minor variations. This is how she told it to the Committee:

On the morning of April 15, 1920, sometime between 11:00 and 12:00 she was walking on Pearl Street. Mr. Tracy was walking ahead of her, and as they neared Mr. Tracy's building she saw a man whom she recognized as Sacco leaning against it and talking with a man across the street whom she afterward identified as Vanzetti when shown a picture of him.

The man across the street called to Sacco and said, "Hurry up there, I've got to get through at 3:30, I have some clams to dig." (5122)

An automobile stood between Sacco and herself, and Vanzetti was at the front of it.

When she saw Sacco on the street she said to herself, "That fellow looks familiar. Well, I wonder where did I see that fellow.

1 This may be a misprint for 1918.

My goodness, I think that that's the fellow that worked here in 1918 during the strike."

When she went back to work that noontime, she spoke to Frank Jackson and said:

"You know who I seen this noontime?"

"No, I haven't the slightest idea."

"I think I saw this Sacco or whatever they call him."

"Good Lord," he said, "I don't think so. I don't think you saw that fellow. I don't know where he is, but I don't think he's been around here since the time of the strike."

Frank W. Jackson, who had charge of the lasting room in the Rice & Hutchins factory, told the Advisory Committee that the following conversation occurred after the crime:

She said, "I met this Sacco that day out in front of Tracy's."

He said, "Why don't you tell it to the District Attorney and not to me?"

She said, "I was standing there talking to Sacco and told him, 'You better lean somewhere else, because if Tracy finds you leaning on that building it won't be well for you.' Sacco said, 'To hell with Tracy.' "

She also told Jackson at that time that when Sacco had worked there she had been out with him.

Asked by the committee to explain what she meant by being "out with him," Jackson said, "I don't know, those are the words she used and I think I can draw my own conclusions and you can draw yours." (5195)

According to Miss Packard's testimony, after the arrest she also told her story to John Shea, a police officer in Braintree. Shea was going down the street in the morning with a newspaper and she was looking over his shoulder going to work.

She said to Mr. Shea: "What is Sacco's picture in the paper for?"

"How do you know Sacco?"

"He worked in our factory in *1918;* he joined the strike."

"It seems to me I remember that man."

"I will never forget that man, he threw a last at little John Den-ehy and I don't know whether he hurt him or not. . . . What has Nick Sacco done now?"

A search of the records of Rice & Hutchins had been made by the Commonwealth before the trial. The records for two years had been burned, and Sacco's name did not appear on the record still extant. When Sacco was on the stand he revealed that he had worked at Rice & Hutchins under an assumed name, Mosmacotelli, in October 1918. I have found nothing in the record fixing the date of the strike.

At the conclusion of her testimony and after she had left the room, Ranney explained to the Committee that, although the Commonwealth had known about her testimony, they did not call her to the stand because they were not able to verify her story about Sacco's employment at Rice & Hutchins. Also they felt that, because of her excitable disposition, they would not be able to control her conduct if she took the stand. They also knew about her reputation for immorality.

We do not know how Lottie Packard impressed the Governor. The Advisory Committee questioned her very closely and came to the conclusion that, although the woman was eccentric and not unimpeachable in conduct, they believed that her testimony was well worth consideration.

Miss Packard's charge that Moore tried to bribe her to leave the state was not supported by Miss Preed's transcript of the inter-rogation, which Miss Preed said included all the conversation ex-cept a few preliminary remarks. Miss Preed's recollection was that she heard and recorded everything that was said, but this does not exclude the possibility that she was not present when the proposal was made. The Commonwealth tried to locate Mirra but failed. Moore's actions in the Andrews and Goodridge cases lend credence to the bribery charge here.

The record does not show who sent Miss Packard to the Gov-ernor. It was surely not the defense, and it is unlikely that the Commonwealth would have sent her there after deciding not to call her at the trial. I suggest the possibility that one of the other witnesses told the Governor about her. She had talked with several of them and with several police officers. She may, of course, have gone on her own motion, feeling that she could tell her story in private to the Governor without fear of the reprisals she would expect if she took the stand.

Thompson's theory was that she had tried to extort money from Moore and not that he had tried to bribe her. A colloquy between Thompson and Lowell reveals that the latter thought differently. Thompson also tried to get Ranney to admit that Katzmann kept Miss Packard off the stand because he had no faith in her story, but Ranney denied this.

Miss Packard was the only identifying witness who claimed a prior acquaintance with Sacco. If she could have told her story on the stand as coolly as she did to Moore in November 1920, and then identified Sacco and Vanzetti face to face in the courtroom, her testimony might well have been believed. If the Commonwealth had known before they closed their direct case that Sacco had worked at Rice & Hutchins, they might have risked using her, although she might have been uncontrollable on the stand and introduced confusing irrelevancies.

The defense certainly can find no comfort in her testimony nor reason to criticize the decision of the Commonwealth to keep her off the stand. This "suppression" was not listed by Thompson as misconduct on the part of Katzmann. On the other hand it seems to me further proof of Katzmann's conscientious behavior, for Miss Packard's identification testimony, with all its weaknesses and all of hers, might well have appealed to the jury as it did in some measure to the Advisory Committee.

CAPTAIN PROCTOR'S TESTIMONY

CAPTAIN WILLIAM H. PROCTOR was head of the State Police and, as such, took an active part in the investigation of both the Bridgewater and the South Braintree crimes. He testified in the Bridgewater case but not as an expert. After the conviction of Vanzetti at Plymouth for the Bridgewater holdup, Katzmann put Michael E. Stewart, the Chief of Police of Bridgewater, in charge of the investigation of the South Braintree crime, although this had occurred in another town and county. This was resented by Proctor; at least, Katzmann thought it was. (5085) In the South Braintree case, Proctor testified as an expert. Immediately after the close of his testimony, Proctor sent a bill for $500 to Katzmann, which the latter refused or failed to pay. When a second bill came in after the conclusion of the trial, Katzmann asked Judge Thayer whether the bill should be paid. Thayer took it up with the Chief Justice of the Superior Court and then advised Katzmann not to pay it. It was never paid. This caused a coolness, and for a time Proctor refused to speak to Katzmann. (5085)

Another cause of coolness was the employment by Katzmann of Captain Van Amburgh as a ballistics expert. This, as Judge Williams (assistant district attorney during the trial) and Stewart both told me on July 16, 1958, was done upon the advice of Dr. Magrath, medical examiner for Suffolk County, who told Katzmann that Proctor was still using a low-power microscope, although microscopes of much greater power were available which would give more positive results. As a result of this advice, Williams went to Connecticut and employed Van Amburgh.

At the trial, Captain Proctor was asked by Williams whether he had an opinion whether bullet No. 3 was fired from Sacco's pistol. He answered that his opinion was "that it is consistent with being fired by that pistol."

In cross-examination, no question about this opinion was put to Proctor, and his testimony was not mentioned by anyone in the argument to the jury. Judge Thomas F. McAnarney told the Advisory Committee that he and his brother Jeremiah had been willing to let this inconclusive answer stand rather than take the risk that Proctor would give a more positive opinion if he asked him questions. And it is apparent that the answer had very little that was positive or probative.

In a charge that fills twenty-seven printed pages, Judge Thayer devoted only two paragraphs to the firing of the No. 3 bullet through Sacco's pistol and only two sentences to the expert opinions. After stating the Commonwealth's claim that No. 3 was fired through Sacco's pistol, he said:

> To this effect the Commonwealth introduced the testimony of two witnesses, Messrs. Proctor and Van Amburgh. And on the other hand, the defendants offered testimony of two experts, Messrs. Burns and Fitzgerald, to the effect that the Sacco pistol did not fire the bullet that caused the death of Berardelli. (2254; my italics.)

He then goes on to say: "Now, gentlemen, what is the fact, for you must determine the question of fact. . . ."

Under the Massachusetts statutes the Court is expressly forbidden to deal, in its charge to the jury, with the weight and probative effect of testimony. That is for the jury, which has heard the testimony and the arguments of counsel analyzing and appraising it, to settle. Yet, because Judge Thayer used the words "to this effect" and did not call attention to the precise wording of Proctor's opinion, he has been charged by Frankfurter and others with having misled the jury into believing that Proctor's opinion was a positive and definite one to the effect that bullet No. 3 had been fired from Sacco's pistol.

But the defense at the trial did not think so. They took no exception to the charge. In argument they could have pulverized Proctor as an expert if they had thought that his testimony was in any way damaging to them. Proctor's knowledge was limited and his methods of identification were inadequate; for these reasons he would not testify that bullet No. 3 *had* passed through Sacco's pistol but only that on his examination it was simply *consistent*, i.e., not inconsistent, that it had. On the one hand he had not found enough affirmative evidence to justify a definitely affirmative conclusion; on the other, he had not found evidence to justify a definitely negative conclusion.

It is my belief that the jury paid no attention at all to the expert testimony and would have paid no attention to Proctor's even if Thayer had misinterpreted it to them as a positive one.

The jury's appraisal of Proctor's opinion may be inferred from what juror Dever said to Edward B. Simmons, staff writer of the New Bedford *Standard-Times*, in the interview cited on page 85.

> You know I was just out of the Army and I was pretty familiar with a Colt pistol. I remember Proctor was asked if he could disassemble one and he replied he could not. As a juror, that made an impression on me. I suspected he did not know as much about guns as the prosecution claimed. If those who believe Sacco and Vanzetti did not have a fair trial are interested, I can tell them right now, Sacco and Vanzetti were not convicted on a basis of Proctor's evidence.

On October 20, 1923, Proctor swore to an affidavit before Justice of the Peace William G. Thompson, in which he said that during the preparation for the trial his attention was repeatedly called by the District Attorney and his assistants to the question whether he could find any evidence which would justify the opinion that the particular bullet taken from the body of Berardelli, "which came from a Colt automatic pistol," came from Sacco's pistol. Proctor's reply had been that at no time had he been able to find any evidence that the particular bullet had come from Sacco's pistol.

At the trial, he continued, the District Attorney did not ask him whether he had found any such evidence, nor was he asked that question on cross-examination. The District Attorney had wanted to ask him that question, but Proctor had told him repeatedly that if he did he would be obliged to answer in the negative; consequently,

> he put to me this question: Q. Have you an opinion as to whether bullet number 3 was fired from the Colt automatic which is in evidence? To which I answered, "I have." He then proceeded. Q. And what is your opinion? A. My opinion is that it is consistent with being fired by that pistol.

Proctor then goes on to say:

> That is still my opinion for the reason that bullet number 3, in my judgment, passed through some Colt automatic pistol, but I do not intend by that answer to imply that I had found any evidence that the so-called mortal bullet had passed through this particular Colt automatic pistol and the District Attorney well knew that I did not so intend and framed his question accordingly. Had I been asked the direct question: whether I had found any affirmative evidence whatever that this so-called mortal bullet had passed through this particular Sacco's pistol, I should have answered then, as I do now without hesitation, in the negative. (3642)

Proctor's version was contradicted by Katzmann and Williams in affidavits of October 31, 1923, Williams using the following words:

> I asked him if he could tell in what pistol this so-called mortal bullet was fired and he said he could not although the marks upon it were consistent with its having been fired in the Sacco pistol. He said that all he could do was to deter-

mine the width of the landmarks upon the bullet. His attention was not repeatedly called to the question, whether he could find any evidence which would justify the opinion that this bullet came from the Sacco pistol. I conducted the direct examination of Captain Proctor at the trial and asked him the question quoted in his affidavit, "have you an opinion as to whether bullet number 3 was fired from the Colt automatic which is in evidence?"

This question was suggested by Captain Proctor himself as best calculated to give him an opportunity to tell what opinion he had respecting the mortal bullet and its connection with the Sacco pistol. His answer in court was the same answer he had given me personally before. (3682)

And so the matter stood until 1927, when the defense developed the theory that Proctor's real opinion was exactly the opposite of his testimony at the trial and in his affidavit of October 20, 1923, to wit, that it was *inconsistent* (not *consistent*) that bullet No. 3 was fired from Sacco's pistol.

On July 11, 1927, *after Proctor's death,* Elias Field, then or soon thereafter one of the defendants' attorneys, testifying before the Advisory Committee, recalled a conversation he had overheard in an automobile between Albert H. Hamilton, ballistics expert for the defense, and Proctor on August 7, *1923,* in which Proctor was heard to say that he thought that it was consistent with its going through that kind of gun but that he did not think it had passed through that gun. Proctor then went on to say, as Field remembered it:

> "Katzmann and Williams had been at me for a long time to get me to express an opinion that the bullet went through that particular gun, and I told him after my experience or examination that I didn't think it did and thereupon they got this man, Van Amburgh. Van Amburgh did come up and when he came the first time I had to show him how to measure a bullet." (4975, 5413)

Hamilton, in his appearance before the committee on July 12, 1927, remembered this conversation somewhat differently and summarized it as follows:

> [Proctor's] opinion was not only that it was *inconsistent* but it was not fired through the Sacco pistol. He admitted to me so that I understood him to impart to me that he knowingly testified what was not so and was misleading to the court. (5007; my italics.)

This would make Proctor a perjurer and Katzmann and Williams suborners of perjury, because, according to this version of the conversation, Proctor's real opinion was that bullet No. 3 did not go through Sacco's pistol; that it was *inconsistent,* not consistent, for it to have done so, and Thompson so charged:

> Mr. Proctor was in the difficult position of trying to evade direct perjury. He knew that it wasn't fired through that gun. I had been at him a long time trying to get the affidavits. I saw him time after time. Thank God he repented but he lied before I regret to say. Perhaps you don't realize the whole depth of what he did and I call attention to the fact that even if he did only confess to me half the truth he is better off than those who induced him to do it. (4977)

The affidavit which Thompson got from Proctor two months after this conversation has already been referred to. *In that affidavit he stated that his opinion was exactly the same as the one expressed at the trial.*

No one has ever explained why the evidence of Hamilton and Field about a conversation of August 7, 1923, was not brought forth at once, while Proctor was still alive and could be interrogated, or at the latest when in his affidavit of October 20, 1923, he confirmed the opinion he had given at the trial. Thompson had tried hard to get Proctor to confess to perjury but had failed, getting nothing except charges by Proctor that Katzmann and Williams had repeatedly asked him if he had found any affirmative evidence, and a confirmation by Proctor of his former opinion.

Was Proctor confronted with the Hamilton conversation and by Field and Hamilton? If not, why not? If so, and he still denied his perjury, why did Thompson withhold the testimony of Hamilton and Field for four years?

My respect and liking for Elias Field makes it impossible for me to believe that he was guilty of deliberate falsehood. I have no doubt that he did overhear a conversation between Hamilton and Proctor in which the latter showed his hostility to Katzmann and his jealousy of Van Amburgh and in which he probably said exactly what he was to say two months later in his affidavit.

But Field's sympathies were engaged; he believed that Sacco and Vanzetti were innocent, and he was then or soon afterward to become a defense lawyer. His recollection of a conversation nearly four years old may unconsciously have been colored. Certainly his recollection should not be substituted for Proctor's own affidavit made two months after the conversation.

It is significant that, when Frankfurter published his book in 1927, he had not heard of the Hamilton-Proctor-Field conversation of August 1923 but based his criticism of the Proctor testimony on his suspicion that Proctor's "consistent" opinion, joined with Thayer's linking of Proctor and Van Amburgh in his charge, misled the jury into believing that Proctor's opinion was a positive one. This quibble would not have been used if Frankfurter had been able on the faith of the conversation to make a direct charge of perjury in that Proctor had used the word "consistent" when his real opinion required the word "inconsistent."

The Advisory Committee disposed of the conversation as follows:

> It seems to us improbable that Captain Proctor, who has since died, should have stated both at the trial and in his affidavit that his opinion was consistent with the firing of the bullet from Sacco's pistol, and in the meanwhile should have said in conversation that his opinion was exactly the oppo-

site. One of the witnesses, Field, merely overheard Proctor's conversation with Hamilton about a subject with which he was not familiar; and the latter stated also to the Committee that Proctor told him that he believed before the trial the bullet was not fired through the Sacco pistol, which would be an admission not of a misleading statement but of deliberate perjury. This charge is inconsistent with Proctor's later affidavit, and we do not believe Hamilton's testimony on this point. (5378u)

Captain Proctor's testimony is the only part of the expert testimony mentioned by Frankfurter in his book. No attempt is made to meet the Van Amburgh opinion or to support Burns and Fitzgerald or to dispute the evidence of the obsolete bullets and what could be clearly seen by the naked eyes of the jury. One would think that Proctor was the only expert witness, and his opinion as "misinterpreted" by Thayer the only evidence. The thoroughgoing Musmanno follows Frankfurter about Proctor, brushes Van Amburgh off, and expresses his confidence in Hamilton.[1]

Morgan's treatment of the Proctor testimony is headed "Misconduct of the Prosecutor; the Arrangement with Proctor." He has swallowed Hamilton's version of the Hamilton-Proctor conversation hook, line, and sinker, and prefers to believe Hamilton, a thoroughly discredited witness,[2] and Field's four-year-old recollection against Katzmann, Williams, Proctor himself, and all the probabilities.

Morgan should not have done this. He had lived long enough in Massachusetts to know the absurdity of charging Harold P. Williams, one of the most respected lawyers of his generation, now a justice of the Supreme Judicial Court, with subornation of perjury, framing testimony, perjury, evasion, or professional misconduct of any kind.

The Proctor opinion need not concern us in determining the guilt or innocence of Sacco. Whatever his true opinion was, it

[1] Musmanno, *op. cit.*, p. 176.
[2] See for Hamilton's lack of qualifications and trustworthiness chapters 10, 19, and 26 of this book.

would have little probative value unless backed up by measurements or markings consistent or inconsistent with the firing of the fatal bullet through Sacco's pistol. If, in his conversation with Hamilton, Proctor had told what measurement or mark had put him in doubt, the defense would have had something substantial, but there is no suggestion of that. And, as we have seen, the jury paid as little attention to Proctor as it did to the other experts—that is, no attention at all.

And, so far as the fairness of the jury trial is concerned, we may accept the conclusion of Judge Riddell: "Whatever Judge or Counsel may have thought of Proctor's evidence, there was no misrepresentation of it to the Trial Jury." [3]

[3] William Renwick Riddell, *op. cit., ubi supra.*

26 THE SHIFTING OF THE GUN BARRELS

AFTER THE TRIAL, in an effort to confuse the ballistics issues, the defense tried a bold maneuver.

Sometime before the hearing of the Hamilton-Proctor motion, Hamilton filed an affidavit and with it deposited with the Clerk of the Superior Court at Dedham two new Colt pistols of .32 caliber belonging to him.

The hearing was held November 8, 1923, and at that time Hamilton disassembled his pistols and the Sacco pistol. Sometime after he had finished his explanation and comparison, he reassembled them. All this was done in the presence of the Court and of counsel on both sides. Then, by order of the Court, he delivered all three pistols to Willard Everett, the Assistant Clerk of the Court. The two new pistols had been brought to the Clerk's office in separate boxes, and Everett put them back in the same boxes after they had been reassembled.

At the close of the hearing, Moore said he would reserve the right to be heard on a request to fire one hundred cartridges through the Sacco pistol. This request was made with a view of showing that the location of the firing pin indentation on the primer surface established an individuality of the firing pin in the pistol. Williams said at that time that he would oppose it until he had communicated with Van Amburgh. Sometime afterward Van Amburgh came to the judges' lobby, examined the then-supposed Sacco barrel, and told Williams that it was not the Sacco barrel.

On February 13, 1924, Williams informed Judge Thayer of what Van Amburgh had told him, and counsel for the defendants were then notified.

On February 15, 1924, the two boxes, in the presence of Van Amburgh, Hamilton, and counsel on both sides, were opened by Thayer, and therein were found Hamilton's two pistols. One of them had a rusty and foul barrel, and in the Sacco pistol there was a new barrel which Hamilton immediately recognized as the barrel which belonged in his new pistol. Hamilton claimed, however, that the old, rusty, foul barrel found in his new pistol was not the Sacco barrel but one which had been substituted by someone while the new pistols were in the custody of the Clerk. Van Amburgh on the other hand said that it was the Sacco barrel, and the Commonwealth claimed that the substitution had been made by Hamilton himself at the hearing.

Thayer thereupon instituted an investigation, not open to the public, to which three weeks and two days were devoted, with daily hearings. Williams represented the Commonwealth; Moore (and Thompson for a very short time) represented the defendants. Hamilton's charge that the substitution had been made while his new pistols were in the custody of the Clerk led to the examination and cross-examination of the Clerk and all courthouse employees. In his decision, Judge Thayer said at this point:

> Taking into consideration all of the evidence heard at Dedham I am unable to find a single fact that would warrant me in finding that there was any substitution of barrels after they were delivered into the custody of Mr. Everett by Mr. Hamilton. This being true, the substitution would seem to have been made during the time Mr. Hamilton reassembled them in court. But notwithstanding this evidence obtained at Dedham, which seemed to me to be convincing, Mr. Hamilton still maintained that the barrel in the new Hamilton pistol is not the Sacco barrel.

The finding that Hamilton had made the substitution himself would settle for most people Hamilton's stubborn claim that the barrel in the new Hamilton pistol was not the Sacco barrel, but Hamilton was always tenacious in falsehood. So Thayer thought it necessary to hear him and other witnesses on this question and, in his decision, to state at great length the evidence, some of it very technical, and his conclusion. His findings and order read as follows:

> I find that the old rusty and foul barrel that was in Hamilton's new pistol is the original Sacco barrel and the new barrel in the Sacco pistol belongs in Mr. Hamilton's new pistol. It is therefore ordered that these two barrels be transferred to their respective pistols.

Now here, if ever, a prejudiced judge actuated by murderous hate and malice could have dealt the defendants a series of stunning blows. He could have held public hearings which would have made headlines. Instead, he insisted on a private investigation, with only counsel and witnesses present, and forbade newspaper interviews. He did not punish Hamilton for contempt or insert sensational findings in his decision. He did not mention the incident in any of his written decisions on the motions for a new trial. He may have told the Governor or the Advisory Committee about it, but if so, he did the defendants no harm, for by that time Hamilton was already thoroughly discredited as an expert and as a truthful witness.

Thayer's reason for this forbearance is high-minded and kindly. He did not wish the defendants to be deprived of any legal right by a condition which was not of their making. In a part of his decision not quoted by Morgan he says:

> Connected with this investigation the evidence in some respects has been very disturbing. Conditions have arisen that have been very distressing to me, but they were not of my creation, and neither were they created by the defendants themselves. Therefore there should not be in any quarter whatsoever the slightest prejudice against them nor should their legal rights in the remotest degree be affected thereby.

The substitute-barrel proceedings were not included in the Holt Transcript, nor was Thayer's long decision, although it had been in the files of the Superior Court in Dedham since March 25, 1924, and docketed "Decision in re substitution of gun-barrels." [1]

Nor was the incident mentioned by anyone reviewing the case until Morgan devoted a whole chapter to it, with copious quotations from the decision. This was greatly to his credit, but he should have gone further and taken the incident as final proof that Hamilton could not be trusted when he blackened the reputations of Proctor and Williams. And with this demonstration of Thayer's fairness, he should not have ended his chapter with a reference to the "demonstrated prejudice of the trial judge."

[1] This docket entry is copied in the Holt Transcript at 5542 and should have excited the curiosity of the editors.

THE MADEIROS
CONFESSION AND HOW
IT GREW

CELESTINO F. MADEIROS, of Portuguese descent, born March 9, 1902, in the Azores, was brought by his parents to New Bedford when he was two or three years old. He attended school in New Bedford until some time in 1917 and from then on lived a life of vice and crime. At school he was regarded as subnormal in intelligence, and all his life he suffered from epilepsy.

The New Bedford police had Madeiros under surveillance during the month of April 1920, and on May 1 they arrested him at the home of his parents in New Bedford on charges of impersonating a Naval officer and of breaking and entering. He was out on bail until May 25, when he was again arrested for breaking and entering and for the theft of a small sum of money, less than $100. He did not get bail for this but was sentenced to five months in the House of Correction, a sentence which he served from June 20 to November 20, 1920.

From March until October 1924 he was employed by Barney Monterio, first as a carpenter, then as a chauffeur, and finally as a bouncer at a disreputable roadhouse, the Bluebird Inn, in Seekonk, Massachusetts.

His proposal to Mrs. Monterio that they elope terminated the employment, and in October Madeiros went to live with a man named James F. Weeks, alias James F. Croft, in a house just off Oak Street, in a wooded section of Randolph, Massachusetts. Oak Street is a short cut between South Braintree and Randolph and was a part of the getaway route used by the South Braintree murderers on April 15, 1920. The Weeks house was about three and one-half miles from the scene of the murders and about half a mile from the home of a family named Driver. At this time, October 1924, Weeks and Madeiros came to know eighteen-year-old Thomas Driver, who was to be mentioned in the confession.

On November 1, Madeiros, Weeks, Alfred W. Bedard, and Harry Goldenberg made an attempt to rob a bank in Wrentham, during the course of which Madeiros shot and killed the cashier, James A. Carpenter.

On November 11, Madeiros was arrested at a lodging house at 180 North Main Street, Providence.

On December 4, Madeiros, Weeks, Bedard, and Goldenberg were indicted for the murder of Carpenter.

Goldenberg was not apprehended and was never tried. The Commonwealth accepted pleas of guilty of murder in the second degree from Bedard and Weeks, and they were sentenced to life imprisonment. Madeiros was tried alone in the Superior Court and was convicted of murder in the first degree. He alleged exceptions, and they went to the Supreme Judicial Court, which ordered a new trial on a technical point.

At the second trial, Madeiros was again convicted of murder in the first degree and again Madeiros went to the Supreme Judicial Court. This time the Court made short work of his case, and he was given the mandatory death sentence.

The evidence against Madeiros, which included his confession, was very strong, and there could be no doubt that he would be convicted of first-degree murder sooner or later. He could not have felt at any time that the legal maneuvers of his counsel would do any more than defer his execution by giving him an extra trial or so. His confession must therefore be regarded as virtually a deathhouse one.

THE CONFESSION

While waiting for the decision from the Supreme Judicial Court after his first trial, Madeiros remained in the Dedham jail and had some opportunity to converse with Sacco. Sacco's story, as told in his affidavit of May 22, 1926, was that on several occasions prior to November 18, 1925, Madeiros had said to him in the bathroom of the jail, "Nick, I know who did the South Braintree job." But Sacco, thinking that Madeiros was just fooling him, said nothing.

During the afternoon of November 16, 1925, a trusty, Edward J. Miller, came to Oliver J. Curtis, the deputy master of the jail, with the request that Madeiros be allowed to take the Financial Report of the Sacco-Vanzetti Defense Committee, stating that Sacco said he might have it. The deputy master gave Miller the report, which was in pamphlet form, and Miller took it to Madeiros. After thirty or forty minutes Miller returned with the pamphlet and an envelope addressed "News Editor Boston American Paper Boston, Mass." and endorsed "C. F. Madeiros, 43 Village av. Dedham, Mass." Inside the envelope was the following:

> Nov. 16, 1925
> Dedham
> Mass.
> 43 Village Av.

Dear Editor

I hear by confess to being in the shoe company crime at south Braintree on April 15, 1920 and that Sacco and Vanzetti was not there.

(signed) Celestino F. Madeiros

Curtis did not mail the confession to the *Boston American* and did not communicate with the defense counsel about it.

On the afternoon of November 18, 1925, Miller got a rap from the cell of Madeiros. He went to the cell, where Madeiros handed him a slip of paper and asked him to give it to Sacco. Miller read it. It was a small, oblong piece of paper, on which the following words were written:

I hear by confess to being in the south Braintree shoe company crime and Sacco and Vanzetti was not in said crime.

(signed) Celestino F. Madeiros

Miller afterward said:

> A few minutes later, I went to Sacco's cell and he was standing leaning against the wall trembling, with the paper in his hands sent to him by Madeiros, and tears in his eyes. He asked me, "What is this?" I said, "Can't you read English?" He said he would telephone his friend and get him to take the paper to Thompson. (4497)

Immediately after receiving the confession, Sacco asked the jail authorities to send word to Amleto Fabbri, a member of the Defense Committee, and the next day, November 19, Fabbri came to the Dedham jail, saw Sacco, and at once took the slip of paper to the office of William G. Thompson and handed it to him.

About 7:00 o'clock in the evening of the same day, Thompson came to the jail and had a conversation with Madeiros and Sacco.

Thompson took penciled notes during the conversation, and from them dictated a statement upon his return to his office. On the following Monday, November 23, he wrote to Ranney, enclosing a photostatic copy of the confession and a copy of the penciled notes, which read as follows:

> —4 Italians picked him up Apl. 15, 1920 on N. Main St., Prov., in open Hudson 5 p. car about 4 A.M. at his room 181 N. Main St., landlord being a Jew.
> —One of my sisters lived there—Mary Bover, then a widow, since again married. She now lives 735 Bellville Ave., New Bedford.
> —Also Arthur Tatro, suicide in New Bed. House of Correction.
> —I was then Lieut. in Am. Rescue League and he was Capt.
> —Two or three privates lived there.
> —At Randolph changed to Buick open car, brought there by another man.
> —Left Hudson car in woods and took it again after job, leaving Buick in woods in charge of one man who drove it off.

—A boy named Thomas in Randolph saw us go by in Hudson after job.

—His father lives on Prang (?) St. , in window metal bus.

—I became acquainted with him 4 yrs. later when I went to live in Randolph with Weeks on same st.

—Thomas told me he saw car that did So. B. job going thro' R. very fast.

—We went from Prov. to Boston and then back to Prov., and then back to So. B. getting there abt. noon.

—Spent some time in a speak easy in So. B., leaving car in yard.

—In Andrews Square I stayed in car.

—This was 2 or 3 miles from job.

—I had never been there before.

—They persuaded me 2 or 3 nights before in a saloon in Prov.

—It was also a poolroom near my boarding house.

—They talked like professionals.

—Sd. had done lots of jobs—freight cars.

—2 young, 20 to 25, one abt. 40, other 35.

—All had caps—can't remem. shaved.

—2 of them did shooting.

—Old one and another did shooting—left on street.

—Went to Boston to see if money shipped.

—Arranged to meet in Prov. saloon next night to divide, but they did not come.

—I sat on back seat of auto.

—Had Colt auto. 38, but did not use it—to hold crowd back.

—Curtains flapping—don't remem. shot-gun.

—Talked lot about N.Y.

—As soon as I got enough money I went to N.Y. and Chicago to find them in cabarets but never found them.

—They had been stealing silk, shoes, cotton, etc., from cars and sending to N.Y.

—Two lived So. Main St. and 2 on No. Main St. in lodging houses.

—I had known them 3 or 4 months.

—Old one—"Mike" "Williams" ("Bill"), don't know others.

—Money in black bag—think.

—I was scared to death.

—Thomas' sister saw us go by.

—Both cars Mass. numbers. (4543-4544)

This story was an obvious fabrication, inconsistent on its face and with the evidence at the trial. It is apparent that, when he lived with Weeks on Oak Street, Madeiros had learned about the boy named Thomas, the Randolph woods, and the rapid getaway of the murder car along Oak Street; from his experience in the Wrentham crime he derived the Buick and the Hudson, the change of cars in the woods, the South Boston speakeasy, his Colt .38, and his own North Main Street address in Providence. What he learned from Sacco in the bathroom and in the conversation with Sacco and Thompson on November 20, 1925, we will never know. Putting the money in a black bag instead of two black metal boxes was a wild and unfortunate guess which should have impeached the confession forthwith and forever.

All this was apparent on the face of the confession to anyone who knew the Sacco-Vanzetti record as thoroughly as Thompson did, and if he made any investigation or cross-examination in November, he must have found falsehood in several details to add to the improbabilities.

THE WEEKS AFFIDAVIT

On May 12, 1926, the Supreme Judicial Court affirmed the conviction of Sacco and Vanzetti, overruling all the exceptions taken at the trial and sustaining Thayer's denials of motions for a new trial filed thereafter.

Unless they could find new evidence or new theories upon which to base new motions, the defendants were at the end of their legal resources. And there was need for hurry, because within a few days the defendants would be given the mandatory death sentence and under Massachusetts law a motion for a new trial in capital cases comes too late if it is made after sentence has been pronounced. (5500)

It was at this juncture that Thompson brought forth the Madeiros confession, and on May 26, 1926, a motion for a new trial was filed on the basis of it. The motion was not accompanied by a Madeiros affidavit, because Madeiros was unable or unwilling to amplify his story by naming his confederates or, indeed, to add a single name to the "Bill" and "Mike" of his statement. This failure would have made a Madeiros affidavit a weak reason for a new trial, and Thompson in his effort to get a complete story was forced to resort to hearsay evidence of a confession supposedly made by Madeiros to Weeks. The story of the Weeks affidavit is an interesting one.

On Friday, May 21, 1926, Thompson went to the State Prison at Charlestown to see Weeks, who was then serving a life sentence for his share in the Wrentham murder.

Ehrmann in his book[1] states that Weeks refused to talk to Thompson, but Thompson in an affidavit says that Weeks refused to give him any information as to statements made to him by Madeiros beyond stating that he knew that the confession of Madeiros was true.

On the next day, Saturday, after a visit to the Bluebird Inn, Ehrmann went to police headquarters in Providence, where he learned that in 1919 and 1920 there had indeed been a group of criminals in Providence engaged in robbing freight cars. This group was known as the Morelli gang, because a number of Morelli brothers belonged to it.

On the following Monday Ehrmann returned to Providence, accompanied by Mrs. Ehrmann. During the day, Ehrmann made a call on John J. Richards, a Providence lawyer who had been a United States marshal in 1920. Richards' interest was instant, and

[1] *The Untried Case, The Sacco-Vanzetti Case and the Morelli Gang*, New York, 1937, p. 68. Soon after Thompson was employed as chief defense counsel, he enlisted the services of the young Boston lawyer, Herbert B. Ehrmann, who took charge of the investigation of the Madeiros confession and the development of the Morelli hypothesis and afterward wrote his book about them.

from then on he cooperated actively with Ehrmann. From him, Ehrmann at once learned a great deal about the Morelli gang which coincided closely—mistakes, omissions, and the rest—with what was to find its way the next day into the Weeks affidavit.

While Ehrmann was making his calls, Mrs. Ehrmann went to the office of the Clerk of the Federal Court and found the records of an indictment with fifteen counts returned December 8, 1919, against Frank, Joseph, Fred, and Pasquale Morelli. The eighth count charged that on a certain day between August 6, 1919, and October 18, 1919, at Providence, they had unlawfully and feloniously bought, received, and had in their possession seventy-eight pairs of men's shoes, which on August 6 had moved as a part of an interstate shipment of freight from the consignor, Slater & Morrill, Inc., at South Braintree, to the consignee, The Potter Shoe Company, at Cincinnati. (4413)

The first, second, third, and fourth counts made the same charge about 605 pairs of ladies' shoes, unlawfully possessed in Providence, which had been shipped in July and August 1919 from Rice & Hutchins, at South Braintree, to Chicago. (4438)

These 683 pairs of men's and women's shoes are absolutely the only evidence linking any member of the Morelli gang with South Braintree. The whole Morelli hypothesis is built on the coincidence that in the fall of 1919 a gang had in its possession in Providence some shoes which had been shipped in interstate commerce from South Braintree. By a parity of reasoning, the other ten counts of the indictment would have qualified the gang, in Ehrmann's estimation, for participation in any holdup or armed robbery which might have occurred in 1919 or 1920 in Middleboro, Brockton, or Canton, Massachusetts, or Slatersville or Bellefont, Rhode Island.

So, on the morning of May 25, 1926, Thompson set out for Dedham jail to see if Madeiros would admit that it was the Morelli gang who had been in the murder car. Upon his arrival, Sheriff Samuel H. Capen telephoned to Assistant District Attorney William P. Kelley and told him that Thompson was at the Dedham jail and had told Capen that he wished to talk to Madeiros. Capen then asked Kelley whether or not he should permit the interview. Kelley asked Capen to put Thompson on the telephone. Thompson then told Kelley over the telephone that the Sacco-Vanzetti case was cleared up, or would be cleared up within a few days, and that Weeks had made a full confession of the South Braintree holdup. Thompson then asked Kelley for permission to ask Madeiros one question, "Wasn't it the Morelli gang?", and Kelly gave him permission. (4666)

Obviously, it would have helped if Madeiros could be induced to name the Morelli gang as a part of his confession, so that a Madeiros affidavit could be filed the next day with the motion for a new trial, instead of a hearsay statement of what Weeks said Madeiros had said to him. But Madeiros "refused to say," and Thompson had to go in the afternoon to the State Prison with an affidavit for Weeks to sign. This was signed and filed the next day with the motion for a new trial. (4428)

Thompson in his affidavit of July 15, 1926, and in his argument gave another version of his morning's activities and conversation with Kelley. According to his version, he did not go to Dedham at all that day but did go to the State Prison for a second interview with Weeks, a message having come to him that Weeks was now ready to talk. He also thought that Kelley was mistaken in placing his questioning of Madeiros on May 25, 1926, but that it was some other date.

Here there is a regrettable difference in the recollection of two lawyers, which I think we must decide in favor of Kelley. It seems unlikely that Thompson would have waited until after he had filed his motion for a new trial before asking Madeiros about the Morellis, and more unlikely that Kelley would have been mistaken in the day Capen and Thompson talked with him from the jail when, as a consequence of those talks, he went immediately to interview Weeks with a stenographer, who recorded the day of the interview as May 25.

On the same morning that Kelley was informed over the telephone by Thompson that Weeks had made a full confession of the Braintree holdup, and before the Weeks affidavit was executed, he went to the State Prison in company with Lieutenant Michael F. Fleming and another State Police officer, Lieutenant Henry A. Plett, who was a stenographer, to interview Weeks. The stenographer's notes show that the interrogation of Weeks began at 11:45 A.M., and later Weeks told Thompson that the three men were with him from 11:40 to 12:22. (4431) When Weeks came into the rotunda, Fleming had a few words in private with him. These were not recorded by the stenographer but were reported by Fleming substantially as follows:

> FLEMING: Has there been somebody over here to see you, Jim?
> WEEKS: Yes, there was somebody over here, I think it was last Friday. [Weeks has already forgotten the "second" interview which, according to Thompson, had occurred that very morning.]
> FLEMING: Did you make a full confession in regard to the holdup in South Braintree?
> WEEKS: Jesus, no, I didn't make any confession like that.
> FLEMING: I have been informed that you made a full confession in regard to that robbery.
> WEEKS: Well, I did not.
> FLEMING: I'm glad you didn't. You would be foolish to make a statement of that kind with the intent of helping some other person out of a scrape.
>
> Now I have come here with the Assistant District Attorney and a stenographer, and if you want to do so, I will have the stenographer take down what you said to *this man who came here last Friday.* (4599; my italics.)

Through the promptness of Kelley and Fleming we have what Weeks said between 11:40 A.M. and 12:22 P.M. on May 25, as compared with the affidavit he signed at 3:55 that afternoon.

In the morning, Weeks told Fleming that he had met Madeiros in 1924 and did not know him in 1920, (4593) but in the afternoon he said in his affidavit, "I have known Celestino Madeiros for about six years." (4400)

Why Weeks signed an affidavit containing this statement, which he had denied in the morning and which Madeiros was later to deny, is explicable only if we believe that Weeks was willing to sign anything put before him.

In the morning interview, Weeks did not mention the freight car thefts, but in the afternoon he swore as follows:

> Madeiros also told me that some of these Morellis had been arrested some months before the South Braintree job for stealing from freight cars in Providence, but were out on bail. (4402)

From 11:40 to 12:22, the Joe Morelli gang consisted of three Morelli brothers (Joe, Butsy, and Patsy), Gyp the Blood, and Bibber. There was no Mike, no Fred, no Bill, and no mention by name or nickname of the men who did the South Braintree job. (4597)

At 3:55 there were five Morelli brothers, a man called Bill (who Weeks said may have been one of the brothers, or Bibber), and Gyp the Blood; and Madeiros had told Weeks that four of the gang who did the job were Mike, Joe, Bill, and *Butsy*. (4401-4402)

These differences in the Weeks story between noontime and afternoon are bewildering, but they become less so if we compare the listing made by Richards in his affidavit of June 10, 1926, filed on June 12:

> The members of this gang were as follows: Joseph Morelli, commonly called Joe, the oldest of the gang and the leader of it; Pasquale Morelli, commonly called Patsy; *Fred Morelli known as Butsy;* Frank Morelli, Michael Morelli, commonly called Mike; Albert Barone, commonly called Bibba; Joseph Imondi, commonly called Gyp the Blood; Paul Rossi, and Tony Mancini. In addition there were a number of others against whom no evidence [of freight car thefts] has been found. (4448)

I have emphasized the references to *Butsy* in the Weeks and Richards affidavits because soon afterward it was found that Fred (the *Butsy* of the Richards and the Weeks lists) was in fact in jail on April 15, 1920, and had to be excluded from the murder party. Richards, after his affidavit was filed, found that he had made a mistake, that it was Frank, not Fred, who was *Butsy,* and corrected it in an affidavit dated July 14, but Weeks never explained why he made the same mistake. (4530)

On this record we must conclude that the affidavit signed by Weeks in the afternoon of May 25 *was not based upon his recollection of what Madeiros had told him but upon what Ehrmann had learned the day before from Richards and the court records.* This dependence upon Ehrmann's information as to May 25 explains why Mike, who was to become the man in the woods on May 27 when Ehrmann visited New Bedford, remained in the Weeks affidavit as an active participant in the crime. It also explains the omission, in the Weeks affidavit, of Tony Mancini, whose name seemingly was not known by Ehrmann until Tony was mentioned by Joe Morelli on June 1 during the visit of Richards and Ehrmann to Leavenworth. And, clearest giveaway of all, it explains why Fred was *Butsy* both to Richards and to Weeks.

EHRMANN VISITS NEW BEDFORD

On May 27, 1926, Ehrmann went to New Bedford and procured an affidavit from Sergeant Ellsworth C. Jacobs of the New Bedford police. The sergeant, with the aid of his 1920 notebook, remembered that a short time before April 15, 1920, he saw a new Buick touring car in which was a man he knew as Michael Morelli. The second time he saw the car was on April 15, when, between 5:00 P.M. and 5:30 P.M., he caught a rear view of the same car as it passed him going to the post office. He caught no view of any occupant of the Buick. He never saw this Buick car again. (4419)

On this startling disclosure Ehrmann built an excited conjecture:

Click! Mike Morelli was in the picture. This member of the gang was landed with the possession of a Buick automobile of the same type and age as the murder car at precisely the critical time. Moreover, this Buick vanished after April 15, 1920. Why? My mind reverted to the scrub oak in the Randolph woods and I could see Mike Morelli, the New Bedford brother, bring the Buick to the meeting place. I could picture the hasty return of the Buick from South Braintree, the switching of the money boxes and number plates, and then Mike Morelli's leisurely and unsuspected drive from Randolph to New Bedford. Under cover of night the pleasant roll to the Manley Woods would be accomplished with another car trailing to take Mike away from the abandoned evidence of his complicity.[2]

THE MADEIROS AFFIDAVIT

The affidavit signed by Madeiros on May 29, 1926, embodied the penciled notes taken by Thompson with some additions, the most significant of which was a postscript reading as follows: "I know the last names of the gang but I refuse to tell who they are." (4418) And he never did.

EHRMANN VISITS LEAVENWORTH

On June 1, 1926, Ehrmann and Richards went to the federal prison at Leavenworth, Kansas, and had an interview with Joe Morelli in the presence of the warden.

Reconstructing the conversations from the paraphrase of them in the Ehrmann-Richards affidavit of June 5, 1926, we have the following:

> RICHARDS [in a few hasty words at 11:00 A.M. in the outer office to the warden before Joe came in]: Morelli was accused of a murder in Massachusetts.

2 Ehrmann, *op. cit.*, p. 60.

WARDEN BIDDLE: You want this man to take the murder on his shoulders?

RICHARDS AND EHRMANN [remonstrating in unison]: Such is not our purpose.

BIDDLE [excitedly]: Morelli is a trusty and might make a break if he got all stirred up. . . . You can see Morelli at 1:30 P.M. I do not care now to hear what you have to say to him. He does not have to talk unless he wishes to.

At 1:30 P.M., Morelli was sitting in the outer office when Ehrmann and Richards came in.

Morelli did not greet Richards but glared at him in a hostile manner and his whole demeanor indicated that he had been advised of the purpose of our visit.

RICHARDS: Allie Crowell has been to see me about your application for parole.

JOE: I do not know Allie Crowell.

RICHARDS: Some of your friends have been to see me about your parole.

JOE: I didn't tell anyone to see you.

RICHARDS: You have been accused in Massachusetts of taking part in the murder of the paymaster and guard in South Braintree in 1920.

[No answer.]

RICHARDS: Do you remember Zack's place on No. Main Street?

JOE: Never knew it.

RICHARDS: Do you know Nathan Remmer's place, near Zack's place?

JOE: I remember Remmer's place.

RICHARDS: Do you know Mancini?

JOE: Mancini? Mancini? Which Mancini?

RICHARDS: I think it was Tony, the one who was sent away for twenty years for killing a man.

JOE: I never heard that.

RICHARDS: I understand Mancini, you, Mike Morelli and a Portuguese—

JOE [rudely interrupting]: I never knew any Portuguese.

RICHARDS: The charge in Massachusetts is that you and others robbed the paymaster and killed him and the guard.

JOE: I never worked with others, always alone. You are trying to put me away, another frame-up like the charge I am serving twelve years for.

RICHARDS: You know better than that. At the end of the trial you suddenly sprang a frame-up plea. Later you said the Judge had not given you a fair trial and that the District Attorney and I had received $5,000. I have known you since you were a boy. Your record in Providence—

JOE [greatly excited and in a voice that whined and wept]: You are trying to spoil my record with my warden.

BIDDLE: You must not have a heated argument. Mr. Richards, how would you like remarks like you made about Morelli made about you?

EHRMANN: Morelli has something more serious to think about than the frame-up in Providence.

MORELLI: There is a just God who knows of the wrongs done against me and he will judge me.

EHRMANN: It might come to that.

RICHARDS: Did you ever hear of Sacco and Vanzetti?

JOE: Sacco and Vanzetti? [repeated several times] Were those the men I read about in the papers? Sacco? Sacco? *See Mancini about that.* [My italics.]

RICHARDS: Do you know the Rice and Hutchins Shoe Factory in South Braintree?

JOE: Never heard of it.

RICHARDS: Did you know that four counts of the indictment against you were for stealing shipments of the Rice and Hutchins Shoe Factory?

JOE: There were fifteen counts, that was six years ago and I can't remember what was in them.

EHRMANN: Did you ever hear of Jimmie Weeks or Croft?

JOE: Never.

EHRMANN: Didn't you steal whiskey with Croft or Weeks?

JOE: Never been in a whiskey job.

EHRMANN: The whiskey may have turned out to be vinegar. [Joe made no comment, from which fact Ehrmann inferred that Joe had a good sense of humor.]

MORELLI: Prove the charges against me and send me to the electric chair. I have nothing to say.

BIDDLE: If Morelli declines to talk the interview is over.

Ehrmann then outlined to Biddle the substance of the evidence against Morelli, leaving out the names of witnesses and the names of Morelli's alleged accomplice. Then:

EHRMANN: There are hundreds of thousands of people who believe Sacco and Vanzetti innocent. If you, whether you did the actual shooting or not, know the facts and help to prove their innocence, you would earn the gratitude of all these people. It is an opportunity for you if you know anything to do a most praiseworthy act but if you do not make a statement until you are publicly accused of the crime, you will get no credit.

[No answer.]

EHRMANN: General Richards and I will be at the Westgate Hotel, Kansas City, until tomorrow if you want to say anything.

MORELLI: I have nothing to say and will have nothing to say tomorrow. (4452-4454)

The interview ended, *exeunt* Richards and Ehrmann, leaving Biddle and Morelli in the warden's office. Richards and Ehrmann waited until evening, hoping that Joe's better nature would prevail over his selfish fear of the electric chair, and then went back to Boston. They were not disheartened, because there had again occurred a startling, astounding, and highly meaningful event. Ehrmann says:

At the mention of the words "Sacco and Vanzetti" Morelli asked whether these were the men he read about in the papers. He then exclaimed, "Sacco? Sacco? *See Mancini about that!*" [Ehrmann's emphasis and punctuation.]

The entire trip to Leavenworth was worth this admission, coming as it did after an earlier attempt to deny knowledge of Mancini. At least Mr. Richards and I thought this slip was full of significance, but, like most of the evidence which our investigation unearthed, it came to be completely ignored.[3]

That *admission,* which was also a *slip,* brought Mancini, who had not been mentioned by Madeiros or Weeks, into the case. He had been too late to be included in the Weeks list of the Morelli gang, but he could be included by Richards when his affidavit of June 10 was prepared.

FERRARI INTERROGATION OF JOE MORELLI

On June 20, 1926, Joseph Morelli was interrogated by Joseph F. Ferrari, a Massachusetts state detective, at Leavenworth. Morelli denied knowledge of Madeiros, the South Braintree crime, and Weeks and supplied an alibi for April 15, 1920, which I will discuss later. The following interchange is of interest:

FERRARI: On June 1, 1926, if you recall, were there two men here to see you and talk with you in the warden's office?
MORELLI: Yes.
FERRARI: Who were they, if you know?
MORELLI: One was formerly U.S. Marshal, John J. Richards that sent me away for the twelve years for interstate, the other was a man whom he called Robinson (and whom now I find his name is Herbert B. Ehrmann).
FERRARI: Will you state what they said to you and what you said to them?
MORELLI: They told me about a murder case that had happened in Boston after they explained to me which murder it was I told them I read it in the paper. John J. Richards

3 Ehrmann, *op. cit.,* p. 111.

took a letter out of his pocket stating he had evidence against me that I done this killing and wanted me to sign a confession to it.

I told him I wouldn't do it because I didn't know anything about it.

He says it is best for you to sign it; it will make it easier for you.

I told him I would not do it.

Well he says the Boston Police is going to indict you for that murder next week.

I says thanks.

Then he tried to bulldoze with the warden telling the warden what a bad fellow I was and so on and so forth.

I told the warden I refused to speak with or see them any longer.

Then the warden said he wouldn't stand for any bulldozing and trying to get me to sign something I wouldn't do.

Mr. Robinson also tried to get me to sign a confession for that murder and I told him I wouldn't do it, because I didn't know anything about it, only what I read in the papers.

He said I would be a good fellow if you sign a confession and save these two fellows battling for life.

I says I would be a poor fool to take the blame for something I didn't do to save the lives of somebody else. (4603-4605)

THE DEPOSITION

The deposition[4] of Madeiros was taken June 28, 1926. Madeiros proved to be a very bad witness, and Thompson soon found that,

[4] The deposition was taken pursuant to an agreement of counsel to provide for the possibility that Madeiros might not be available to testify at a new trial of Sacco and Vanzetti if one were ordered. As we have seen, Madeiros had been convicted of murder in the first degree and was awaiting the outcome of a bill of exceptions which had been taken to the Supreme Judicial Court on his behalf. If this failed, as seemed likely, he might be executed before the new trial of Sacco and Vanzetti could be held. Ranney's agreement was that the deposition could be offered in evidence at the motion for the

to get any kind of story from Madeiros, he had to resort to leading questions and other questions of a kind which are permissible in cross-examination, if at all, but not in direct.

Thompson did succeed, however, in having Madeiros make a few changes of greater or less significance in the confession, conforming it more closely to the probabilities and to Ehrmann's conjectural history of the crime.

But with all his leading questions and cross-examiner's tricks and all his confronting of Madeiros with the Weeks affidavit and with pictures of the Morelli gang from the rogues' gallery of the Morelli gang, Thompson could not get Madeiros to identify a single picture or add a single name to the "Bill" and "Mike" of his statement of November 20, 1925. *The only support the Morelli hypothesis ever got from Madeiros was his references to Providence and to the freight car thefts.*

Two of the changes in his story made by Madeiros in the deposition are noteworthy.

In the affidavit, Madeiros had himself picked up at 4:00 A.M., by four Italians at his rooming house. In the deposition, he was waiting for the Italians in a saloon on the opposite side of the street from the rooming house, and the four Italians had become three Italians and a kind of slim fellow with light hair, not an Italian but a Pole or a Finn or other northern European. This man was the driver of the murder car. (4630, 4683-4684)

---

new trial. He did not consent to the deposition being used at the new trial, "if there is one," or for any purpose except the motion for a new trial. However, he agreed that, if a new trial were granted to Sacco and Vanzetti, the attorney general and the district attorney would urge the Governor to respite the execution of Madeiros for such time as would enable him to testify orally at the new trial. If the respite was not granted and Madeiros was executed before the new trial of Sacco and Vanzetti, the district attorney would then and only then consent to the deposition being used at the new trial. (4717-4718)

A new trial for Sacco and Vanzetti was not granted, but the sentence of death later imposed upon Madeiros was from time to time respited by the Governor until after Madeiros had been interviewed by the Governor and the Advisory Committee and until after Sacco and Vanzetti had exhausted all their efforts to get a new trial. Indeed, Madeiros was executed the same day and at the same time that Sacco and Vanzetti were executed, giving point to Ehrmann's contribution to the deification of Vanzetti: "History had written that the execution of a thief was necessary to a perfect Calvary."

Why were these changes made? It was surely immaterial whether the gang met at the lodging house or in the saloon or, indeed, whether they met in Providence or somewhere else. Madeiros had, however, committed himself to the early meeting in Providence and at his lodging house. Unfortunately for this story, his sister had told officer Fleming on December 6, 1925, "positively" that Madeiros was not living with her in Providence on April 15, 1920, and had confirmed this by affidavit. (4573)

So Madeiros had to wait for the gang in a saloon across the street. This was awkward, because 4:00 A.M. was a little early for a saloon to be open in Providence, even during Prohibition. The best the defense could do with this was to offer the affidavit of George Hatton, an early-morning patron of this saloon, who affirmed that this particular saloon was always open as early as 5:30; he knew, because he was there every morning and found the porter opening up at that time. (4566-4567)

No 4:00 A.M. witness was found.

The substitution of the slim, light-haired northern European for the fourth Italian was made to conform the confession to the overwhelming testimony at the trial that the murder car was driven by a light-haired man who gave every appearance of being sickly. It would be interesting to know who told Madeiros that his gang must include a light-haired man. (4656)

The cross-examination by Ranney developed, in addition to the items already mentioned and others of the same kind, information about Madeiros' knowledge—or total ignorance—of the South Braintree locale and the details of the shooting.

Madeiros admitted that he could draw and could read blueprints, but although he could draw a sketch of the road in Randolph he could not draw a plan of South Braintree, where the shooting took place: "to tell you the truth, I haven't got the memory of what it looks like." (4686) He wasn't in condition to have a memory at the time, he said; he was not really drunk, but he had had a few drinks. He could not say whether there was a railway anywhere near the scene of the shooting, or any factories or stores or excavation work; or whether it was thickly populated (it was not country); or whether there were swamps, lakes, or water tanks nearby; or whether there was anybody on the street at the time of the shooting. He could not say that they went across a railroad crossing. He stuck to his story about the black bag; he guessed it was a large bag which was thrown under a blanket in the Buick, shifted with the blanket to the Hudson in the Randolph woods, and taken to Providence, which was the last he saw of it. He was not interested in the contents of the black bag at that time. (4688 et seq.)

Efforts of the defense to find corroborative evidence failed to get anything of substance, and all must agree with Morgan that the Madeiros confession began and ended as a wholly worthless story from an utterly untrustworthy source.[5] The Governor and the Advisory Committee found the confession valueless, and only the most faithful supporters of Sacco and Vanzetti have defended it. It has often been said, however, that the Morelli hypothesis, built upon his confession, solved the crime and cleared the defendants.

Frankfurter was sure of this—he thought the proof was positive. Fraenkel is more cautious:

> The Madeiros confession may be as worthless as the Lowell Committee maintained yet the probability that the Morelli gang committed the South Braintree murder was at least great enough to have justified an investigation by government authority free from any connection with the prosecution of Sacco and Vanzetti.[6]

Well, let's see.

[5] *Harvard Law Review*, p. 538, in Morgan's review of the Ehrmann book.
[6] Fraenkel, *op. cit.*, p. 534.

AFTER MUCH TRIAL and error, Ehrmann chose a murder party from these candidates: Michael Morelli (Mike), Joseph Morelli (Joe), Pasquale Morelli (Patsy), Frank Morelli (Butsy), Fred Morelli (the original Butsy), Albert Barone (Bibba or Bibber), Paul Rossi (Pauli), Joseph Imondi (Gyp the Blood), Raymond McDevitt (Ray), Antonio Mancini (Tony; originally Bill), Steve Benkosky (Steve the Pole), and Celestino F. Madeiros.

With the exception of what Madeiros had told about himself, there never was any evidence against any one of these men, and Ehrmann had a free hand in assigning and reassigning seats in the murder car. This proved convenient, because he soon found it necessary to go outside the "Morelli gang," excluding three of the most likely suspects: Patsy, for a reason never clearly stated, and Fred (the original Butsy) and Bibber, because both were in jail on April 15, 1920.

Pauli, another of the freight car thieves, also was dropped. Ehrmann, when he came to write his book, did not clearly remember why Pauli was dropped, but to the best of his recollection Richards suggested the exclusion after he had questioned Pauli in a Rhode Island jail. Perhaps Pauli had an alibi.

Gyp the Blood was excluded because he was disqualified by disposition. He was a peaceable gangster who had been given his ferocious nickname in derision and not in tribute. He was good at prying the locks of freight cars in the night time but was not fitted for important work. At any rate, he was too dark to have been the driver of the murder car and temperamentally unfitted for the place of Bill the Killer.[1]

When the four Italians placed by Madeiros in the murder car became three Italians and one light-haired North European, it was necessary to look outside the Morelli gang of Italians for a chauffeur. Ray McDevitt was provisionally nominated for the job.

> He was a light complexioned young man, slender and rather good looking. He was a thief, a hi-jacker and a holdup man. He was not definitely a member of the Morelli gang, but hailed from their hangout in *Pawtucket* and was engaged in freight car robberies. He corresponded in general appearance to the driver of the car and was at liberty on April 15, 1920.[2] (My italics.)

But Ray was dismissed because, during the deposition, Madeiros hesitated before refusing to identify his picture as that of a person he had seen before. This hesitation told Ehrmann plainly "that McDevitt had nothing to do with the crime or the Morellis, but that after consideration Madeiros had decided not to make any exception" to his refusal to identify pictures.

The driver's seat was not open long. Steve Benkosky, a young desperado of the right complexion and disposition, was available. He was not of the Morelli gang but apparently a member of another circle which included Madeiros, Weeks, a man named Mingo, and Manuel Pacheco.

Thus, by exclusion and by what is known in the theater as type casting, Ehrmann in his book although not in the affidavits arrived at the following murder party:

Joseph Morelli (Joe), the boss of the gang, about forty, one of the men who did the shooting.

Antonio Mancini (Tony) thirty-three, the other shooter.

Steve Benkosky (Steve the Pole), the driver, about twenty.

1 Ehrmann, *op. cit.*, pp. 78-79.
2 Ehrmann, *op. cit.*, pp. 79-80.

Frank Morelli (Butsy), twenty-three, a back-seat rider.
Madeiros, eighteen, another back-seat rider.
Mike Morelli, the man in the woods.
Let us now consider these characters separately.

JOE MORELLI, THE ORIGINAL MIKE

Ehrmann had some difficulty in qualifying Joe Morelli for a principal role in an armed robbery. Joe had no record of participation in crimes of violence. In the opinion of his own counsel he was a blowhard and a coward. He had indeed boasted to Richards that stealing from freight cars was beneath his dignity but that, if it was a bank robbery or a "stick-up" job, that was more in his line; he was a "high-class man." He had shot at a deputy sheriff but missed him, and he had threatened the life of the marshal. In his relations with other criminals he ignored the code of the gangster: he protected himself, he informed on others, he was a stool pigeon for prison wardens, a nasty piece of goods altogether, capable of many crimes but with no record of a crime in which he took life or risked his own. In the end, Ehrmann had to fall back on opinion evidence: "Those who knew Joe well did not doubt that he would be a principal actor at the South Braintree tragedy."

To this opinion that Joe was capable of murder, Ehrmann adds these other items: his possession of a Colt .32; what happened when a rogues'-gallery picture of Joe was shown to eyewitnesses of the shooting; the size of Sacco's hand; and Joe's ability, because he was American born, to use clear and unmistakable English when saying, "What to hell are you holding us up for!" to the gatetender at Matfield crossing.

Ehrmann's theory that Joe was the man who shot Berardelli rests wholly upon Joe's ownership of a Colt .32. A principal trouble with that theory is that on March 8, 1920, Joe's .32 had been taken from his possession by a United States deputy marshal serving a search warrant and turned over to the marshal, and Joe never got it back. This revolver was an exhibit at the freight car theft trial in May 1920, and unless the marshal let Joe have it for the day on April 15, 1920, it could not have been the murder gun. (4423)

This consideration led Ehrmann to imagine that Joe had several Colt .32's. For that inference he relied on the testimony of Gyp the Blood who, at the freight car theft trial, remembered that he had seen another Colt .32 in Joe's house. But as this gun belonged to the Bibber, there was still a gap for the imagination to fill, and it was never filled.

Ehrmann remained convinced, nevertheless, that the fatal bullet found in Berardelli's body was fired by Joe. To this deduction, Ehrmann added his opinion that the fatal bullet supposedly found in Berardelli's body was a false exhibit. By this paradox, I assume that Ehrmann meant that Captain Proctor or someone else had substituted bullet No. 3 for the actual bullet, which was of the kind that would have been fired from Joe's .32 if Joe had been there and had his gun with him.

No eyewitnesses of the crime or of any of the day's events were invited to go to Leavenworth to look at Joe Morelli in person, and there was no face-to-face identification of him or, for that matter, of any member of Ehrmann's murder party by any eyewitness. What "identification" there was, came from witnesses who looked at pictures; and this occurred only in the cases of Joe, Mancini, and Benkosky, no pictures of Mike or Frank having been obtained.

Pictures of Joe were shown in 1926 to Lillian E. Splaine, Lewis L. Wade, and several other witnesses who had testified at the trial. None of these identified the picture as that of the man they saw on April 15, 1920. Miss Splaine expressly denied that she had made a mistake in identifying Sacco as the man she saw instead of the man in the picture. Wade thought the man in the picture "strikingly like the man whom I saw shooting Berardelli." "In my judgment," he said, "the picture also bears a resemblance to Sacco, especially the side view."

A picture of Joe was shown to Dominick DiBona, who had been a defense witness. He thought the picture seemed remarkably like

Sacco's. Four others who had been defense witnesses (two cellar diggers and two railway workers) mistook a likeness of Joe for Sacco, and Frank J. Burke thought the picture of Joe was a remarkable likeness of the man sitting next to the driver who snapped a pistol at him.

That is all the evidence of identification of Joe. The record does not disclose nor does Ehrmann tell us whether the picture was shown to other witnesses or, if so, what they said. It does not appear that the picture was shown to Mr. and Mrs. Monterio to find out whether Joe was one of the men who came to the Bluebird Inn to get the girl named Tessie when Madeiros was there. We know from the book but not from the affidavit that pictures of Sacco and Joe Morelli were shown in 1926 to Mancini, who did not think that they looked at all alike, and we know from the deposition that Madeiros, when shown a picture of Joe on June 28, 1926, refused to say who it was, "for private reasons."

It is obvious that evidence which went no further than to prove a resemblance between Sacco or Sacco's picture and Joe Morelli's picture would be of no value in a trial of Joe, however much it might have been used to impeach the identification of Sacco in his trial. The problem was whether Joe was the man whom the eyewitnesses saw on April 15, 1920, not whether he looked like Sacco.

Miss Splaine at the trial made a positive face-to-face identification of Sacco as the man she had seen leaning out of the murder car. Part of her description of this man was as follows: "I noticed particularly the left hand was a good sized hand, a hand that denoted strength." (222)

On June 12, 1926, at about 11:00 A.M., Ehrmann had Herbert C. Dow, a glove salesman who had measured thousands of hands, come to the Dedham jail to measure both of Sacco's hands for gloves. Dow found that Sacco's left hand wore comfortably a size $7\frac{3}{4}$, smaller than the average (which is between 8 and $8\frac{1}{2}$), and that Sacco had what men in the glove trade would call small hands. (4526)

Obviously Ehrmann here measured the wrong person's hand. His purpose was to establish that Joe and not Sacco was the man in the murder car seen by Miss Splaine. On this point Sacco's hand was not important. The jury had seen it, and if Miss Splaine was wrong about its size they could take that fact into account in appraising her testimony. (1944) Did Joe have a big, strong hand? That was the question to be asked, if the purpose was to put Joe into the murder car and not merely to take Sacco out.

Why wasn't Joe's hand measured? Ehrmann does not give the reason but relies feebly on this:

> As for Joe Morelli, it is at least interesting to know that the Federal District Attorney asked him during the trial in Providence, whether he had not boasted of the great strength of his hand, that he could hang to a freight car with one hand and open the door with the other.

But, as Ehrmann explains in a footnote, this question by the District Attorney was never incorporated into an affidavit because Joe denied that he had made the boast.[3]

The rest of the evidence for identifying Joe as the murderer was his ability, because American born, to use clear and unmistakable English when saying, "What to hell are you holding us up for!" to the gatetender at Matfield crossing.

This point was relevant in Vanzetti's trial. If in fact Vanzetti was unable to speak these nine words in clear and unmistakable English, the jury might infer that the gatetender was mistaken in his identification; and as they had heard Vanzetti on the stand, they could make or reject the inference. In a trial of Joe, the point would be of no value unless the prosecution proved that Joe was the only man in the vicinity capable of clear and unmistakable English.

TONY MANCINI OR BILL THE KILLER

The "Bill" of the Madeiros confession became "Tony" in the Morelli hypothesis, and thereby the role of the second shooter was assigned to Antonio Mancini.

He, it is supposed, fired bullets No. 1, 2, 4, 5, and 6 found in

3 Ehrmann, *op. cit.*, p. 102.

the bodies, using the pistol of foreign manufacture with which he had killed Alberti Alterio on a New York street on February 10, 1921. This weapon, a Star automatic pistol of caliber 7.65, had disappeared by 1926 and was never found.

At the trial no theory was advanced by anyone as to who fired bullets No. 1, 2, 4, 5, and 6, and there was a difference of opinion among the experts at the trial and afterward as to whether the bullets had been fired through a Savage automatic, or a Steyr pistol, "one of the best known foreign automatics," or a Walther, also a foreign automatic, or a Harrington & Richardson.

Ehrmann, rejecting the opinions of Proctor, Van Amburgh, and Hamilton, adopts Burns's opinion that it might have been a Savage *or* a Steyr *or* a Walther as a positive opinion that it was a Steyr. He then takes the further step of imagining that there was a stenographic error on the records of the District Attorney's office in New York whereby the Mancini pistol was recorded as a Star when it should have been recorded as a Steyr.

And that is all that Ehrmann finds to identify Mancini as the murderer, except that, when in 1926 a picture of Mancini was shown to Donato DiBona, who had been a defense witness at the trial, he thought it resembled closely a man he saw beside the driver. DiBona was not taken to the New York State Prison in Auburn to look at Mancini in person, nor was the picture of Mancini shown to Madeiros. Also, as we have seen, neither Madeiros nor Weeks mentioned Mancini in their affidavits.

Ehrmann's interview of Mancini in Auburn did not get into an affidavit because he admits that he came away empty-handed and without a thing of evidentiary value.

STEVE THE POLE

A newspaper picture of Benkosky (Steve the Pole) was shown in 1926 to at least three persons—how many more we are not told— and those three (Donato DiBona, Minnie Kennedy, and Louise Kelly) saw some resemblance between the driver of the car and the picture, but all thought that the driver of the car was thinner and did not have as full a face as the man in the picture. Ehrmann explains this by a suggestion that the Benkosky picture shown to the witnesses was taken five years after the crime and Steve had put on weight during that time and his face had become fuller.

This half-hearted identification by DiBona, Kennedy, and Kelly, plus the Weeks statement that Madeiros had told the South Braintree story in the presence of Steve at the Lime Rock Inn in 1924, plus Steve's light complexion, is *all* the evidence against him. No one on either side seems to have known where he was in 1920, and by the time he was nominated for the driver's seat, he had been killed in a hijacking operation and could not be interviewed. The glimpses we get of him in the affidavits are in 1924.

FRANK MORELLI

Ehrmann deduces "consciousness of guilt" on the part of Frank Morelli from the following incident related by Sergeant Ellsworth C. Jacobs in his affidavit:

On May 27, 1926, Sergeant Jacobs remembered that on April 24, 1920, he had seen a big, black, dull-looking touring car, a Cole "8," standing at the curb in front of Fiore's restaurant in New Bedford. This car bore the same number plate, 154E Rhode Island, as the Buick in which he had seen Mike Morelli a few days before April 15, 1920.[4] Jacobs went into the restaurant and found Frank Morelli at a table with three other Italians. Jacobs was worried because he was unarmed. As he approached the table, one of the Italians (not Frank) reached for his hip pocket. This action made Jacobs believe that the man was going to draw a gun, but he didn't. (4419)

Frank asked Jacobs

why I was picking on him all the time and what I wanted with him.

I asked Frank how it happened that the Cole car below had the same number as the new Buick which I had seen Mike driving and Frank replied that he was in the auto-

[4] See Chapter 27 ("The Madeiros Confession and How It Grew").

mobile business and that the plate was a dealer's plate which he transferred from one car to another. (4419)

The other affidavits are equally unsatisfactory. Weeks had an impression that Madeiros had also mentioned Frank as being in on the South Braintree job, but was not sure. This was when Richards and Weeks thought that Fred, not Frank, was "Butsy." Frank bet on the races and on baseball games and lived by his wits. He always had plenty of money. He was in the freight car case and was sentenced to five years in Atlanta. He was out of jail on April 15, 1920, but not out on bail.

In his book, Ehrmann explains his choice of Frank as follows:

> Frank Morelli, or Butsy, certainly qualified for the job. He was generally regarded as the most dangerous of the brothers. During the trial he had threatened to kill his associate, Joe Imondi (Gyp the Blood), and one of the fences who turned state's evidence told me he was in constant terror for fear of Frank. Frank later figures in a stabbing affray. He was a bird of passage, shifting about among Providence, New Bedford, or New York. Sergeant Jacobs had already described Frank's guilty actions in Joe Fiore's restaurant in New Bedford. As Frank had surrendered himself directly to the Federal authorities, we could procure no rogues' gallery likeness from the Providence police or anyone.[5]

Thus, in Ehrmann's book, Frank gets in on his reputation and the guilty action of an associate at a restaurant, without identification by any eyewitness and without other evidence of any kind.

MIKE, THE MAN IN THE WOODS

Mike Morelli, second in age of the Morelli gang, had moved from Providence to New Bedford several years before 1920. He was a gambler, a pimp, and a white slaver but, so far as appears, had no reputation for violence.

Madeiros in his confession named Mike as the oldest of the four

5 Ehrmann, *op. cit.*, p. 76.

Italians in the murder car with him and as one of those who did the actual shooting. Weeks did not mention him to Kelley and Fleming in the morning interview of May 25, but in the afternoon affidavit he knew that Mike was one of the Joe Morelli gang, that he and Frank followed the races and bet on them and on baseball games, that he always had plenty of money, and that his real headquarters was Providence. In the afternoon, though not in the morning, Weeks was quite sure that Madeiros had named Mike, Joe, Bill, and Butsy as four of the gang who were in the South Braintree job.

So, for a day or two Mike, although he had not been indicted for the freight car thefts, was cast for a seat in the car and a leading part in the shooting. On May 27, 1926, however, Mike lost his leading role and became the man in the woods who shifted the cars. This change came when Ehrmann, with the aid of Sergeant Jacobs' notebook and his own imagination, reconstructed the day's events and gave Mike, the pimp, a role more suited to his disposition and record than that of a desperado.

Sometime during the morning, says Ehrmann, the bandits went in the Hudson to the Randolph woods, where they met an Italian (Mike) with a Buick. They exchanged cars and left Mike in the woods with the Hudson. The others then took the Buick to a South Braintree speakeasy to eat and drink until it was time to do the job. The Buick, which several witnesses saw in the street of South Braintree as early as 9:30, and off and on during the morning and early afternoon, simply wasn't there. It was in the woods until the exchange was made, and it did not get into South Braintree until noon, when it was parked in a yard before a speakeasy in South Braintree until the time to do the job arrived and Madeiros had become half drunk.

The getaway, Ehrmann goes on, was in the Buick as far as the Randolph woods. The murderers then changed back to the Hudson and gave the Buick back to Mike, who had brought it. At first it was supposed that he had abandoned it in the Randolph woods, but this supposition proved untenable when it was learned that there had been no Buicks of this type abandoned in Randolph in

1920. (4587) Ehrmann then adopted the theory that the Buick followed the Hudson out of the woods, went to New Bedford, where it was seen at 5:30 or thereabouts by Jacobs, and presumably was taken back after nightfall and abandoned in the Manley Street woods. (The murder car had been found in the Manley Street woods on April 17, 1920.)

It would seem that, if the Buick was going to show itself immediately, the change from Buick to Hudson in the woods was an unnecessary precaution against detection. And if the Buick had escaped suspicion throughout the ride from Randolph to New Bedford, why did Mike think it necessary to abandon his new Buick in the Manley Street woods? Had he had enough of Buicks?

The efforts of Thompson to have Madeiros name, or acknowledge acquaintance with, the Italian who brought the Buick and took it away failed, for, here as elsewhere, Madeiros would not name or adequately describe any of his companions in the South Braintree crime.

MADEIROS-MORELLI AND SACCO-VANZETTI

The Madeiros confession and that part of the Morelli hypothesis which had been developed before Ehrmann wrote his book were presented to the District Attorney as a reason for a *nol pros* of the Sacco-Vanzetti case, to Judge Thayer as a reason for a new trial, and to the Governor and the Advisory Committee as a reason for executive clemency. All the data supporting them were made a part of the record which went to the Supreme Judicial Court on exceptions to Thayer's denial of the motion for a new trial.

The argument was that a better case of murder could be proved against Madeiros, Joe, Frank, Tony, Mike, and Steve the Pole than the case that had been proved in court against Sacco and Vanzetti. In support of this argument, the defendants' brief in the Supreme Judicial Court printed in parallel columns a comparison of the Morelli gang and the defendants. (4791 *et seq.*) These parallel columns were reprinted by Frankfurter in his book and by Ehrmann in his, and they must be regarded as the best they could do with the argument. Fraenkel also reprints the columns but refrains from comment. Morgan has too much sense or too keen a sense of the ridiculous to quote them in his discussion.

	Madeiros-Morelli	*Sacco-Vanzetti*
Character of accused	Typical gangsters and gunmen of the worst type.	One of them an industrious workman with a family and a savings bank deposit, and no previous criminal record. The other a fish peddler never before his arrest accused of crime. Both unpopular as pacifists and extreme radicals.

But, as we have seen, Ehrmann's murder party, with the possible exception of Mancini, were not "typical gangsters and gunmen of the worst type" at all. It is only by repeated assertion that the world has come to believe that this group of petty thieves, pimps, gamblers, and receivers of stolen goods were gangsters and gunmen.

Nor was the murder party, as finally selected in the hypothesis, a gang. Madeiros, Mancini, and Benkosky were not members of the Morelli gang of freight car thieves. The most that can be said for Mike's membership in that gang was that he bore the name of Morelli, but he had been living as a pimp and petty criminal in New Bedford for several years and was not connected with the freight car thefts at all, so far as the record shows. This leaves only Joe and Frank as members of the Morelli "gang."

As for the "Sacco-Vanzetti" column, we may grant a slight margin of probability in favor of murder by a group of petty criminals and pimps as against murder by an industrious worker and a fish peddler never before accused of crime, but this margin disappears quickly where there is no evidence against the group and a great deal against the worker and the fish peddler.

	Madeiros-Morelli	*Sacco-Vanzetti*
Motive	Desperate need of funds for lawyer and bail before trial for serious Federal offense. Source of income through robbing freight cars blocked by U.S. Marshal and R.R. Police.	Robbery for private gain alleged. No claim or evidence that either defendant ever received or had any part of the stolen money.

The need for bail applied only to Joe, because Madeiros, Mike, Frank, Steve, and Tony were not out on bail; they were just out. Nor was it ever proved that any one of them, including Joe, was in desperate need of funds for any purpose. Nor, so far as the record shows, did Madeiros, Mike, Steve, or Tony have anything to do with the freight car thefts. Frank did, but the uncontradicted evidence was that he always had plenty of money.

As for the motive ascribed to Sacco and Vanzetti, I find no allegation by the Commonwealth that the robbery was for private gain in the sense that they were robbing to add to their savings or their spending money. Where, as in this case, robbery was obviously the motive, it was no part of the Commonwealth's case to prove what the defendants wanted or needed the money for; their guilt would not depend on whether the robbery was carried out for private gain or to get money for the poor or for bail or to pay lawyers or to promote the revolution.

There was evidence that Sacco and Vanzetti were in possession of the stolen money immediately after the murder and during the getaway. There is no evidence that any of Ehrmann's murder party had it at any time. Where it went after the crime remains a mystery so far as the record is concerned, but it was never proved that any of the Morellis or Madeiros or Mancini or Steve the Pole ever had any of it.

	Madeiros-Morelli	*Sacco-Vanzetti*
Opportunity to plan crime	Had been repeatedly stealing large shipments from Slater and Morrill and Rice and Hutchins of South Braintree after a member of the gang had "spotted" them in that place.	None alleged.

The only evidence that any of Ehrmann's murder party had been stealing large shipments from Slater & Morrill and Rice & Hutchins was their unlawful *possession in Providence* of 683 pairs of shoes, shipped in the fall of 1919 *from* South Braintree in interstate commerce. The "spotter," another figment of Ehrmann's active imagination, was never named, nor did the defense place any member of the murder party in South Braintree at any time. The freight car thieves were not stealing in South Braintree or at other points of origin but from cars in Providence or otherwise enroute to out-of-state destinations. If the shipments had been of money, diamonds, or other very valuable merchandise, a "spotter" at the point of shipment would have been helpful, but it is ridiculous to suggest that the Morellis "spotted" relatively small shipments of shoes from a small town and thereby learned the day and hour when the Slater & Morrill payroll would be on the street.

Nor was a "spotter" necessary. Anyone who lived in South Braintree or had worked there or could ask a question knew or could readily find out that on payday the money would be on the street in midafternoon.

Sacco, who lived within a few miles of the South Braintree factories and *had worked in one of them,* was in at least as good a position to know about this as any "spotter" from Providence.

	Madeiros-Morelli	*Sacco-Vanzetti*
Accusation by confederate	Direct testimony of participant.	None

The only direct testimony of a participant is the worthless confession of the untrustworthy Madeiros. As we have seen, he did not even clearly implicate himself and never did include an accusation of anyone else by name or adequate description.

On the other hand the lies told to Katzmann by Sacco and Vanzetti on May 6, 1920, were eloquent of their guilt.

	Madeiros-Morelli	*Sacco-Vanzetti*
Identification by others	Opportunity restricted, but Joe, Mancini, and Benkosky identified from photographs by Government as well as defense witnesses. No available photographs of Mike or Frank. Undoubted resemblance of Joe Morelli to Sacco in many particulars.	Some identification of Sacco; very slight of Vanzetti at the scene of the murder. Identification open not only to doubt, but to the gravest suspicion owing to unprecedented manner of displaying these defendants, previous identifications of other criminals by same witnesses, changes in stories, suppression of testimony, manifestly impossible details such as the man identified as Vanzetti using "clear and unmistakable English," and the man identified as Sacco having an unusually large hand.

The "identification" from pictures of the members of the Ehrmann murder party is fully discussed earlier in this chapter and the face-to-face identification of Sacco and Vanzetti in previous chapters.

It is true that identification at the trial by some of the witnesses followed identification at the police station, where there was no line-up. This is not unprecedented and does not open the identification to suspicion where the witnesses are honest.[6]

Similarly, it is true that previous identification of the pictures of other criminals by some of the witnesses did occur before the arrest. This was certainly a proper subject for cross-examination and for the jury to consider in appraising the face-to-face identification on the stand.

The same should be said about changes in stories.

The point is that it is the face-to-face identification on the stand that counts, and one would certainly have to hear it before discarding it on the ground that it was inconsistent with what the witness had done or said before. A good example is Pelser, who lied to the state, lied to the defense, and yet, in the mind of one of the jury, was the most impressive of the identification witnesses.

As we have seen, Sacco's hand size and "the clear and unmistakable English" were relevant in appraising the testimony of Miss Splaine and Austin T. Reed (the gatetender at the Matfield crossing) about Sacco or Vanzetti, but Sacco's hand and Vanzetti's English are not proof that Joe was in the getaway car unless we are to believe that Joe was the only person anywhere who had a large hand or who could speak clear and unmistakable English.

	Madeiros-Morelli	*Sacco-Vanzetti*
Alibi	Full of contradictions as to Morellis. None by Madeiros.	Testified to by many reputable witnesses.

I find it difficult to follow Ehrmann's reasoning here. If he means that a weak or nonexistent alibi is some proof of participation in a crime, he is indulging himself in another fallacy like the fallacies of Sacco's hand and the clear and unmistakable English. There were doubtless many thousand people who in 1921 could not account for their whereabouts on April 15, 1920, but that

---

[6] See Chapter 9 ("The Eyewitnesses").

would not place any of them in South Braintree shooting at a pay-master on that day.

If, however, Ehrmann meant only that the Madeiros-Morelli alibis would not have been a good defense, his point is of no consequence, for unless there is evidence of participation in the crime the alibis do not become relevant.

Whatever his point may be, it is obvious that it was of very limited application.

No alibis were offered for Steve the Pole or for Mancini. Ehrmann, the only person to interview Mancini, neglected to ask about his whereabouts on April 15, 1920, and no one seems to know where Steve the Pole was at any time before 1924.

The alibis of Frank and Mike depended on the statements of Fred, Patsy, and Frank. These statements are not full of contradictions nor were they contradicted.

The testimony of the sister of Madeiros gave him a pretty fair alibi with some corroboration, not too definite, from the New Bedford police.

Joe had three alibi witnesses—himself; his Providence attorney, Daniel E. Geary; and his housekeeper. I do not find that he or his housekeeper contradicted themselves. Geary did. On June 4, 1926, he told Ranney that, although he could not state where Joe was on April 15, 1920, he did know that Joe was in his office daily during the month before the trial and became a nuisance. Later, when he had been employed by the defense to find a missing transcript which might implicate Joe in the South Braintree murder, Geary could only "presume that Joseph Morelli was in my office occasionally in the month of April 1920, but when I have no means of telling."

Pauline Gray swore that she had been employed by Joseph Morelli as a housekeeper during the month of April 1920. He was at home every night before 12:00 and did not leave until 10:00 the following morning. If he had left the house at any time between midnight and 10:00 the next morning she would have known it, and he did not leave. (4608)

Thompson, who spared no one, took care of this testimony,

which Miss Gray never changed, by annexing to his supplemental affidavit of July 15, 1926, (4541) certified copies of court records showing that Pauline Gray had been convicted of being lewd and wanton, of being a common nightwalker, and of having illicit sexual intercourse. We need not inquire whether these convictions destroyed the Gray testimony or made it more credible.

	Madeiros-Morelli	*Sacco-Vanzetti*
Consciousness of guilt	Alleged motion to draw gun on officer uncontradicted. Falsehoods consistent with nothing but consciousness of guilt of crime charged. Confession by Madeiros.	Alleged motion to draw gun on officer contradicted. Falsehoods explained by terror felt by radicals and draft evaders at time of persecution of "reds" two days after murder or suicide of a friend while in the custody of Department of Justice officials.

The gun in question was not drawn by Frank himself but by an unnamed Italian in his company at Fiore's restaurant in New Bedford when the police inquiry was about an automobile on the street and not at all about the April 15 murder. The falsehoods alleged are denials by Joe and others of statements made by Madeiros, Weeks, Richards, and Ehrmann. To make anything of these denials as consciousness of guilt, Ehrmann should first have proved that they were falsehoods, and he did not do that.

The confession by Madeiros was more consistent with consciousness of advantage to be gained by the confession than with consciousness of guilt of the crime.[7]

[7] The scanty and inaccurate summary of the consciousness-of-guilt evidence in the Sacco-Vanzetti column should be compared with the evidence itself as given in Chapter 13 ("Consciousness of Guilt"). See for the "persecution" Chapter 32 ("The 'Red Scare'") and for the death of the friend Chapter 17 ("The Death of Salsedo").

	Madeiros-Morelli	*Sacco-Vanzetti*
Bullets	One fired from pistol of type owned by Joe Morelli (Colt .32) and five from type owned by Mancini ("Star" or "Steyr," 765 mm.).	One only claimed to have been fired by weapon of Sacco, and none by Vanzetti. Sharp disagreement of experts, but if real opinion of one of the Government's experts had been known at the time of the trial he would have proved a *defense witness.*

This is surely making much of Joe Morelli's Colt and Mancini's Star and very little of the ballistics evidence at the trial, which was never met by the defense except by claiming without evidence that the exhibits were false. Joe Morelli's Colt .32 was, on April 15, 1920, in the possession of the marshal. Sacco's Colt .32 was in his waistband when he was arrested, and in his pocket were obsolete bullets of the type found in Berardelli's body and not found elsewhere. The defense connects Mancini with the case because he owned a Star 765, which was never found and which by a stenographic error might have been a Steyr.

Proctor's evidence has been fully discussed elsewhere. See Chapter 25.

	Madeiros-Morelli	*Sacco-Vanzetti*
Other corroborative matter	Morellis were American born and could have used "clear and unmistakable" English. *Every member of the murder party accounted for.* Unwillingness of Morelli lawyer to state any-	Testimony shows that cap claimed to be Sacco's was *not* identified by Kelley, and effort to connect Vanzetti's popular make of revolver with Berardelli's supported by most remote type of evidence, in-

Madeiros-Morelli	*Sacco-Vanzetti*
thing tending to implicate his former clients in the South Braintree murder.	cluding confused records of gun shop offered by an ex-agent (unrevealed) of the Department of Justice.[8] Does not account for other members of the party.

I have mentioned the "clear and unmistakable English" as relevant to an impeachment of the identification testimony but surely not proof that Joe was in the car, unless it is shown that he was the only person anywhere who could speak clear and unmistakable English.

"Every member of the murder party accounted for" is a large claim for the manner in which five men were included without a scrap of evidence against any of them.

The last sentence relating to Geary, the Morellis' lawyer in the freight car prosecution, is inexplicable. Geary *should* have been unwilling to state anything tending to implicate his former client in the South Braintree murder, and no inference from his silence should be drawn. As a matter of fact he did try to implicate Joe by trying to find a missing transcript.

Sacco's cap and Berardelli's gun are treated in earlier chapters.

The failure of the prosecution to fill the murder car was due to the fact that, unlike the defense, it was unwilling to name persons against whom it had insufficient evidence. If the prosecution had

---

8 The unrevealed ex-agent of the Department of Justice was Lincoln Wadsworth, an employee of Iver-Johnson, who testified from the record that a .38 Harrington & Richardson revolver, "property of Alex Berardelli," had been brought to Iver-Johnson for repairs and that Exhibit 27 (the revolver found on the person of Vanzetti at the time of his arrest) was of the same description as the gun left for repairs. Wadsworth had been an agent of the Bureau of Investigation of the Department of Justice before being employed by Iver-Johnson, but we have never been told what that has to do with his testimony. See Chapter 12, "Berardelli's Gun."

been as facile as the defense, it could have named Boda, Orciani, and Coacci with much more plausibility. It is to the prosecution's credit that it did not make accusations it could not prove but proceeded cautiously as the evidence became available.

	Madeiros-Morelli	*Sacco-Vanzetti*
Stolen money	Madeiros's possession of $2,800 immediately thereafter (about his "split" of the total sum stolen).	None. On the contrary, when arrested, Sacco and Vanzetti, supposed to be in possession of over $15,000, and ex-hypothesi, to be accomplished automobile thieves, were using streetcars after an unsuccessful attempt to borrow a friend's six-year-old Overland.

Madeiros never admitted that he received any part of the South Braintree money. He claimed throughout that he was double-crossed, and for a while the defense gratefully accepted this claim, because the double cross fitted into its case against Bibber Barone. When Bibber went out of the cast because of his alibi (he was in jail), the double cross was no longer of service and the agile defense adopted the theory that Madeiros came into immediate possession of $2,800 (about a one-sixth share of the money stolen) but felt that he had been double-crossed because the gang had estimated his share at $4,000 or $5,000.

The immediate possession of $2,800 by Madeiros rests entirely upon what Ehrmann calls "a chance remark" by a man who thought he was a fellow lodger of Madeiros in April 1920. The remark proved to Ehrmann's satisfaction that Madeiros on April 16, 1920, wanted to be sure that his door was locked.[9]

9 Ehrmann, *op. cit.*, p. 146.

But, although in this revised theory Madeiros had the money, he did not begin to spend it immediately or change his mode of living. He went on collecting for the American Relief Society and indulging himself in minor crimes until his arrest on May 25, 1920. Nor did he spend any of it after his release from the House of Correction on November 20, 1920, until in January 1921 he started south with it all intact.

This, the defense contrasts with Sacco and Vanzetti's situation. They were supposed to be in possession of $15,000 (all the booty, with nothing for the others in the car) and still, three weeks after the crime, were using streetcars to go to a place where they could borrow an old automobile. Madeiros, then, could wait nine months with $2,800 in his pocket before spending any of it, but Sacco and Vanzetti must within three weeks buy themselves a car or steal one, and their failure to do so must be taken as proof that they got no part of the stolen money.

It is quite possible that Sacco and Vanzetti did not retain for themselves any share of the booty, and it is perhaps unfair to connect the possession of the money with the changes they made in their mode of living after the crime. Vanzetti, however, did quit work entirely, did not sell a fish from April 15 to May 5, did take a trip to New York, did spend some time in Boston, and did visit with his friends. Sacco did quit work early in May and did prepare to take his family to Italy with a passport dated the day before the arrest.

As to the automobile, Vanzetti did not drive a car, and Sacco was going to leave the country. Neither had any use for an automobile of his own and neither, *ex-hypothesi* or in fact, had ever stolen one. The trip to get the Overland car was taken by streetcar but that fact did not prove that Vanzetti and Sacco had no money. It proved only that they had no automobile and would have none until they "borrowed" the Overland.

What happened to the money stolen at South Braintree remains a mystery. It may have gone to Italy with Coacci or Boda. It may have gone to the support of the cause. It may still be hidden somewhere. That Sacco and Vanzetti did not buy or steal an automobile within three weeks after the crime proves nothing. It surely proves nothing that Madeiros had $2,800 with which to go south nine months after the crime or that he put a chair against his door in April 1920.

And how about Joe and Mike and Frank and Steve the Pole and Tony? Did they also have $2,800 apiece?

	Madeiros-Morelli	*Sacco-Vanzetti*
Attitudes of authorities	Seriously offer statements and affidavits of Morellis denying participation in crime. Declined request of defendants' counsel to interview *all witnesses* jointly to avoid vulgar contest of affidavits. Declined to investigate.	Anti-Red excitement capitalized; highly prejudicial cross-examination as to draft evasion and anarchistic opinions and associations; patriotic speeches and charge by Judge to jury; interference by Department of Justice agents who believed defendants innocent; suppression of testimony favorable to defense; intentionally misleading testimony of expert on vital points.

If Ranney had not offered the statements and affidavits of the Morellis, the defense would have argued that the statements and affidavits of Madeiros, Weeks, Thompson, and Ehrmann were not contradicted. It also would have drawn inferences of guilt. Did the defense want to get that advantage and deprive men who had no connection whatever with the South Braintree crime the right to deny unfounded charges?

The request of defendants' counsel to interview all witnesses jointly came a little late. By the time it was made, Thompson had already interviewed Madeiros and Weeks, and Ehrmann had already interviewed Mrs. Matthews,[10] Richards, and Geary.

Ranney did not decline to investigate. He investigated. Early in December 1925, shortly after he was notified of the confession, he sent Fleming to interview Mrs. Matthews (Madeiros's sister) and the New Bedford police; Kelley and Fleming interviewed Weeks; the Morelli brothers were interrogated in Providence and at Leavenworth; the circumstances under which the confession was made were investigated; Madeiros's deposition was taken, and Van Amburgh was called in to straighten out the "Star"—"Steyr" confusion.

Ranney's investigation led to the inevitable conclusion that the case had been solved by the Sacco-Vanzetti trial and that the confession and the Morelli hypothesis were worthless.

The points mentioned in the Sacco-Vanzetti column relating to the fairness of the trial are discussed at appropriate places in other chapters.

The only possible conclusion is that the Morelli hypothesis was as worthless as the Madeiros confession.

10 In his confession Madeiros had himself picked up on April 15, 1920, at 181 N. Main Street in Providence, where he said one of his sisters, Mary Bover, then lived. Mary Bover was Mrs. Matthews when she was interviewed by Ehrmann and the police about Madeiros's whereabouts on April 15. She denied that she and Madeiros were living in Providence then.

29   MADEIROS-MORELLI IN THE
COURTS AND AFTERWARD

BEFORE the Madeiros motion was heard by Judge Thayer during September 13-17, 1926, many affidavits had been filed. Also he had before him the deposition of Madeiros taken on June 28, 1926.

Under Massachusetts practice, motions for new trials are heard by the judge who presided at the trial, and Thompson made no effort to disqualify Thayer. Indeed it was not until some time later that Thayer was charged with prejudice and hostility by any lawyer for the defendants.

Ehrmann reports that Judge Thayer listened impassively to the argument, which lasted five days, and that he was uniformly courteous, even engaging in an occasional pleasantry.

On October 23, 1926, Judge Thayer denied the motion and filed a long decision. He would have been following the usual procedure if he had denied the motion by endorsing it simply "motion denied," without filing a written decision giving his reasons.

Judge Thayer, however, thought that he should give his reasons in full, and he spent many days in the preparation of a detailed and reasoned analysis. If he was thinking about the public he was in a dilemma, because whatever he did would be wrong. If he did not give his reasons, the mythmakers would tell the public that the case was so strong it could not be answered, and if he did give his reasons in a long opinion he dignified a trivial case and made his decision rather than the Madeiros confession the target of criticism.

And that is what happened. Even before the Supreme Judicial Court had passed on the motion, Frankfurter, unmindful of the ethics governing lawyers when cases are *sub judice,* published his *Atlantic* article carrying this extravagant and outrageous abuse of Judge Thayer to the public:

> I assert with deep regret, but without the slightest fear of disproof, that certainly in modern times Judge Thayer's opinion stands unmatched, happily, for discrepancies between what the record discloses and what the opinion conveys. His 25,000 word document cannot accurately be described otherwise than as a farrago of misquotations, misrepresentations, suppressions, and mutilations. The disinterested inquirer could not possibly derive from it a true knowledge of the new evidence that was submitted to him as a basis for a new trial. The opinion is literally honeycombed with demonstrable errors, and infused by a spirit alien to judicial utterance.[1]

One looks in vain in Frankfurter's book for a single specification of misquotation, misrepresentation, suppression, mutilation or demonstrable error, and the defendants in their brief and Ehrmann in his book found nothing of consequence. Frankfurter does mention Thayer's use of the phrase "lego-psychic neurosis" and of the word "approved" instead of "affirmed," but that is all. As Wigmore demonstrated, Frankfurter misstated his first point and took advantage of a trivial slip in his second.[2]

There is little to criticize in Thayer's statement of the evidence or in his logical processes. There is justice in the charge that the spirit of the opinion was that of an advocate and that the tone was in some parts of it somewhat alien to judicial utterance. This was unfortunate, and if the Madeiros confession had deserved serious consideration or the evidence and the arguments had presented a close or doubtful question, the tone of the decision might

---

1 Frankfurter, *op. cit.,* p. 104.
2 See Chapter 34 ("The Frankfurter Book").

well have been used by the Supreme Judicial Court as some evidence of an abuse of discretion.

The exceptions to rulings made in denying the motion for a new trial were the basis of the second resort by Sacco and Vanzetti to the Supreme Judicial Court. These exceptions were embodied in an amended bill of exceptions which contained all the data (affidavits, the Madeiros deposition, exhibits, and stipulations) which Thayer had before him and the full text of his decision. Under the Massachusetts rule the question presented to the Supreme Judicial Court was whether the trial judge could conscientiously, intelligently, and honestly have reached the result he had reached. Many assertions to the contrary notwithstanding, this does not mean that the Supreme Judicial Court was precluded from an examination of the entire record or barred by law from upsetting Thayer's decision. On the contrary, the Court had to examine the entire record to find out whether an impartial, intelligent, and honest judge would be justified in finding, as Judge Thayer did, that the confession and the additional facts fell "far short of furnishing adequate proof of their [the Morellis' and Madeiros's] guilt or of establishing reasonable doubt of the guilt of the defendants."

Judge Thayer's denial of the motion was upheld by the Supreme Judicial Court on April 5, 1927. In the opinion, it was expressly stated that the Court had studied the statements in Judge Thayer's decision and all the affidavits, exhibits, and records placed before it in the light of all the arguments of counsel for the defendants and the helpful and minute discussion contained in their brief. In a word, the Supreme Judicial Court did examine the whole record and consider every argument before it arrived at its conclusion that an impartial, intelligent, and honest judge would be justified in reaching the conclusions that Judge Thayer did.

We may be confident that, if the members of the Supreme Judicial Court had found any substance in the Madeiros confession or the Morelli hypothesis, they, as honorable and humane men, would have reached another result. But there was no substance there, and they would have been stultifying themselves and doing Thayer a great injustice if they had found that in rejecting these flimsy makeshifts he had acted dishonestly or ignorantly.

When the case came before the Governor by appeal for executive clemency, Madeiros was interviewed by the Governor himself and by the Advisory Committee. The Advisory Committee found the Madeiros confession worthless, and the Governor in his decision of August 3, 1927 made the following finding:

> I give no weight to the Madeiros confession. It is popularly supposed he confessed to committing this crime. In his testimony to me he could not recall the details or describe the neighborhood. He furthermore stated that the Government had doublecrossed him and he proposes to doublecross the Government. He feels that the District Attorney's office has treated him unfairly because his two confederates who were associated with him in the commission of the murder for which he was convicted were given life sentences, whereas he was sentenced to death. He confessed the crime for which he was convicted. I am not impressed with his knowledge of the South Braintree murders.

Ehrmann, in his extended criticism of the proceeding before the Governor, accused Governor Fuller of offering Madeiros a commutation of his sentence if he would recant his confession. In the final paragraph of his book he imagines that some future DaVinci will paint the scene suggested by Madeiros, Vanzetti, and Sacco in the death house at Charlestown:

> In the center, flanked by a uniformed escort, stands the perfectly groomed Governor of Massachusetts smiling blandly at someone in the cage before him. Contrasting strangely with this embodiment of success and power, slouches the figure of Madeiros, doomed, hopeless, and worm-eaten from birth. Yet the genius has depicted upon the face peering through the steel bars an expression of surprise changing to contempt as the friendless epileptic from the Azores realizes

that the great Governor is merely trying to sell him a bill of goods for recantation.

As authority for this serious charge of misconduct and abuse of office, Ehrmann cites part of Thompson's offer of proof in the Canter case. In this, Thompson told of a conversation he said he had had with Madeiros on August 4, 1927, the day after the Governor's decision was made public:

> Madeiros said that Governor Fuller had come down to see him and that the Governor began the interview by saying that he understood that Madeiros said that he had thought he had been given—I think the expression was—"a raw deal" or something indicating double-dealing, or improper dealing by the Government, and that Madeiros said that Officer Ferrari of the State Police had given him a promise of second degree murder if he confessed the [Wrentham] murder, and that was given to Mr. Brooks who was employed at the State House and who had a good deal to do with criminal cases.
>
> The Governor said that if he was satisfied that any such promise had been made he would do something for Madeiros. The Governor then said, before waiting for any reply from Madeiros, *according to Madeiros' statement to me*, "You do not know anything about the Sacco-Vanzetti case, do you?" And Madeiros said he did, and the Governor asked him if he was in the car with the other men who committed the murder in South Braintree, the South Braintree murder, and Madeiros said he was, and the Governor then said, "So you are a double murderer; I will do nothing for you." (My italics.)

By assuming that Thompson had stated what Madeiros told him accurately, completely, and in proper sequence and that Madeiros had for once told a complete and truthful story, Ehrmann could, I suppose, interpret Governor Fuller's question "You do not know anything about the Sacco-Vanzetti case, do you?", following the Governor's conditional promise of clemency, as a subtle invitation to trade a commutation of sentence for a recantation of the confession.

This interpretation is far fetched and violates the probabilities, for it implies that Governor Fuller was lacking in common sense as well as integrity. Trading a commutation for the recantation of a worthless confession would have been a very bad bargain indeed. The confession would have been given new life, not destroyed, and everything that Governor Fuller did about the case from then on would be suspect. Thompson, who knew what a liar Madeiros was, because, as he often admitted in the hearings before Judge Thayer, Madeiros had lied to him time after time, should be censured severely for accepting and repeating Madeiros's account of the interview.

I am trying not to speak in anger, but now and then it is hard to refrain when men I have known and admired and trusted for a lifetime are vilified—called murderers, hangmen, traffickers in pardons, double-dealers, suborners of perjury, suppressors of evidence, shufflers of exhibits, tricksters, conspirators—all because in the face of abuse and threat they faithfully did their duty as they saw it.

On April 30, 1958, after the foregoing was written, Governor Fuller died. The next morning the *Boston Globe* quoted Ehrmann as follows:

> Atty. Herbert B. Ehrmann, Brookline, associate counsel for Sacco and Vanzetti at the time of their execution: "I regret to see a public servant like Gov. Fuller pass away. He had a difficult decision to make in 1927 and I believe he made the wrong one. But he acted according to his conscience and did what he thought was right."

When this appeared I wrote to Mr. Ehrmann, in the hope that he would permit me to insert the following paragraph in this book:

Mr. Ehrmann, a few days after the death of Governor Fuller, informed me that he now thinks that he and Thompson were wrong in believing and stating that Governor Fuller had attempted to trade a commutation of Madeiros's sentence for a recantation of the confession. He now believes that Governor Fuller throughout the case acted honestly and he wishes to apologize to his memory for an unwarranted attack on his integrity.

But Mr. Ehrmann would have none of that. By return mail I had an indignant letter, certified, return receipt requested, in which I was chided for interpreting Mr. Ehrmann's "civil comment" as evidence that he would "deny the authenticity of what has become an historical account of the interview between Governor Fuller and Madeiros." That Governor Fuller had acted according to his conscience, which was the "kindest comment" he could make, was not, in Mr. Ehrmann's mind, inconsistent with an effort to get Madeiros to recant his confession in return for a commutation so that the Governor's decision to allow the men to die would be more palatable to the public.

Thus I learned again that the Myth has its scriptures and may not be abated one jot or tittle, even to do justice to the dead.

30

THE STATE OF MIND AND CONDUCT OF JUDGE THAYER

BEFORE the Advisory Committee, and in its applications to the federal courts and in the final application to the Supreme Judicial Court, the defense made the contention that the state of mind and conduct of Judge Thayer made a fair trial impossible. Judge Thayer, it asserted, "from the very beginning entertained a strong prejudice and hostility against both defendants by reason of their anarchistic views." (5352)

This is shown, say Thompson and Ehrmann in the brief filed with the Advisory Committee, by the affidavits or testimony before the committee, or both, of Professor Richardson, Marquis Ferrante, Messrs. Crocker, Sibley, Benchley, Hill, Beffel, the McAnarneys, and Mrs. Rantoul and Mrs. Bernkopf. Further evidence of Thayer's prejudice was found by the defense in "his constant sneers and hostile tone of voice and expression of face testified to by Mr. John McAnarney, the Marquis Ferrante, Mr. Sibley, and Mr. Thompson, in overruling the objections of Mr. Moore." (5353)

The affidavits and testimony thus gathered were widely used by the radicals for purposes of propaganda and agitation. This was standard practice, for when the Reds take over the exploitation of a criminal trial, the trial judge is always represented by them as a monster of cynicism and cruelty. And so it is that Judge Thayer has come down to this age as a combination of Pontius Pilate and Torquemada, and more the latter than the former.

I believe that this would have happened to anyone who presided at the trial, just as it happened to President Lowell, called a murderer by Heywood Broun, who at the same time called Harvard, Hangman's House. It happened also to Mr. Justice Brandeis, who refused to take any action in the case because members of his family had been sympathetic with the defense. He was called a Pontius Pilate and accused of washing his hands of the case because of the pressures of the Established Order and his own class consciousness. President Stratton was called a nonentity; Judge Grant, because of a humorous remark about an incident on an Italian trip, was accused of racial prejudice; Governor Fuller was called a murderer and a trafficker in pardons; District Attorney Katzmann and Assistant District Attorney Williams were charged with subornation of perjury and conspiracy; Vahey was called a Judas; Stewart was called corrupt and a beast; the women eyewitnesses were called harlots and psychopaths; Attorney-General Sargent and Acting Attorney-General Farnum were accused of conspiracy to murder and concealment of evidence; juror Ripley was charged after his death with misconduct in the jury room; Captain Proctor was charged after his death with perjury, and the whole "Established Order" in Massachusetts were called hangmen in frock coats.

Judge Thayer suffered most in this wholesale assassination of character. He has become, in commentary, literature, and history of the new tradition, a symbol of sadistic fury or, at the best, a hopelessly prejudiced judge. This was a shameful thing; the whole case against Judge Thayer was built long after the trial and based on a tissue of falsehood and triviality which would have been recognized as such by commentators and historians if they had taken the pains to examine the evidence, as the Governor and his Advisory Committee did and as we now shall do.

Let us begin with two witnesses whose testimony is demonstrably false.

WILLIAM G. THOMPSON

Thompson told the Advisory Committee that on the first day of the trial, May 31, 1921, he sat with John W. McAnarney in the courtroom three hours and a half and heard Moore examining witnesses. (4982) He said:

> Katzmann would say something and Moore would object to it, he was jumping up all the time. He would make objection after objection. Judge Thayer would sit there and look at Moore with the fiercest expression on his face, moving his head a little. Moore would say, "I object to that" and Judge Thayer would move his head around and [after] an intense pause, jurors would begin to look at Judge Thayer, after turning his face 90 degrees, he would lean back. I am not a mimic, but I wish you could see it. He would sit back in his chair and say, "Objection overruled." It wasn't what he said, it was his manner of saying it. It looked perfectly straight in the record; he was too clever to do otherwise. I sat there for a while and I told John McAnarney either that day or the next, "Your goose is cooked. You will never get these men acquitted. The Judge is going to convict these two men and see that nothing gets into the record; he is going to keep his record straight and you have no chance." I never went to the trial again; kept away from it. . . .
>
> During the whole of my thirty years experience . . . I have never seen anything conducted as this was. . . . That jury was influenced by the judge; they couldn't help it. (4982)

The principal trouble with this account is that it is a falsehood. As John W. McAnarney told the Advisory Committee, Thompson was in the court for three hours and a half the first *morning* of the trial, coming in before any of the jury was impaneled and remaining while Judge Thayer examined some of the jurors. (4992) No witnesses were being examined and Judge Thayer had no opportunity to communicate his prejudice to a jury which had not yet been impaneled. (5001) Thompson tried to wiggle out of this by saying that it might have been the second day of the trial and that he was sure he had heard Moore examining someone, perhaps it was the deputy sheriffs. (5003) But there was trouble with that, because the deputy sheriffs were not examined until late in the *evening* of the *fourth* day, and then were examined *in the absence of the jury* by Thomas McAnarney, with no objections raised by anyone. (38 *et seq.*)

On August 8, 1927, Thompson was a witness at the hearing in the Supreme Judicial Court on the petition for a writ of error heard by a single justice, Mr. Justice Sanderson, and under oath gave this third and final revision:

> [On June 3, 1920] I went into court. The trial proceeded. I stayed there about three and one-half hours. I observed carefully Judge Thayer's conduct. I at one time thought in making this statement that testimony was going in from witnesses. I now perceive that was an error. There were about seven jurors selected, and what was going on was the selection of some alternate jurors out of a new venire of five hundred men. Somebody was up for examination. Who it was I don't know. *The District Attorney was questioning some possible juror.* There were some men in the jury box and some jurors to be selected. Mr. Moore was objecting from time to time. I noticed nothing offensive in Mr. Moore's manner at that time, but I noticed particularly Judge Thayer's expression of face and his attitude toward Mr. Moore. Whenever Mr. Moore objected to what was going on, Judge Thayer—and this is very clearly and distinctly in my mind—it was the first picture I got—Judge Thayer would look steadily at Mr. Moore for a moment. It is difficult for me to put this in a picture that would be intelligible without using some adjectives. He looked at him with a very intense stare, suggesting he was an object of curiosity. He then turned in his seat slightly, towards the jury-box, and, with what I feel entirely justified in describing as a sneer, certainly a very contemptuous expression, he said: "Objection overruled." That occurred a good many times while I was there. (5380; my italics.)

But this questioning of a venireman by Katzmann did not happen because it could not have happened in a Massachusetts trial, where the trial judge in the examination of jurors asks *all* the questions, including those suggested by counsel. I have never heard of an exception, and the Sacco-Vanzetti case was certainly not one. Thompson was indeed desperate when he told this obvious fabrication under oath to Judge Sanderson in a courtroom filled with Massachusetts lawyers.

JOHN NICHOLAS BEFFEL

John Nicholas Beffel's affidavit of April 28, 1927, was presented to the Governor and the Committee, but Beffel did not appear in person.

Beffel, author of "Eels and the Electric Chair," [1] was in the pay of the Defense Committee, handling publicity, and had been brought to Boston by Moore early in 1921. He also covered the case for the Federated Press, the Communist press service.

In his affidavit Beffel relates an incredible story for which I have found no corroboration. On or about the fourth morning of the trial, he says, while the jury was being impaneled, Marquis Agostino Ferrante, Italian Consul at Boston, was present in court as a spectator. At the close of the session Ferrante dictated to Beffel a brief statement which he wanted to give out to the press, as follows:

> The Italian authorities are deeply interested in the case of Sacco and Vanzetti, and this trial will be closely followed by them. They have complete confidence that the trial will be conducted solely as a criminal proceeding, without reference to the political or social beliefs of anyone involved.

Beffel then, as he said, typed this statement with several carbons which he handed to other newspapermen at the luncheon table. Judge Thayer was sitting in another corner of the room, at his own table. As the judge got up to leave the room, Jack English of the *Boston American* showed him the Ferrante statement

[1] *New Republic,* December 29, 1920.

and asked him what he thought about it. Judge Thayer made a gesture of anger.

"Why," he said, "that fellow came clear out to my home in Worcester and assured me that the Italian government had no interest in this case."

This, says Beffel, was uttered in the presence of several newspapermen, including Jack English, Frank P. Sibley of the *Boston Globe,* Jack Harding of the Associated Press, and, "I think," Charles Folsom of the *Boston Herald.*

Other questions were then asked by the reporters. Mention of Moore's name aroused signs of hostility from Judge Thayer. And here Beffel fixed the date by an irrelevant parenthesis:

> (This was on the day when the special venire of 175 extra talesmen had been gathered in, and all the morning the defense had strenuously opposed the use of any of the talesmen as jurors, on the ground that they had been summoned not from the highways and byways as required by law, *but from special places such as a Masonic meeting.*) (My italics.)

Referring to attorney Moore's objection to the special venire, Beffel quoted Judge Thayer: "And what do you suppose that fellow wanted me to ask those veniremen? 'Are you a member of a labor union? Are you opposed to union labor? *Are you a member of a secret society?*" (My italics to indicate a question invented by Beffel.)

Then, said Beffel, the judge made another gesture of anger and went on, addressing the newspapermen in general: "Did you ever see a case in which so many leaflets and circulars have been spread broadcast, saying that people couldn't get a fair trial in the State of Massachusetts?"

Beffel then tried to tell Thayer that he had issued the statement at Ferrante's request, but, Beffel said, Thayer brushed him aside and, shaking his fist, said to the other newspapermen: "You wait till I give my charge to the jury, I'll show 'em!"

After Thayer left the room, the newspapermen agreed not to

say anything about the incident and, said Beffel on April 28, 1927, "It has never yet been made public." (4929-4930)

This affidavit was obviously for propaganda purposes and for export to Italy. Beffel dragged in the Masonic meeting, Moore's rejected question to the veniremen about labor unions (inventing the one about secret societies), and the leaflets and circulars.

The Italian Consul's statement and Thayer's threat to "show them" in his charge got no corroboration from Ferrante or from Sibley or the other newspapermen and are on their face improbable and incredible. It is inconceivable that the Italian Consul would release a statement through a Communist press agency when there was a representative of the Associated Press in the room. Indeed, it is inconceivable that an Italian Consul would release such a statement to anyone.

However that may be, there is nothing in this affidavit which has any relevance to the issue of Thayer's fairness except the words: "You wait till I give my charge to the jury, I'll show 'em!" These words, if said, were extremely improper and showed bias and prejudice. They should have been reported by Beffel to the defense attorneys at once, and by them to Chief Justice Aiken. The fact that Sibley and the other reporters did not mention them at any time is convincing proof that they were never said.

ROBERT BENCHLEY

Robert Benchley, a classmate of Ehrmann and Ranney in the Harvard Class of 1912, was dramatic editor of *Life* in 1921 and 1927. He had been brought up in Worcester and knew Judge Thayer. Sometime in July 1921 (the exact date was never definitely fixed; Benchley thought it was at the end of the first week) he and Mrs. Benchley came to Worcester and were the weekend guests of Mr. and Mrs. Loring Coes.

During this visit, Benchley, Mrs. Benchley, and Mrs. Coes sat in a car for a short time outside the Worcester Country Club, waiting for Coes. Coes came out and they drove away; the two men sat in the front seat, Coes driving, and the two women in the back.

Neither of the women remembered the incident. In an affidavit dated March 25, 1927, Benchley swore as follows:

> When Mr. Coes came out and got into the automobile he told us what Judge Thayer, who was in the club, had just said, in his presence and in the presence of several others, about Sacco and Vanzetti. Mr. Coes told us that Judge Thayer, whom he referred to as "Web," had just been telling what he, Judge Thayer, intended to do to Sacco and Vanzetti, whom Judge Thayer referred to as "those bastards down there." Mr. Coes said that Judge Thayer had referred to Sacco and Vanzetti as bolsheviki who were "trying to intimidate him," and had said, "he would get them good and proper." Mr. Coes said that Judge Thayer had told him and the other men that a "bunch of parlor radicals were trying to get these guys off and trying to bring pressure to bear on the Bench," and that he, Judge Thayer, "would also like to hang a few dozen of the radicals." Mr. Coes said that Judge Thayer added that "no bolsheviki could intimidate Web Thayer" and that he added in substance that Worcester should be proud of having such a defender as Judge Thayer. (4918)

Benchley then went on:

> I am informed and believe and therefore allege that Mr. Coes has within a few days been requested by Mr. Thompson . . . to make an affidavit . . . and has refused to do so on the ground that it is difficult for him to remember what happened so long ago, and that he is disinclined to make the effort because Judge Thayer is an old friend of himself and his family. I am also informed and believe and therefore allege that in October, 1926, Mr. Coes was thrown from his horse and sustained an injury from which he [has] not yet recovered. (4919)

Benchley had told this story to a great many people but not, apparently, to the right ones until, in the early fall of 1926, he was talking with Mr. Wolker, the dramatic editor of the *New York World*. Wolker said, "Why don't you write a story?" and suggested that Benchley get in touch with the editor of the *World*, which he did. A little later he was visited by Gardner Jackson, of the Defense Committee, who asked him to try to get an affidavit from Coes. Benchley then, during the month of November, went up to Worcester but, finding that Coes had fallen off a horse and was in the hospital, could not get the affidavit. Thompson himself made a try on March 21, 1927, but got no affidavit. On March 25, Thompson got Benchley's hearsay affidavit from which the foregoing quotations came.

On May 5, Benchley's affidavit was printed in the *Boston Evening Transcript,* and on the same day a statement made by Mr. Coes, reading as follows, was also printed:

> I flatly deny the truth of Mr. Benchley's statement that I told him that Judge Thayer had referred to those two men as "bastards," [2] that Judge Thayer said he would like to hang a few more of such radicals, or any of the other statements which Mr. Benchley alleges I told him the Judge had made.
>
> I do not recall any such incident as Mr. Benchley describes in his affidavit. My wife, who is mentioned by Mr. Benchley as being one of the party to whom I repeated the Judge's language, denies any recollection of the entire episode.
>
> I have known Judge Thayer since 1908. I have never heard him use language that he could not repeat in mixed company and I have played golf with him.
>
> Had Judge Thayer, in my hearing, made the statement which Mr. Benchley charges me with repeating to him, I should have remembered it.
>
> I am particularly annoyed by Mr. Benchley's closing statement that I was thrown from my horse and sustained an injury from which I have not completely recovered, insinuating that my memory has been affected. My memory is not affected.

[2] The *Transcript* was rather prim in 1927 and used a blank for the word "bastards."

Mr. Benchley makes the further statement that I was requested by Mr. Thompson, counsel for the two men, to make an affidavit as to the incident and that I declined to do so because of difficulty in remembering and also because of my friendship with Judge Thayer. I was not requested to make an affidavit. Mr. Thompson telephoned me and asked if I recalled telling Mr. Benchley something Judge Thayer had said. I informed him that I did not remember. He did not say what it was that I was supposed to have heard Judge Thayer say. Had he told me that I was supposed to have heard the judge call these two men "bastards" or that he "would like to hang a few dozen of these radicals" . . . I should have been glad to give him an affidavit that such was not the truth, had he cared for such an affidavit. . . .

And I could have done this, for any such statements of Judge Thayer would have remained in my memory. However, Mr. Thompson did not ask me if I remembered any specific statements.

I was also telephoned by a Boston newspaperman who said he had a copy of an affidavit by Mr. Benchley and if I had anything to say about it. When I invited him to read it, he declined. Naturally I had nothing to say.

The Coes statement left very little of the Benchley affidavit. Thompson tried to save something of it by impeaching the credibility of Coes, on the theory, it is to be supposed, that Coes was to be believed when he told shocking things about Judge Thayer but to be disbelieved if he denied saying them. Thompson's effort is found in his letter to Governor Fuller, printed in the *Boston Evening Transcript* of May 7, 1927. In that letter Thompson told the Governor that he had telephoned to Mr. Coes in March 1927 about the Benchley matter; that Coes had told him that he (Coes) had a vague recollection of having talked with Benchley occasionally about the case, that he might have told him some things that Thayer had told him about the case, that whatever Thayer had told him was not in any public place but while driving from the Worcester Country Club to Thayer's home, that he was an old friend of Thayer's and did not want to do anything to hurt him and "in any event he [Coes] couldn't remember anything that had occurred so long ago."

All the foregoing, Thompson went on, had been incorporated in a letter Thompson had written to Benchley immediately after the telephone conversation. Thompson then goes on in his letter to Governor Fuller:

> That this was said to me by Mr. Coes there is no doubt whatever. I remember a further remark of his which I did not put in my letter to Mr. Benchley [written immediately after the telephone call], namely, that Judge Thayer had known him since he (Coes) was a boy in short trousers, and that he would not do anything to injure Judge Thayer. I remember also one further remark that he made, which was that he would not want to remember, even if he could, any remarks of Judge Thayer that might injure Judge Thayer if repeated.

But Thompson did not say that he had asked Coes for an affidavit or had told Coes the nature of the words Thayer was supposed to have said in his presence.

Joseph J. Glancy, a newspaperman, also tried to rescue the Benchley affidavit. On July 13, 1927, Glancy appeared before the Advisory Committee and told of a telephone call he had had with Coes after he knew of the Benchley affidavit. According to Glancy's testimony, Coes admitted that he knew Benchley and recalled the time the conversation happened, but Coes couldn't recall the conversation because it was so long ago. Then, according to Glancy, Coes said:

> "I told Mr. Thompson that. He got in touch with me and I told him the same thing, that I couldn't recall the conversation I had with Mr. Benchley."

> And Glancy said to Coes, "You did have a conversation with him and you are the Mr. Coes referred to."

Coes said to Glancy: "I can't recall what was said at the time." (5023)

In cross-examination, Ranney deflated Glancy with one question:

Q. That isn't the way it came out in the newspaper, is it, Mr. Glancy? I don't happen to have a copy of the paper but my memory is that it was a denial.
A. The interview I had with him was not printed. (5023)

In my effort to find the truth about Thayer's conduct and state of mind, I have given consideration to Benchley's affidavit, although in a court his testimony could not have been used to prove that Thayer did say something in the locker room or to prove what words he used, because it would have been excluded under the rule against hearsay. Evidence of what Thayer said could have come only from Thayer himself or from Coes or from one of the men in the locker room. The common sense of the rule against hearsay has no better illustration than in this case. To accept this hearsay affidavit as evidence of the words spoken by Thayer, we would have to believe that Benchley remembered after five years what Coes had told him and that Coes had told him correctly and with all necessary context what Thayer had said. This is a large order, as is known to everyone who has tried to reconstruct a conversation even a few moments after it has occurred. And there are the intonations to consider. In the companionship of a locker room an indiscreet judge might well say with a smile, or in a Pickwickian sense, words which, reduced to cold print, would be shocking. And finally it would be necessary to know about whom Thayer was speaking: was it the defendants, whom he had treated with scrupulous fairness and courtesy throughout the trial, or were the "bastards" he allegedly had in mind the radicals, bolsheviki, and parlor radicals who were, by abuse and threat, attempting to intimidate and terrify judge, jury, counsel, and witnesses to an extent unprecedented in our history?

Benchley's long delay in telling the defense about his conversation with Coes had never been explained. If the words attributed to Thayer were said about the defendants, they should have been reported immediately to the defense or to the Chief Justice of the Superior Court, for these words were inexcusable in a judge and should have been recognized as such by Coes and Benchley and the men in the clubhouse who are supposed to have heard them. If Benchley was right about the date, the trial was still in progress; it could have been halted or its validity questioned if the unfitness of the trial judge to proceed further had been put in issue forthwith by a motion for a mistrial or by application to the Chief Justice of the Superior Court for appropriate action. The evidence of Coes and the men in the locker room would have been available, Judge Thayer could have been questioned by the Chief Justice, and Benchley could have been heard to impeach Coes if the latter denied the conversation.

The answer must be that, if anything was said by Thayer in the locker room and repeated to Benchley, it did not shock Benchley or make him question the fitness of Thayer to continue in the trial. Thompson's account of his conversation with Coes seems to be of a piece with his account of his three hours in the courtroom —a desperate attempt to make a case against Thayer out of nothing.

THE McANARNEYS

John W. and Thomas F. McAnarney appeared before the Advisory Committee and testified. Jeremiah T. McAnarney did not appear before the committee. None of them made an affidavit. Contrary to the assertion in Thompson's brief filed with the Advisory Committee, John W. McAnarney, who had not participated in the trial but heard much of it, expressed no opinion about Thayer's fairness and gave no testimony about Thayer's sneers. All that Thomas F. McAnarney said was this:

> I think Judge Thayer was—that he couldn't conduct a trial fairly with Attorney Moore on the other side. I have the

highest respect for his character and ability, but this man
Moore got under his skin, as I said before, to such an extent
and so irritated him, so that people around could see his reaction on the jury . . .

PRESIDENT LOWELL: Did the judge treat you fair?

THE WITNESS: Yes, that was one of the things that made it
embarrassing. He would say to Moore, "Why don't you do
the same as McAnarney does?" and Moore was chief counsel.

JUDGE GRANT: Was he rather a disagreeable person?

THE WITNESS: I will tell you now—At the trial, the jury
there, there would be friend Moore, offering his best interests at the trial, on hand with his coat and vest off and his
shoes off in front of the courthouse and I would say to
Moore, "For God's sake, keep that coat on in the courtroom,
can't you?" . . .

PRESIDENT LOWELL: The judge treated you fairly well, you
and your brother.

THE WITNESS: Oh, yes.

McAnarney also got the "impression" that Thayer was convinced of Vanzetti's guilt from the outset because Thayer had sat
at Plymouth and imposed a sentence of twelve to fifteen years
then. (5061-5062) This may well have been, but unless Thayer's
conviction got to the jury in some way (they say it did not) no
harm was done.

MRS. RANTOUL

Mrs. Lois Burnett Rantoul was one of a group of women of position whose help had been enlisted by the Defense Committee.
She attended the trial as a representative of the Greater Boston
Federation of Churches, which had an undisclosed interest in the
case, and wrote a report, a copy of which was annexed to her affidavit of June 10, 1926. (4932 *et seq.*) She appeared before the
Advisory Committee on July 13, 1927.

Mrs. Rantoul thought that Thayer, who had already sentenced
Vanzetti to fifteen years in prison, could not, for that reason, sit

with an unprejudiced mind; that in his charge he had not referred to the witnesses in enough detail; that he had misstated
officer Connolly's testimony; and that his charge showed an extreme desire for the jury "to be loyal and do their duty and stand
up and all this talk." This last was particularly bad because "you
were dealing with the type of intelligence that would eat that
stuff up." (5026)

It is noteworthy that Mrs. Rantoul, who sat throughout the trial,
said nothing about Judge Thayer's sneers, bad manners, or hostility to Moore.

The point she made about officer Connolly's testimony was
this: Thayer in his charge, referring to that testimony, said, "The
Commonwealth claims that Vanzetti put his hand into his hip
pocket." No, says Mrs. Rantoul, the record shows that Connolly
testified that Vanzetti made a motion with his hand toward his
hip pocket. "Quite different from being in his hip pocket." (4944)
But it is Mrs. Rantoul who is mistaken. Connolly did testify that
Vanzetti put his hand in his hip pocket; it was Sacco who merely
reached. (751)

Mrs. Rantoul tells of two interviews she had with Judge
Thayer. The first was at Thayer's request in the judge's room at
the conclusion of the Commonwealth's case:

> I told him [she says in her report] that I had not yet heard
> sufficient evidence to convince me that the defendants were
> guilty. He was much disturbed at this, showing it in both
> voice and gesture [in her affidavit, "words, gestures, tone of
> voice, and manner"], and said that after hearing both argu-
> ments and the charge I would come to him feeling differ-
> ently. (4943)

In the second interview, at which again no third person was
present, George T. Kelley's testimony was discussed. Mrs. Rantoul
praised Kelley's testimony because he had given Sacco a good
character; this, coming from an employer, had great weight. But
Judge Thayer, she said, expressed scorn for this view and told her
that Kelley did not mean what he said because he, Judge Thayer,

had heard that on the outside Kelley had said that Sacco was an anarchist and that he couldn't do anything with him.

Mrs. Rantoul seems to have misunderstood the purpose of Kelley's testimony. He was not a character witness at all but testified about Sacco's alibi and Sacco's cap. In connection with the alibi, he did say that Sacco was a steady worker and had to be because he was the only worker in the plant who was skilled in his specialty. This was evidence to prove steady attendance at work and not to prove good character. Mrs. Rantoul seems to have recognized this, for she or the draftsman of her affidavit changed "character" in her report to "steady character" in her affidavit and to "fine worker" in her testimony before the Advisory Committee.

The variances in Mrs. Rantoul's accounts of the second interview suggest that we should not accept any of her accounts as exact quotations of what was said by Thayer. We may be sure that she did not intend to make misstatements, but her report shows that in several instances she did not understand what was going on, and she may well have been at cross-purposes with Judge Thayer in her conversations with him.

But even if we take Mrs. Rantoul's account literally, the first interview proves only that Judge Thayer had made up his mind about the guilt of the defendants at the close of the Commonwealth's case and was disturbed that Mrs. Rantoul did not agree with him. It was not wrong for Judge Thayer to believe that the defendants were guilty if he kept his belief away from the jury, which the jurors say he did. It was a breach of decorum for him to communicate his belief to Mrs. Rantoul even in a private conversation, but no harm was done to the defendants and his remarks did not prove prejudice, hatred, or abhorrence. They proved merely his appraisal of the Commonwealth case.

As to the second interview, it seems reasonable to believe that Judge Thayer was not discussing Sacco's character but was discussing Kelley's identification of Sacco's cap. As we have seen, the identification seems to have been more positive outside the courtroom than it was on the stand. In a discussion of that evidence with Mrs. Rantoul, Thayer might reasonably refer to what

Kelley said off the stand about the cap or about Kelley's fear of violence.

Kelley knew that Sacco had radical opinions; Kelley had discussed them with him when he told him that he was being investigated by Federal agents, but it is unlikely that Thayer was interested in telling Mrs. Rantoul that Kelley had called Sacco an anarchist off the stand; he might well have been indiscreet enough to tell her about the difference between Kelley off the stand and Kelley on the stand when the identification of the cap was in issue. But if Mrs. Rantoul had relied on Thayer's indiscretion in telling her about Kelley's cap testimony on and off the stand, she would have had to include in her report a mention of Sacco's cap, which she chose to ignore entirely.

AGOSTINO FERRANTE

Marquis Agostino Ferrante was the Italian Consul in Boston from November 15, 1920, until after the execution. He attended the Dedham trial nearly every day, sometimes accompanied by his wife, who understood English better than he did. Before the Advisory Committee he had this to say about Thayer.

> I met Judge Thayer. Now, probably Mr. Thompson will disagree with me on this point: I always considered Judge Thayer as a gentleman. . . .
>
> But he was sure that those two men were guilty, he was absolutely confirmed in his soul that those two men are guilty, and this feeling of his was evident all through the trial. You can read the trial, you can read the record that you have, and you will find sometimes an answer, sometimes a question that is all right, but you can see sometimes that you have the general impression, and the jury had it. Suppose I ask you, "This is a pencil?" and you say "No." I ask you, "This is a pencil?" and you say "No." That would be very different to me.[3]

[3] I suppose that Ferrante varied the pencil question by accent or tone of voice and that when he quoted Thayer's "question excluded" he mimicked him.

I remember one day a question asked by Moore to the witness. I don't remember which one . . . and Judge Thayer turned to the side, looked at the jury. "Question excluded. . . ." That gave me the feeling that Judge Thayer don't like Mr. Moore. That was my feeling, but because I never like this man. One of the last days of the trial, I think when Katzmann made his last speech before the jury on the last day, you had the feeling that the lives of two men were at stake, and Judge Thayer had an enormous bunch of flowers on his desk. I thought that was bad taste, I think. (5245-5246)

Ferrante was obviously an honest witness, and in spite of his language difficulties his impression that Thayer was prejudiced is entitled to consideration, but the specific instances he cites, that is, the tone of voice in overruling Moore and the flowers on the desk, show at most a prejudice against Moore and questionable taste.

GEORGE U. CROCKER

George U. Crocker, a Boston lawyer and one-time Treasurer of the City of Boston, lived during the summer of 1921 at the University Club in the Back Bay. Judge Thayer was also there, but Crocker had never been introduced to him. One evening Thayer forced himself on Crocker and volunteered the information that all the talk to the effect that the men were anarchists and that the Government was prosecuting them for that reason was utter nonsense, and he went on to tell why he thought so.

This seemed to Crocker to be manifest impropriety.

One morning at breakfast Thayer again forced himself on Crocker and immediately began to talk about the case, pulling out of his pocket a portion of the charge he was going to deliver on that day. Thayer would say, "Counsel for the defense said so and so yesterday, and this is my reply," and then he would read part of the charge and say, "I think that will hold him, don't you?" [4]

The points about which Thayer talked to Crocker and which Crocker remembered in 1927 were the failure of the defendants to establish an alibi, the fact that they were draft dodgers and anarchists and entitled to no consideration, and some evidence about their identification. Crocker's memory was not vivid as to details, because he was annoyed at what seemed to him the impropriety of Thayer's conduct. (4946-4947)

Crocker did not come forward with this information until long after. He then told Thompson in confidence and prepared a statement, to which he did not swear, for the attention of the Governor or Attorney General only. This statement was sent to the Governor and to the Advisory Committee, before which Crocker appeared on July 11, 1927. (4968)

On August 6, 1927, when the motion for revocation of sentence and for a new trial was filed, an unsigned document entitled "Affidavit of George U. Crocker" [5] was also filed. In this document Thayer is not quoted as saying that as radicals and draft dodgers the defendants were entitled to no consideration. In

[4] I am told by several judges of the Superior Court that Thayer liked to submit his writings to them and to discuss them. He took pride in his work, and using the phrase "That will hold them, don't you think?" meant no more to him than "It is well written and sound, isn't it?"

[5] Ehrmann in an affidavit of August 6, 1927, explains Crocker's failure to sign the affidavit as follows:

"On November 18, 1926, George U. Crocker, Esquire, sent an unsigned statement to Mr. Thompson, and on July 11, 1927, the said Crocker testified before Messrs. Lowell, Stratton, and Grant, who were acting as a Commission of Inquiry appointed by the Governor of this Commonwealth. The draft of an affidavit annexed herewith contains the substance of Mr. Crocker's statement of November 18, 1926, and of July 11, 1927. I know of my own knowledge that William G. Thompson, Esquire, on July 26th requested Mr. Crocker to sign the affidavit, draft of which is hereto annexed, and that Mr. Crocker declined to do so for personal reasons having no reference to the accuracy of the statement." (5410-5411)

This is one of several instances where Thompson or Ehrmann made an affidavit where the witness refused to. In some cases the "testimony" was incorporated in the lawyer's affidavit; in others, a draft affidavit prepared for the witness but not signed was annexed.

place of this quotation of specific language an "impression" gained from language vaguely remembered is substituted:

> I cannot remember all that Judge Thayer said, and very little definite language that he used, except the matter of the arguments of the defendants' lawyers, and his thinking that his answer would hold them. . . . In these conversations with me Judge Thayer was excited, especially on the last morning when he read parts of his charge. He conveyed to me by his words and manner the distinct impression that he was bound to convict these men because they were "Reds." I remember that Judge Thayer in substance said to me that we must stand together and protect ourselves against anarchists and "Reds." He also said that these defendants were draft dodgers. (5472)

There undoubtedly was evidence of a lack of decorum here, but on the merits it does seem that Crocker's vague and varying impressions of conversations six years old are trivial ground for the inference that Thayer was strongly prejudiced against the defendants and that he intended to see that they were convicted because they were Reds and draft dodgers. On this point, the "affidavit" adds another item of some significance. Crocker here states for the first time that in 1921 he had heard Judge Thayer talk about the case to Judge Crosby of the Supreme Judicial Court "in much the same way as he had talked to me," but that Crocker, in his memorandum of November 18, 1926, sent to Thompson and by Thayer to the Governor, had omitted all reference to Judge Crosby—

> as I did not wish to go any further than was absolutely necessary in involving other judges in this matter; but the facts in relation to Judge Thayer's conversation with Judge Crosby were drawn from me by questions, and for that reason I feel at liberty to incorporate them in this affidavit. (5412-5413)

It must be clear that if Thayer had uttered words to Judge Crosby that showed prejudice and the intention of convicting the defendants because they were "Reds," and because as radicals and draft dodgers they were not entitled to consideration, Judge Crosby would have been moved to action of some kind, but apparently neither he nor Crocker considered that Thayer's state of mind was such that it should be reported immediately to someone.

The long silence of Crocker, his desire for secrecy, his refusal to swear to the affidavit, and the silence of Judge Crosby seem to me to be proof that whatever Thayer said in 1921 to Crocker or Crosby did not shock them enough to make them fear a miscarriage of justice because of prejudice on the part of Thayer.

FRANK P. SIBLEY

Frank P. Sibley, a reporter for the *Boston Globe,* was in attendance at Dedham every day during the trial. His affidavit about Judge Thayer's conduct was dated April 5, 1927.

In his affidavit Sibley justly criticized Judge Thayer for discussing the case with reporters at lunch time. The specific instances of lunch-time indiscretion show that Judge Thayer was critical of Moore and the defense attorneys generally and showed too much interest in how the case was reported.

During the early stages of the trial, the affidavit said, when the talesmen were being examined Judge Thayer had proceeded to discuss Moore with Sibley and exclaimed, "I'll show them that no long-haired anarchist from California can run this court!"

During the progress of the trial he frequently referred to the counsel for the defense as "those damn fools." On several occasions he said, "Just wait until you hear my charge."

On one occasion Judge Thayer approached the table at which the reporters were at lunch and made the following statement: "I think I am entitled to have a statement printed in the Boston papers that this trial is being conducted in a fair and impartial manner."

Sibley's criticism of Judge Thayer in the courtroom concerned two incidents. On one occasion, a conference between the judge and an attorney was about to begin at the bench. The jury was not present. A stenographer was moving around with his book to take notes, and Judge Thayer turned sharply to him and said in a low voice, "You get the hell out of here."

The other incident took place during the cross-examination of Sacco when Judge Thayer, to an objection by Mr. McAnarney, said, "Are you going to claim that your client in collecting this literature, was acting in the interest of the United States?" [6] (4924-4925)

On July 11, 1927, Sibley was brought before the Advisory Committee and questioned by Thompson and Ranney. Sibley, in response to Thompson's questions, repeated part of what he had said in the affidavit and added his "impression" that Judge Thayer had acted in an undignified way. He also told about the armed guards and the protection of the courtroom.

> I have seen the judge sit in his gown and spit on the floor. I don't know whether there was a spittoon there or not. I have heard him swear. His conduct was very improper. What affected me more than anything else was his manner. It is nothing you can read in the record. In my thirty-five years I never saw anything like it. When I went there, officers who knew me felt me over to see if I had a gun. His whole manner, attitude seemed to be that the jurors were there to convict these men. (4956)

On cross-examination Sibley admitted that the only words spoken by Judge Thayer in the presence of the jury that were prejudicial or unfair were the words about the interest of the

[6] The relevancy of this question and the reason for its repetition was this: Katzmann was cross-examining Sacco about his love of this country, which he had testified to in direct examination. McAnarney objected to one of Katzmann's questions, and Judge Thayer, before passing on the objection, asked McAnarney whether he claimed that Sacco in gathering the literature was acting in the interest of the United States. McAnarney evaded a direct answer, and Judge Thayer had to ask this question several times. Thompson chose to interpret this appropriate question as a sarcastic one designed to prejudice the jury. Sibley followed Thompson in this, but probably because he misunderstood the purpose of the question. Judge Riddell, *op. cit.*, *ubi supra*, reviews this incident at some length and concludes that Judge Thayer's question was a proper one and that he did not repeat it unnecessarily.

United States. (4959) He also admitted that the swearing and the spitting were not in the presence of the jury (4961) and that it was a wise thing to protect the courtroom. (4962)

To me, the most significant thing about Sibley's testimony is that he did not support Thompson's account of the examination of the talesmen or Beffel's account of the press release by the Italian Consul. If they had been truthful accounts, Sibley would surely have corroborated them, for he was admittedly partial to the defense and did his best to discredit Judge Thayer.

ELIZABETH R. BERNKOPF

We now turn from testimony about incidents at the time of the trial to events remembered in 1927 as having occurred in 1923 and 1924.

Mrs. Elizabeth R. Bernkopf, a Smith College graduate, was a reporter for the International News Service in 1923 and the early part of 1924 and covered the hearings in the motions for a new trial. She had not attended the trial. She invariably took the train to Dedham in the morning from the Back Bay station and often rode with Thayer. "Once, on his own initiative, he presented me with an autographed picture of himself."

Mrs. Bernkopf could not remember the exact language Thayer used in his frequent discussion of the case, but the burden of it was that he was not going to be intimidated by anyone; that the defense would find that they could not hoodwink him; that he represented the integrity of the courts; that he distrusted and had no sympathy for the kind of people who were supporting the defense financially and otherwise; and that he disliked and was suspicious of attorney Moore, whom he generally called that "long-haired anarchist from California." He also stated that, if they appealed from his decision to the Supreme Judicial Court, they would see how far they would get." (4926-4927)

Mrs. Bernkopf's affidavit is dated March 26, 1927, and she appeared before the Advisory Committee on July 11, 1927. (4963)

Of course, Thayer should not have talked so freely with reporters while there were motions still pending before him, but by this time he had good reason to dislike Moore, who had made several efforts to hoodwink the court and to bribe, intimidate and blackmail witnesses.[7] But this was a prejudice against Moore, not against Sacco and Vanzetti, and was a prejudice shared by Sacco himself and by Mrs. Sacco.

ARTHUR D. HILL

Arthur D. Hill, a prominent Boston lawyer, was brought into the Sacco-Vanzetti case by Thompson on March 14, 1924, and remained connected with the case (he had to do with the Ripley motion)[8] until October 3, 1924, reentering it in 1927. He was abroad when the case was tried. He knew Judge Thayer slightly and had a high opinion of Katzmann. During the period between March 15 and October 3, 1924, Hill saw Thayer very often at hearings and on the train to Dedham. Hill did not quote Thayer —he could not remember the exact words. Nor could he recall the subject matter of the conversations further than that there were a good many generalities in it

> about the danger to our institutions from foreigners and radicals, and the importance of respect for the law and of a firm hand in the administration of justice. His manner indicated to me a strong feeling of prejudice both against the men themselves, their opinions and their counsel, Mr. Moore.

Judge Thayer, he said, was under great nervous tension in 1924; he was obsessed with the case, he could talk of nothing else, and he could not refrain from talking about it. (5206)

> . . . I argued the presence of the bullets in the jury room [the Ripley motion]. . . . The impression I got at that time was that Judge Thayer was absolutely impervious to any argument whatever and that it was a waste of time to

7 See Chapter 23 ("Lola R. Andrews"), Chapter 21 ("Louis Pelser"), Chapter 22 ("Carlos E. Goodridge"), and Chapter 26 ("The Shifting of the Gun Barrels").
8 See Chapter 19 ("Alleged Misconduct of the Jury: the Ripley Motion").

make them. . . . One thing that shocked me a good deal was his evident pleasure in being photographed by the newspapers in connection with the case. . . . Mind you, he was always perfectly kindly and gracious to me out of court, and he did nothing in court except to show, as a judge can show, that he is strongly against you from the beginning in everything that you say. But I felt rather sorry for the man. I felt that he had been subjected to more of a strain by threat of political excitement, of emotion, and of consciousness of his own position and importance than he had been able to bear.

This analysis by Hill of the mental condition of Judge Thayer in 1924 will, in several particulars, meet with an affirmative response from many who knew him. Thayer did become obsessed with the case, he did talk about it on every occasion, and he did live under nervous tension. He told me in the 1930's that every day at noon he telephoned his home in Worcester to learn whether it had been bombed. Whether this was before or after it was actually bombed, I do not recall. (To the end of his life he lived in fear of a second bombing.) That he showed his prejudice against the adherents of Sacco and Vanzetti who had threatened his life and the lives of his family and later did blow up his house, and who had by their lying tongues destroyed his reputation is not surprising. Nor is it surprising that he showed from the start what the result of the Ripley motion would be. Hill had to argue a trivial case, fully answered by the affidavits of the surviving jurors, and could not have expected to win it from any judge.

It is apparent that Hill's testimony about his experience in 1924 adds nothing of any consequence about the state of mind and conduct of Judge Thayer at the trial in 1921.

PROFESSOR RICHARDSON

On April 19, 1927, James P. Richardson, Parker Professor of Law and Political Science at Dartmouth College, a lawyer by profession who had lived and practiced in Massachusetts, wrote to Governor Fuller endorsing the suggestion that the Governor appoint an impartial commission to aid him in a review of the case, ending his letter with these sentences:

> I know of my own personal knowledge that Judge Thayer's mental attitude during the progress of this case was such as to make him liable to prejudge it in many of its later stages. I had a personal conversation with him in Hanover at a date which was either in the fall of 1924 or in the fall of 1925 (I regret that I cannot place it more accurately) in which it was very evident that Judge Thayer regarded these men with a feeling which can only fairly be described as abhorrence. (5068)

After this letter was written, Thompson communicated with Richardson and asked for a more definite statement. Richardson then went to the registry of the Hanover Inn, found that Thayer had been registered there in November 1924 but not in November 1925, and so decided that the conversation had taken place in the fall of 1924.

The more definite statement that Richardson then made relates that he met Thayer on the crowded athletic field in Hanover.

> He spoke to me by name. He has known me for a long time. He immediately went into the subject of the Sacco-Vanzetti case. He referred at once to the motions which had been pending before him and which he within a short time disposed of. My recollection is that some of the motions had been decided on shortly before this conversation.
>
> Judge Thayer said, as near as I can remember, "Did you see what I did with those anarchistic bastards the other day? I guess that will hold them for a while. Let them go to the Supreme Court now and see what they can get out of them." There was more of the same sort. I think he used the words

"sons of bitches." He said, "They wouldn't get far in my court." (5418-5419)

On July 12, 1927, Richardson appeared before the Advisory Committee and gave his testimony orally. (5064-5069)

This conversation followed by a month or more Thayer's decision of October 1, 1924, overruling various motions for a new trial (including the Ripley, Gould, Pelser, Goodridge, Andrews, and Hamilton-Proctor motions), and was therefore at a time when Thayer had nothing before him or under consideration. The unethical conduct of Moore and others in the Pelser,[9] Goodridge,[9] and Andrews[9] matters may well have disgusted Thayer with the radicals who were directing the defense and exploiting the case, and it is my belief that, if he did call anyone "anarchistic bastards" or "sons of bitches," he referred to Moore, Van Vaerenwyck, and Biedenkapp, not to Sacco and Vanzetti.

However that may be, we are led to ask why Richardson waited so long to tell about this. He was a Massachusetts lawyer, and if he really thought that the words Thayer used did indicate violent prejudice or deep abhorrence, he should have reported it at once. Judge Thayer's decision obviously was going to the Supreme Judicial Court, and the defense should have been informed about his prejudice. The answer must be that the words used and the manner of expression were such as not to shock Richardson in 1924.

After Richardson had written his letter to the Governor, the letter was made public, and in consequence an alumnus of Dartmouth sent a telegram to Dartmouth President Ernest M. Hopkins promising, if Hopkins would discharge Richardson, to make a check out for $10,000. Hopkins then wrote a letter to Richardson telling him about the offer and treating it humorously. The letter from Hopkins to Richardson was read to the Advisory Committee, and the incident was used by Thompson to show that his

[9] See Chapter 21 ("Louis Pelser"), Chapter 22 ("Carlos E. Goodridge"), and Chapter 23 ("Lola R. Andrews").

witness had been subjected to attempted intimidation. This made good propaganda, with a special appeal to the academic men who had rushed to the defense of Sacco and Vanzetti and the assassination of the character of Thayer.

And that is the sum of the criticism of Judge Thayer. It does not add up to much, and if we exclude the fabrications of Thompson and Beffel and the disputed hearsay upon hearsay of Benchley, we have nothing except triviality and ambiguities. The Advisory Committee's conclusion is a just one:

> From all that has come to us we are forced to conclude that the Judge was indiscreet in conversation with outsiders during the trial. He ought not to have talked about the case off the bench, and doing so was a grave breach of official decorum. But we do not believe that he used some of the expressions attributed to him, and we think there is exaggeration in what the persons to whom he spoke remember. Furthermore, we believe that such indiscretions in conversation did not affect his conduct at the trial or the opinions of the jury, who indeed, so stated to the Committee. . . ." (5378)

WHAT OTHERS THOUGHT

Jeremiah J. McAnarney in his closing argument said the following words, which seem to me to be more than a conventional compliment to the Court:

> I want to say on behalf of these men—I say it to those men and to their friends—that they have had every opportunity here, they have had every patience, every consideration. I want them to know that we have done—that everything has been done as Massachusetts takes pride in doing, granting to any man, however lowly his station, the fullest rights to our Massachusetts Commonwealth laws. (2175-2176)

It is significant that, when Thompson made his attack on Thayer before the Advisory Committee, Jeremiah J. McAnarney, who had uttered these words, did not appear to join in that cruel assassination of character. Nor did Moore, throughout his connection with the case, accuse Thayer of bias or prejudice. In fact I have heard from what I regard as reliable hearsay—Thayer to a justice of the Supreme Judicial Court to me—that Moore, while waiting for the verdict, told Thayer, "Well, I at least have the satisfaction of knowing that the defendants had a fair trial."

The Governor in his decision used this language:

> I have consulted with every member of the jury now alive, eleven in number. They considered the judge fair; that he gave them no indication of his own opinion of the case. Affidavits have been presented claiming that the judge was prejudiced. I see no evidence of prejudice in his conduct of the trial. That he had an opinion as to the guilt or innocence of the accused after hearing the evidence is natural and inevitable. . . .
>
> I have read the record and examined many witnesses and the jurymen to see from a layman's standpoint whether the trial was fairly conducted. I am convinced that it was. (5378)

The Advisory Committee said:

> It has been said that while the acts and language of the Judge, as they appear in the stenographic report, seem to be correct, yet his attitude and emphasis conveyed a different impression. But the jury do not think so. They state that the Judge tried the case fairly; that they perceived no bias, and indeed some of them went so far as to say that they did not know when they entered the jury room to consider their verdict whether he thought the defendants innocent or guilty. (5378k)

Mr. Justice Oliver Wendell Holmes, to whom everything had been presented from the record and elsewhere that the defense could produce relevant to Judge Thayer's conduct, and who had read Frankfurter's book with sympathy and without doubting its good faith, summed it all up in this excerpt from his letter to Harold Laski, dated July 10, 1930:

> But I have not had a very high opinion of the intellectual powers of such extremists as I have known or know about. All of which is painfully near rudimentary twaddle—but I say it because little things once in a while make me wonder if your sympathies are taking a more extreme turn as time goes on. I always am uncertain how far Frankfurter goes. But I notice that he and you are a good deal more stirred by Sacco and Vanzetti, who were turned into a text by the reds, than by a thousand worse things among the blacks. Indeed, so far as I can judge without having read the trial I doubt if those two suffered anything more from the conduct of the judge than would be a matter of course in England.[10]

[10] *Holmes-Laski Letters,* edited by Mark DeWolfe Howe, Harvard University Press, 1953. Quoted by permission.

31

ALLEGED CONSPIRACY
BETWEEN KATZMANN
AND THE DEPARTMENT
OF JUSTICE

AFTER the Madeiros deposition had been taken on June 28, 1926, Thompson must have realized that with a worthless confession and a rather silly hypothesis on his hands he had a pretty poor case.

So, although his motion for a new trial had been based solely on the Madeiros confession, he in something like desperation threw into the case two additional contentions.

The first of the additional contentions was that a conspiracy between the Department of Justice of the United States and the prosecuting officers of the Southeastern District of Massachusetts was shown to have existed which rendered their trial unfair.[1] It was a conspiracy either to secure the conviction of the defendants of murder as charged by the indictment or to prove that they were dangerous radicals subject to deportation or punishment under the laws of the United States.

This contention was made before Judge Thayer at the hearing of the motion for a new trial and before the Supreme Judicial Court, the Advisory Committee, and the Governor. Ostensibly in support of it, the affidavits of former agents of the Department of Justice and private detectives were introduced. In them are to be found reckless charges, unsupported opinions, and suspicions asserted as fact, but not one scrap of evidence in support of

---

[1] The second additional contention, that Katzmann had suppressed identification evidence, has already been discussed at appropriate places herein. See Chapter 9 ("The Eyewitnesses") and Chapter 20 ("Roy E. Gould").

the conspiracy charge. The contention on its face was absurd and outrageous. To accept it one would have to believe:

That the Department of Justice suspected but could not prove that Sacco and Vanzetti were dangerous radicals who should be deported or punished as such under Federal law; and

That the Department had in its possession evidence that Sacco and Vanzetti were not guilty of murder; and

That, nevertheless, above all the radicals in the country, the Department feared or hated these two obscure men so much that it conspired with Katzmann to have them indicted and tried for murder so that they would be convicted of murder or, failing that, the United States would in the course of the trial for murder get proof that they were dangerous radicals subject to deportation or punishment as such; and

That the Department was not satisfied to have Sacco leave the country voluntarily with the passport he had obtained or to have Vanzetti in the State Prison for twelve to fifteen years, but insisted that the murder trial go on until the defendants were sent to the electric chair, not because they were murderers but because they were radicals; and

That the conspiracy was carried on for years after the trial into a new administration and resulted in the concealment by Attorney General Sargent of evidence which, if disclosed, would have led to a new trial and acquittal of the defendants; and

That Stewart and Katzmann committed perjury in the affidavits in which they disclaimed any assistance from, or correspondence with, the Department of Justice in the preparation and trial of the case; and

That the Department of Justice misrepresented the contents of its files to representatives of the defense and withheld evidence which would have saved the defendants from death.

In dismissing this contention of conspiracy after it was argued before him as a part of the Madeiros motion, Judge Thayer used language which has been criticized as being infused with a spirit alien to judicial utterance. The provocation, however, was great. This is what he said:

Since the trial before the Jury of these cases, a new type of disease would seem to have developed. It might be called "lego-psychic neurosis" or "hysteria," which means: "a belief in the existence of something which in fact and truth has no such existence."

This disease would seem to have reached a very dangerous condition, from the argument of counsel, upon the present Motion, when he charges Mr. Sargent, Attorney General of the United States, and his subordinates, and subordinates of Former Attorney-General of the United States Mr. Palmer and Mr. Katzmann and the [present] District Attorney of Norfolk County, with being in a conspiracy to send these two defendants to the electric chair, not because they are murderers but because they are radicals. (4748)

When the contention of conspiracy got to the Supreme Judicial Court, it was dismissed summarily, and it is significant that, as to this particular contention, the Court did not rely on the discretionary power of Judge Thayer. Rather, it said that a judge would be *compelled* to find that no substantial evidence appeared that the Department of Justice of the United States had in its control any proof of the innocence of the defendants, or had conspired to secure their conviction by wrongful means.[2]

There is no mention of this contention in the Governor's decision, and I like to think that this was a way of treating it with the contempt it deserves.

The Advisory Committee, in its report, describes the affidavits and disposes of the conspiracy contention as follows:

In one of the motions for a new trial Mr. Thompson, now counsel for the defense, contended that between the District Attorney and officers of the United States Secret Service engaged in investigating radical movements there had been collusion for the purpose either of deporting these defendants as radicals or of convicting them of murder, and thus of getting them out of the way; that with this object Mr. Katz-

2 *Commonwealth v. Sacco*, 259 Mass. 128, 141. (4893)

mann agreed to cross-examine them on the subject of their
opinions, and that the files of the Federal Department of
Justice contain material tending to show the innocence of
Sacco and Vanzetti. In support of these charges he filed affidavits by Ruzzamenti, Weyand, Letherman and Weiss which
declared that the files of the Federal Department of Justice
would show the correspondence that took place in the preparation of the case; but none of these affidavits states or implies that there is anything in those files which would help
to show that the defendants are not guilty. For the Government to suppress evidence of innocence would be monstrous,
and to make such a charge without evidence to support it is
wrong. Mr. Katzmann in answer to a question by Mr.
Thompson stated to the Committee that the Federal Department had nothing to do with the preparation of the
case, and there is no reason to suppose that the Federal
agents knew the evidence he possessed. He stated also that
he made no agreement with them about the cross-examination. A spy named Carbone was, indeed, placed in the cell
next to that of Sacco, and it was stated in an agreement of
subsequent counsel that this was to get from him information relating to the South Braintree murder; but Mr. Katzmann, in answer to a question by Mr. Thompson, informs
us that that is a mistake; that the Federal authorities wanted
to put a man there with the hope of getting information
about the explosion on Wall Street. To this he and the
sheriff consented, but no information was in fact obtained.

. . . . We agree wholly with the remark of Mr. Justice
Wait in the opinion of the Supreme Judicial Court that "an
impartial, intelligent and honest judge . . . would be compelled to find that no substantial evidence appeared that the
Department of Justice of the United States had in its control
any proof of the innocence of these defendants, or had conspired to secure their conviction by wrongful means."
(5378l-m, t-u; my italics.)

THE MOST SWEEPING criticism of the fairness of the trial is that in Massachusetts in 1921 two Italian anarchists could not, because of hatred and hysterical fear of Reds, get a fair trial for murder.

Arthur Schlesinger, Jr., in explaining the falsehoods told by Sacco and Vanzetti at the time of their arrest and subsequent conviction, expresses it thus:

> These were the days of the red scare: Nicola Sacco and Bartolomeo Vanzetti, not knowing why they had been stopped, hardly able to understand English, acted confused and guilty. Eventually brought to trial on the murder charge, they stood little chance as confessed radicals, aliens, and draft-dodgers in a time of hysteria. The trial judge, who soon boasted of what he had done to "those anarchistic bastards," completed the design of Massachusetts justice. So in 1921 Sacco and Vanzetti were sentenced to death—two obscure immigrants about whom no one cared.[1]

If space permitted, it would be interesting to analyze the distortion and falsehood of the sentences quoted. The most amazing is the statement that no one cared about the two obscure immigrants. How, in the face of the worldwide support of the defense by law professors, lawyers, law students, college presidents, col-

[1] *Op. cit.,* p. 140.

lege professors, journalists, preachers, poets, playwrights, authors, labor unions, civil liberties unions, church councils, picketers, demonstrators, dynamiters, and do-gooders, Schlesinger had the effrontery to write that "no one cared" would pass my comprehension if I knew less than I do about his standards of scholarship.

The contention about the Red Scare, if well founded, should have been raised at the outset by a motion for change of venue, and if another Massachusetts venue were regarded as equally hysterical, there should have been a motion for a postponement until the atmosphere had cleared. But no one thought of this at the time, nor was this contention raised in any court proceedings—not even when the defense tried to persuade the Supreme Court of the United States that the trial was so unfair that the proceedings were not a trial at all within the due process clause of the Fourteenth Amendment. This shows clearly that there was no proof supporting the contention; if there had been, it would have been adduced to show that the proceedings were void in a legal sense. But as Moorfield Storey, who had written the preface to the Post book,[2] upon which, as we shall see, Thompson relied as proof of the Red Scare, wrote to the Attorney General of Massachusetts in 1927, "there was no crusade against Reds in Massachusetts at the time this case was tried."

It is true that many who lived in Massachusetts in 1921 were uneasy and fearful about the violence which had accompanied some strikes, as well as the May 1, 1919, riots in Roxbury and elsewhere, the bomb outrages of June 2, 1919, and the Wall Street explosion of September 16, 1920, but this uneasiness had not been converted into hysteria or into fear or hatred of two obscure anarchists on trial for murder.

Moreover, it was not until long after the trial, if at all, that Sacco and Vanzetti confessed to radical activities or opinions that would have subjected them to hatred, deportation, or punishment or caused them to be feared. When arrested, Sacco denied that he was an anarchist. He told Stewart and testified on the stand

2 *Deportations Delirium of 1920*, Louis F. Post, Chicago, 1923.

that he did not believe in the overthrow of the government by force or violence. Vanzetti, when asked by Stewart whether he was an anarchist, was not sure: "I am a little different." He, like Sacco, said that he did not believe in the overthrow of the government by force and violence.

Ostensibly as proof that there was a Red Scare in 1920, but obviously to smear the Department of Justice, Thompson presented to the Advisory Committee but never to a court two documents he had received from Frankfurter, and made the following statement:

> I asked him to let me have anything that would bear on this matter. One is a book entitled, "Deportations Delirium of 1920," by Louis F. Post. Then I desire to present to the Commission a report on the Illegal Practices of the Department of Justice, belonging to Mr. Frankfurter personally, because I see his name is stamped upon it. . . . (5252)

In his argument before the Advisory Committee, Thompson also relied on the case of *Colyer et al. v. Skeffington*, Commissioner of Immigration,[3] which I summarize below.

The Post book is a history of the raids of January 2, 1920, and the deportation proceedings which followed it. These raids, conducted jointly by the Department of Labor and the Department of Justice, resulted in the arrest of several hundred aliens suspected of being Communists. At that time, membership in the Communist Party was regarded by the departments as sufficient cause for deportation. Sacco and Vanzetti had nothing to fear from these raids and were not arrested. They were anti-Communists and called themselves Libertarians, opposed to every theory of authoritarian communism and socialism, sharing their ideas, as they said, with Christ (a "political anarchist"), Thomas Jefferson, Thomas Paine, Ralph Waldo Emerson, Abraham Lincoln, and Benjamin Franklin. (4921) Thompson, in his offer of proof in

3 265 Fed. Rep. 17 (District Court, District of Massachusetts, Opinion dated June 23, 1920).

the Canter case, said they hated communism as much as capitalism.

After the arrests, hearings were held before Immigration inspectors, with an agent of the Department of Justice in attendance, with varying results: some of the persons arrested were released, some were ordered deported, and some were held for further proceedings.

Twenty of the aliens who were ordered deported brought petitions for writs of habeas corpus, which were heard by Circuit Judge George W. Anderson. Lawrence G. Brooks and Morris Katzoff appeared for the petitioners, and Lewis Goldberg, Assistant United States Attorney, for the respondent. Felix Frankfurter of New York City and Zechariah Chafee, Jr., of Cambridge, Massachusetts, appeared as *amici curiae*. The case was heard at great length on fifteen days, with a record of 1600 pages and a large mass of exhibits.

The petitioners made three main contentions.

The first contention was that the deportation warrants, although signed and issued by the Acting Secretary of Labor, were void, because grounded on investigations and proceedings initiated and conducted by the Department of Justice and not by the Department of Labor, to which Congress had delegated the power of investigating and deporting aliens of the prescribed classes. This was an important point for the Communists, who preferred the treatment they received from the Department of Labor to the vigorous enforcement of law by the Department of Justice and investigation by its Bureau of Investigation (now the F.B.I.). The contention was rejected, however, by Judge Anderson, who held that the Department of Labor could, if it chose, avail itself of investigations made and evidence obtained by the agents of the Department of Justice or by any other governmental department or even by unofficial volunteers.

The second contention was that the Secretary of Labor was wrong in holding the Communist Party within the purview of the Act of October 16, 1918, so as to make mere membership therein cause for deportation. Judge Anderson decided that this question was open to the Court and that the Secretary of Labor was wrong in his decision which made membership in the Communist Party a sole cause for deportation. On this point, the most important one in the case, Judge Anderson was reversed by the Circuit Court of Appeals for the First Circuit. That Court found in the platform and manifesto of the Communist Party substantial evidence that the Communist Party "teaches and advocates the overthrow of the government by force and violence." [4]

In connection with this second contention, the ingenious friends of the court asserted that "under-cover informants" or government spies placed in the Communist Party by the Department of Justice had slyly given form and color to the party platform and other documents upon which the Secretary of Labor had based his ruling that membership in the Communist Party was membership in an organization which advocated the overthrow of the Government by force and violence. Judge Anderson could find no evidence that the spies did this, nor could he, as he said, make a finding that they did this, nor could he, as he said, make a finding that they did not. So, in all seriousness, he asked the Department to explain the nature and extent of its "under-cover informants," a revelation which obviously would have made further investigation of communism by the Department of Justice as ineffective as it became in 1925, when Congress was persuaded to discontinue appropriations granted to the Department of Justice for the investigation of radical activities, and as it is now by force of judicial decisions and executive hostility.

The third contention was that the records on which the Secretary of Labor based his decisions adverse to the aliens were vitiated by lack of due process. On this part of the case, testimony was produced to show arrests without warrants, arrests on telegraphic warrants received after the event, unwarranted searches and seizures, police brutality, invasion of homes, unduly long detention of persons afterwards released, hardships due to bad conditions at the prison on Deer Island in Boston Harbor, and

---

4 *Skeffington v. Katzoff*, 277 Fed. Rep. 129 (1922); Judge Anderson's opinion is in *Colyer v. Skeffington*, 265 Fed. Rep. 17.

lack of due process in the hearings before the inspectors. On this branch of the case Judge Anderson found lack of due process in the hearings with respect to sixteen of the petitioners, and this finding of fact was not appealed. Frankfurter in his book on the Sacco-Vanzetti case makes a point of this, arguing that the failure to appeal was a confession of illegal tactics on the part of the government. This may be so, but another reason appeals to me. Judge Anderson's decision was not a final adjudication protecting the aliens against deportation; it merely held that the proceedings up to that time were void. All the government had to do was to start over, give the aliens a new hearing, and deport or not deport as the Secretary of Labor might decide. It would have been a waste of time and money to appeal when the record could be corrected in a few days by administrative action.

However all that may be, it is obvious that the Post book and the Skeffington case are in no way concerned with public hysteria or fear but only with alleged misconduct of the Department of Justice and the Department of Labor.

THE TWELVE LAWYERS

The other document presented by Thompson to the Advisory Committee was Frankfurter's own copy of the "Report Upon the Illegal Practices of the U. S. Department of Justice." This report was issued May 27, 1920, by Judson King, director of the National Popular Government League, a publicity bureau for various organizations represented on its directorships, which included the American Civil Liberties Union, the League for Industrial Democracy, and several others closely affiliated with them.

The report was signed by twelve lawyers: Felix Frankfurter, Ernst Freund, David Wallerstein, Jackson H. Ralston, Francis Fisher Kane, Zechariah Chafee, Jr., R. G. Brown, Alfred Niles, Swinburn Hale, Frank P. Walsh, Roscoe Pound, and Tyrrell Williams.

In the report, the Department of Justice is charged with continual illegal acts in its campaign for the suppression of radical activities. Thirty-one affidavits very much like the affidavit of

Roberto Elia, referred to in Chapter 17, are appended to the report, and if they were to be believed (the Department disputed them), some agents of the Department were guilty of illegal conduct, but what that has to do with the state of mind in Norfolk County in 1920 is beyond understanding.

The Red Scare was a red herring, and if we conclude that it was dragged into the case in bad faith by Frankfurter and Thompson for its value as propaganda and to help the American Civil Liberties Union and the International Labor Defense Committee in their war with the F.B.I., would we be far wrong?

ON JULY 3, 1926, Thompson sent a letter to Attorney General
John G. Sargent. In that letter he asked:

> that William J. West, now a Special Agent of the Depart-
> ment of Justice in Boston, be authorized to talk with me
> concerning the Sacco-Vanzetti Case and to show me what-
> ever documents and correspondence are on file in his office
> dealing with the investigations made by the Boston agents
> before, during, and after the trial of Sacco and Vanzetti,
> which occurred in June and July, 1921." (4719)

Thompson asserted that he received no reply to his letter, and
because of that he severely criticized the Attorney General.
(4542)

However, this appears from Thompson's affidavit:

> On July 13, 1926, Mr. Dowd, the agent in charge of the
> Boston Branch of the Department of Justice, called me on
> the telephone and stated that although he had no personal
> knowledge of the Sacco-Vanzetti Case, having been ap-
> pointed comparatively recently, he had been instructed by
> the Attorney General "to get in touch with me" and to in-
> terview me accompanied by Mr. West, "for the purpose of
> ascertaining what I wanted." I replied that what I wanted
> had been accurately stated in my letter of July 3rd to the

Attorney General and I repeated it, namely, that I wanted *truthful answers* to such questions as I might see fit to put to Mr. West concerning the connection of the Boston Agency of the Department of Justice with the Sacco-Vanzetti case and an inspection of all letters and other documents on file in the Boston Office relating to that case. He [Dowd] said he had no authority to permit Mr. West either to give me the information desired, or to show me any papers whatever. I then stated under those circumstances I did not desire to confer with him as it appeared that what he was seeking was, in effect, not to give information but to obtain it from me. (4542; my italics.)

As Judge Thayer noted, Thompson did not ask Dowd whether or not there was any information in the file that would in any way tend to prove that Sacco and Vanzetti were innocent of the crime charged.

And so the matter rested, until the decision of the Supreme Judicial Court overruling the exceptions taken to the denial of the Madeiros motion.

After this decision came down, on April 5, 1927, Thompson tried to persuade the Governor and the Advisory Committee that the conspiracy did exist and that the files of the Department of Justice contained important information. He did not, however, make any further attempt to get access to the files or to produce additional affidavits or testimony.

When the Governor's decision denying clemency was made public on August 3, 1927, Thompson withdrew from the case and Arthur D. Hill became the new chief counsel. Musmanno tells us that on the morning of August 5, 1927, Hill called into his office for a conference a group which included Ehrmann, Francis B. Sayre (President Wilson's son-in-law), Felix Frankfurter, and himself, later joined by Elias Field and Richard C. Evarts. This group agreed upon a five-point program of action which, as listed by Musmanno, did not include another attempt to get access to the Department of Justice files. Musmanno himself, however, and a Citizens Committee organized for the sole purpose of securing an examination of the files did make the attempt: Musmanno by application to Acting Attorney General George R. Farnum, and the Citizens Committee (acting through Arthur Garfield Hays, Francis Fisher Kane, and Frank P. Walsh) by application to Sargent and then to Farnum.[1]

Musmanno's application was made to Farnum in Washington on a date in August 1927, not clearly fixed.

When Musmanno called, Farnum told him that, as he had made the trip all the way from Pittsburgh, he was willing to receive him but that the Sacco-Vanzetti case was a state matter in which the federal government had no concern and about which he, Farnum, had very little information. Musmanno assured him that he did not intend to quote Farnum, and there was some conversation, but at no time did Farnum say or hint or in any way give Musmanno reason to believe that there was anything in the files of the Department of Justice relevant to the case.[2]

After Musmanno's visit to Farnum, the next step was taken by a committee of three: Arthur Garfield Hays, Francis Fisher Kane, and Frank P. Walsh. As representatives of the Sacco-Vanzetti Citizens' National Committee, they went to Ludlow, Vermont, and saw Attorney General Sargent, who was then on vacation. Sargent referred them to Farnum who, in the absence of Sargent, was Acting Attorney General. Sargent informed Farnum by telephone that he had referred the committee to him, and he told Farnum that he might expect a visit from the committee. Soon thereafter a telegram was received by Farnum from the committee announcing their intention to come to his office at 9:00 A.M. on Sunday, August 21.

After the Ludlow conference and before the Sunday morning

---

1 Musmanno, *op. cit.*, pp. 291-292.
2 Musmanno's account of this interview is in his book *Twelve Years After*, at pages 320-322. On June 18, 1958, I sent Mr. Farnum a copy of this account and a few days later talked with him at his office in Boston. He characterized Musmanno's account as a tissue of distortion and gave me his version as in the text. Mr. Farnum also supplied me with a memorandum which supports the statements made in this chapter.

conference, a conspicuous editorial appeared in a Baltimore paper distorting what the Attorney General had said to the committee and misrepresenting his position. Farnum determined to avoid a similar occurrence and during the Sunday morning conference dictated a statement which he handed to the committee and immediately released to the press. It read as follows:

Last night I received a telegram from Vermont signed by Arthur Garfield Hays of New York City and Francis Fisher Kane of Philadelphia stating that they would be at the Department of Justice this morning at 9 o'clock to interview me with reference to the Department of Justice files relative to the Sacco-Vanzetti case.

They called this morning at 9 o'clock and I accorded them the courtesy of an interview which lasted four hours. They were accompanied by Frank P. Walsh of New York City. They stated that they were representatives of an organization which they described as the Citizens' National Committee and also represented counsel for Sacco and Vanzetti.

They requested that the Department of Justice files be opened. I stated that I had been informed, after a thorough and recent re-examination of the files at Washington, New York and Boston, that they contained no evidence tending to establish the guilt or innocence of Sacco and Vanzetti, or either of them, of the crime for which they were convicted in the Massachusetts courts, nor any evidence whatever of any collusion whatsoever between the State and Federal authorities prior to the arrest of Sacco and Vanzetti or prior, during or subsequent to the trial of these two men. I explained that the Federal Government had no jurisdiction whatever over this case and that it was solely a matter for the State authorities of Massachusetts.

I declined to permit access to the confidential files of the Government to representatives of unofficial organizations or counsel on behalf of Sacco and Vanzetti as requested, but did say:

"While I do not authorize you to convey to the authorities of the Commonwealth of Massachusetts any suggestion or message in any shape or form on my behalf, I do say to you that, if it should happen that a request is received from Governor Fuller, the Attorney General of Massachusetts or the Lowell Commission appointed by the Governor for access by them to our files it will be immediately accorded."

In reference to a suggestion that some one attorney be selected by me to examine the files, I stated that I saw no purpose to be served at this late date as the files had already been checked and rechecked under conditions which tended to insure as impartial an examination as could be obtained.

No request to examine the files came from the Governor or the Attorney General or the Advisory Committee.

It is impossible to believe that there was anything in the files which would have helped the defendants in the murder case or that Attorney General Sargent or Acting Attorney General Farnum would have concealed or conspired with anyone to conceal relevant evidence. It is not unlikely that the American Civil Liberties Union and the International Labor Defense Committee would have found the files interesting, because they might have learned the names of some undercover informants in them.

However that may be, Thompson's action in bringing this issue into the case helped the radicals in their unceasing warfare with the F.B.I. and in their use of the Sacco-Vanzetti case for propaganda and mass agitation.

34

**THE FRANKFURTER
BOOK**

A FRANKFURTER ARTICLE in *The Atlantic Monthly* for March
1927 was expanded into a book published the same month under
the title, *The Case of Sacco and Vanzetti, a Critical Analysis for
Lawyers and Laymen.*

There are significant differences between the article and the
book. For example, in the magazine article there is no mention at
all of two important items, Berardelli's gun and Sacco's cap. In
the book, Berardelli's gun and Sacco's cap are mentioned but
only as items of evidence too insignificant for notice.

Two sentences in the articles are given to the Bridgewater case.
They occur in a footnote which dismisses it as only a part of the
South Braintree affair and fails to mention that Vanzetti did not
take the stand at Plymouth. This footnote was expanded in the
book to contain an inaccurate and incomplete account of the
Bridgewater trial, which has been discussed in the first chapters
of the present book.

In the consideration of the article and the book, serious questions have arisen.

In March 1927 the motion for a new trial based on the Madeiros
confession, the alleged conspiracy between the Department of
Justice and the Massachusetts authorities, and the alleged suppression of evidence had been taken to the Massachusetts Supreme Judicial Court and was awaiting decision. Under those
circumstances and at that time it was a breach of journalistic

ethics for the *Atlantic* to publish Frankfurter's argumentative survey of the case and a breach of Canon 20 of the Canons of Professional Ethics for a lawyer, whether connected with the case or not, to publish such an article.

Frankfurter has denied that he ever was counsel for the defendants. Thompson has also denied that Frankfurter was counsel and I think we may be sure that Frankfurter never received any fees for his services. There is evidence, however, that from the time that Thompson came into the case Frankfurter was in active charge; at least he had control of the purse. A court stenographer who reported part of the proceedings after Thompson came into the case wrote me in 1958 that he asked Thompson several times to approve extra charges for the reporting work,

> and on more than one occasion he [Thompson] said he would have to speak to Frankfurter about the matter, and later told me that Frankfurter said it was all right. Frankfurter was apparently running the whole show.

We also know from Musmanno's book that, in the last stages of the case, Frankfurter attended a conference of the defendants' lawyers; he is named by Musmanno as one of them.

However that may be, Frankfurter as a member of the National Committee of the American Civil Liberties Union had been active in the defense from March 1921, if not before, and at the time his article was published he was an active member of the Sacco-Vanzetti Defense Committee.

Frankfurter and the *Atlantic* should not have concealed from the public his close association with the defense. Whether he was, in the strict sense of the word, counsel for the defense or not, he should not have been represented by the *Atlantic* as a disinterested lawyer making a complete, accurate and impartial survey of a case then pending before the Supreme Judicial Court.

A more serious question of ethics and patriotism is presented. By March 1927 Frankfurter knew that, whatever he might think of the merits of the defense and the fairness of the trial, the case was being used by the international Red organization, directed from Moscow, by the International Labor Defense, by his own American Civil Liberties Union, and by Communists, anarchists, and radicals generally as a means of mass agitation.

Throughout this book I have from time to time, under appropriate headings, compared Frankfurter's statements of the facts with the real facts; it is my opinion, which these various instances fully support, that the Frankfurter book is unreliable in its statements of fact and its conclusions of law.

The book has done incalculable harm because of a plausibility gained from misstatements, artful distortion, and deliberate suppression. President Lowell himself said that, after reading it and before his own investigation, he had some doubts about the trial. Certainly the book was the basis for the faith of intellectuals, academicians, and clergy who could not but be impressed by what seemed on its surface to be an impartial and accurate survey by a professor of law at Harvard.

THE WIGMORE-FRANKFURTER LETTERS

Shortly after the publication of Frankfurter's book, John H. Wigmore, Dean of the Northwestern University Law School, one of the leading legal scholars in the country and author of a great book on the law of evidence, wrote a letter to the *Boston Evening Transcript* which initiated the much-discussed Wigmore-Frankfurter correspondence of April and May 1927.

Limitations of space forbid the publication of this correspondence in full, but the following summary will, I am sure, be found sufficiently complete so far as the trial was concerned. Wigmore's contentions were that the Frankfurter article was neither fair nor accurate nor complete in vital details of the trial and that it misrepresented the law of Massachusetts about the scope of review in a capital case.

Under his first head, Wigmore dealt with Frankfurter's charge that the jury was specially selected and picked, a point which has been discussed in Chapter 8 of this book.

From this, Wigmore went on to discuss the charge that Judge

Thayer in his decision on the Madeiros motion had made two misrepresentations.

The first of these was that Judge Thayer had written that the Supreme Judicial Court had "approved" the verdict. Wigmore's answer to this was that Thayer had referred to the verdict four times, using the proper word "affirmed" three times and not using the improper word "approved" at all. Unfortunately Wigmore had overlooked one passage where Thayer had slipped and had used the word "approved." Frankfurter jumped gleefully on this oversight and in his reply contended that this one use of the wrong word justified his statement that Thayer had been guilty of having given meretricious authority to his self-justification by misrepresenting the action of the Supreme Judicial Court on the verdict.

Wigmore then re-read Thayer's decision and found that the verdict had been referred to nine times. In four of these, Thayer used the proper word "affirmed," in four he used an equally proper phrase, "sufficient evidence to warrant," or the like, and in one only he erroneously used the word "approved." Wigmore then asked this question:

> Since the critic (as we must suppose) himself had read that memorandum of the judge, and seen those nine references, eight of which were correct, how could the critic as an honorable member of the Bar dare to pick out that one single slip and tell all the world that the judge was an official liar?

Frankfurter's reply to this question was that Thayer had actually used the word "approved" and that it was not a "slip" but a "knowing falsity," in other words a deliberate lie.

To the nonquibbling mind, the use of "approved" for "affirmed" when speaking of a verdict which the Supreme Judicial Court has refused to upset seems to be a rather innocent way of representing what the Court did. Of course, the Court did not put itself in the jury box and pass on the facts; nor, in a strict sense, did the Court *approve* what the jurors did. What it did was to say that on the record the evidence was sufficient to warrant the verdict. Technically, this is not an approval of the verdict, but I do not believe that many laymen, or lawyers either, would be misled by this use of the wrong word or that its use once in nine chances is evidence of deliberate falsehood.

Wigmore then took up Frankfurter's other charge of misrepresentation, namely, that Thayer had characterized Thompson's activities "on behalf of these two Italians as 'lego-psychic neurosis.' " Wigmore's reply was that Thayer had not used these words to characterize Thompson's activities "on behalf of these two Italians" but had applied them to a single part of this *argument* on the 1926 motion for a new trial. This was the part alleging a conspiracy between the Attorney General of the United States and the local authorities to convict the accused because they were radicals and not because they had committed murder. Whether Thayer was justified in characterizing Thompson's suspicion of conspiracy as lego-psychic neurosis or hysteria may be debated, but Frankfurter was certainly not justified, Wigmore pointed out, in attributing Thayer's characterization to all of Thompson's activities on behalf of the two Italians. To this, Frankfurter made no reply.

Wigmore then went on to consider the evidence which Frankfurter claimed he had "fairly placed before the reader." He first mentioned two items of evidence which Frankfurter had suppressed. One of these was Sacco's cap, the omission of which by Frankfurter has already been discussed in this book.[1] The other was the passport in Sacco's pocket at the time of the arrest, which Wigmore said discounted any fear he might have had about deportation.

Frankfurter's reply to this was a claim that he had not suppressed the passport, because in his book he had stated that Sacco's alibi was based on the fact that on the day of the crime "he was in Boston seeing about a passport to Italy whither he was planning shortly to return to *visit* his recently bereaved father." (My italics.) Sacco, he goes on, did not fear *return* to Italy; he

---

[1] See Chapter 11 ("Sacco's Cap") for the interchange between Wigmore and Frankfurter about Sacco's cap.

feared *deportation,* because deportation to him meant the fate of his radical friend Salsedo, "found crushed to death the day before Sacco's and Vanzetti's arrest."

Wigmore in his rejoinder did not think that "seeing about a passport" and "planning shortly to return" were the same things as having a passport already in his pocket when arrested, with his passage fixed for two days later, and so the passport point was left.

In the debate about the passport, Frankfurter scored on Wigmore on an incidental point. As proof that Sacco had in his pocket a passport, Wigmore, who did not have the complete transcript before him, relied upon the following passage from Judge Thayer's decision:

> Mr. Katzmann, in his cross-examination, brought out that Sacco said that he was afraid of deportation, that he did not want to go back to Italy and that he had told falsehoods because of this fear and then he asked this question: "Mr. Sacco, you say you feared deportation and that is why you told all these lies and why you did what you did?" and Mr. Sacco said "Yes." Then came the next question: "Mr. Sacco, at the very time when you were telling these lies, you had already secured a passport for Italy on which you, your wife, and two children were to sail two days after the night of your arrest?" and the answer was "Yes." (4771)

A careful examination of the transcript itself was made for Frankfurter, and he was able to say, correctly, that it did not appear that Katzmann had asked Sacco the two questions Thayer had incorporated in the foregoing passage.[2] Accordingly Wigmore

---

[2] The error here, if there is one, is chargeable to Judge Thayer and not to Wigmore. I have not yet found the reason why there is the variance between the transcript and the passage from Judge Thayer's decision quoted above. The two questions attributed to Katzmann would come naturally in a cross-examination on this point, but they certainly do not appear in the Holt Transcript or in the transcript at the State Library in Boston. Judge Thayer may have relied on his memory or on his own notes, or the stenographer may have missed the questions. The misstatement of the evidence, if it is one, is not serious, because there was other evidence upon which Katzmann could argue, as he did, that Sacco with a one-way passport in his pocket could not have feared deportation.

could not rely on the cross-examination for proof that, when arrested, Sacco did have a passport in his pocket and intended to sail with his family two days after his arrest. But Frankfurter did not supply a complete answer to Wigmore's point, for there was conclusive evidence apart from the cross-examination that Sacco did have a one-way passport for himself and family and did intend to sail shortly. In his argument to the jury, Katzmann made the following argument about Sacco's fear of deportation:

> Sacco, who, on the exhibit that he himself has put in this case, was going on a one-way passport, a passport that would take him from Boston to Italy and would not take him back, the Foglio di Via. (2200-2201)

Wigmore's final point was that Frankfurter had misstated the Massachusetts law about the scope of the review of facts by the Supreme Judicial Court where the verdict of a jury or the disposition by a trial judge of a motion for a new trial is in issue. Frankfurter's assertion was that the Supreme Judicial Court of Massachusetts could not inquire whether the facts set forth in the printed record justified the verdict but could only review the conduct of the trial judge.

This, said Wigmore, was completely false, and he showed that the Supreme Judicial Court had passed upon the sufficiency of the evidence to warrant a verdict of guilty and upon the insufficiency of the evidence to upset the denial by Thayer of the various motions for a new trial.

In this legal argument Wigmore, as it seems to me, had much the better of it. But, however that may be, he was certainly right in his common-sense assertion that the court, regardless of the technical ground of its decision, would not have failed to direct a new trial had it seen any reason to distrust the correctness of the verdict.

35

THE MURDER AND THE
MYTH

SACCO-VANZETTI as myth is a murder engineered by a decadent
ruling class ("hangmen in frock coats") to eliminate two radicals
("goddam agitators") who were interfering with their betters
and obstructing their exploitation of the proletariat. Eugene V.
Debs charged the mill-owning, labor-sweating malefactors of Massachusetts with having Sacco and Vanzetti framed, pounced upon,
thrown into a dungeon, and sentenced to be murdered by their
judicial and other official underlings.

William G. Thompson presented and seriously argued to the
Supreme Judicial Court and to the Advisory Committee the monstrous contention that there was a conspiracy between the Department of Justice and the Commonwealth of Massachusetts to have
Sacco and Vanzetti put to death not because they were murderers
but because they were radicals. In the Canter case he offered to
prove that Governor Fuller, though not a murderer in the ordinary sense of the word, was morally responsible for the murder by
Massachusetts of two innocent men.

In the myth, Harvard College became Hangman's House because President Lowell headed the Advisory Committee which
found that the defendants were guilty beyond a reasonable doubt
and that the trial was fair.

In Russia the myth took another turn. There, Sacco and Vanzetti were honored because as agents of the revolution they had
murdered a paymaster and his guard.

But Sacco-Vanzetti was not a frame-up. On May 5, 1920, three weeks after a brutal murder in South Braintree, Sacco and Vanzetti, one a shoe worker, the other a fish peddler, under no suspicion of crime and wholly unknown to the police of Bridgewater, West Bridgewater, and Brockton, fell into a trap set by the police for a man named Boda and were arrested. When arrested, Sacco had in his pocket six obsolete bullets which could not be matched elsewhere except by the fatal bullet found in the body of Berardelli, which was of the same rare and obsolete type. In the waistband of his trousers Sacco had the pistol through which the mortal bullet was fired.

When Vanzetti was arrested he had in his pocket Berardelli's revolver and four shotgun shells of the kind and gauge fired through the shotgun in the Bridgewater holdup.

The day following the arrest, after they had been viewed by thirty or thirty-five eyewitnesses of the two crimes, Sacco and Vanzetti were interrogated by District Attorney Katzmann. Then and there both defendants told a series of falsehoods which established their consciousness of guilt of murder and wrecked the alibis afterward fabricated for them. No criticism of these interrogations can be made. Radicalism and draft dodging were not mentioned at all. The prisoners knew that Katzmann was interested in a holdup and a murder and in the events of December 24, 1919, and April 15, 1920. There were no language difficulties, because there was an interpreter present. There was no doubt about what the questions and answers were because they were transcribed by a stenographer. The accuracy of the transcript was admitted on the stand by the defendants. The prisoners were not bullied or badgered—they were treated "as a gentleman ought."

Sacco was asked what he was doing on April 15, 1920, and although this date was only three weeks in the past he lied and told Katzmann that he was at work all that day. Later, when his employer denied that he was at work at all on that day, Sacco was to recall that he had gone to Boston early in the morning and spent the day there seeing about his passport. This lie about April 15,

1920, which could have no possible connection with his radical opinions or his draft dodging, would not have come from an innocent man who had actually been in Boston on that date. And if Sacco's recollection was innocently at fault, why did his alibi witnesses Guadagni, Bosco, Williams (the ad collector), Monello (the theatrical enthusiast), Affe (the grocer), and Andrower (the consular clerk), not come forward immediately and contradict him and tell the District Attorney that they had seen Sacco in Boston on that date?

This single lie, which destroyed Sacco's alibi, with several other equally damaging lies made the verdict inevitable. Vanzetti's lies were equally significant, and his alibi was so ridiculous that it laughed itself out of court.

These circumstances, supported by the testimony of eyewitnesses and the later discovery that it was Sacco's cap which had been left at the scene of the murder, gave the Commonwealth a case which convinced the jury, the trial judge, the Governor, and the Advisory Committee.

Much of the debate about the guilt of the defendants has concerned itself with the testimony of the eyewitnesses, and if identification were the sole evidence, one who did not see and hear the witnesses could not, from reading the record, arrive at a positive conclusion about guilt. Whether on that hypothesis the jury or the Governor, who did see and hear the witnesses, would have found that guilt had been proved beyond a reasonable doubt, is of course a matter of conjecture. The jury seems to have placed reliance chiefly on the circumstantial evidence and less on the identification than the Governor did. After the trial, as we have seen, the defense spent much time and money in an attempt to weaken the identification evidence. A temporary recantation of the testimony of Mrs. Andrews was obtained by blackmail and browbeating, and Louis Pelser also recanted, while he was drunk, repenting of it the next day. The attempt to blackmail Goodridge into a recantation failed. A "newly discovered" eyewitness, Gould, was brought forth to deny that Sacco was the man who shot at him during the crime, according to his first story, or during the get-away according to his second.

The defense was unable to do much with the circumstantial evidence at the trial or after it. The evidence of the obsolete bullets which appealed so strongly to the jury and the Advisory Committee has been generally ignored by commentators. The comparison of the obsolete bullets in Sacco's pocket with the mortal bullet taken from Berardelli's body was obvious and could be made without the aid of expert opinion by the naked eye. In the end, Thompson was led to the desperate claim, unsupported by any evidence, that the bullet produced at the trial as the mortal bullet was a false exhibit which Captain Proctor, who had died before the contention was made, had substituted.

Proof that the mortal bullet was fired from Sacco's pistol depended at the trial upon expert opinion, about which, as we have seen, there was much controversy. After the trial the fact was one which could, by the use of Colonel Goddard's compound microscope, be determined by the eye of a layman without expert assistance. In our search for the truth we are justified in relying on the Goddard experiment, although it was not a part of the trial or of the posttrial record. The test was, however, conducted in the presence of counsel for the defendant and of a defense expert who was convinced by it.

When John W. and Thomas F. McAnarney were before the Advisory Committee, both acknowledged that the conduct of the defendants at the time of the arrest and the falsehoods they told to the District Attorney left them no defense to the murder charge unless the falsehoods could be explained as consciousness of the guilt of something else. For this reason, the defendants were advised by their counsel to tell the jury about their radicalism and their draft dodging and to give as a reason for getting Boda's automobile at the Johnson house the gathering and concealment of radical literature. Thus the defendants introduced radicalism into the trial, and if it created any emotional issue (the jury said it did not), it was not the fault of the Commonwealth or the trial judge who had advised against it. As we have seen, the story of the radical literature failed as a defense, because it was vague, varied, inconsistent, improbable, and even if believed did not explain the most significant of the falsehoods. What, for example did the hiding of radical literature have to do with Sacco's lie about his whereabouts on April 15, 1920?

Five years after the trial, someone found a man named Madeiros who, facing execution for another murder and having everything to gain and nothing to lose, was willing to confess the South Braintree crime. This "worthless confession from an utterly untrustworthy source," to quote Professor Morgan, was built up by the perjured affidavit of another murderer and the excited conjectures of a defense attorney into the hypothesis that the murder had been committed by the Morelli gang of Providence, against whom there was never produced a single shred of evidence of any kind connecting them with the crime.

By ignoring the circumstantial evidence, the obsolete bullets, Sacco's pistol, Berardelli's gun, Sacco's cap, the defendants' falsehoods upon arrest, the weakness of the alibis, the worthlessness of the Madeiros confession and of the Morelli hypothesis, the fraudulent action of the defense expert Hamilton in shifting the gun barrels, and the bribery, intimidation, and blackmail of witnesses by the defense—by ignoring all those, some adherents of the defense have vehemently insisted upon the innocence, even the saintliness, of the defendants. Two idealistic anarchists were, they contend, quite incapable of a brutal murder. Murder was out of character for them but not for Governor Fuller, Attorney General Sargent, President Lowell, President Stratton, Judge Grant, and Massachusetts judges, juries, and prosecutors.

Other builders of the myth brush the question of guilt aside and assert that whether guilty or not the defendants, because of the unfairness of the trial, the sadistic fury of the trial judge, the intolerant patriotism of the jury, the public hatred and abhorrence of radicals, and the crimes and conspiracies of the Department of Justice and officers of the Commonwealth of Massachusetts, were swept off the board without a valid checkmate.

In the chapters relating to the fairness of the trial, I have had to lead the reader through a maze of perjury, irrelevance, triviality, disputed hearsay, distortions, innuendo, falsehood, and character assassination upon which the myth of unfairness was built. I cannot see how any candid inquirer can reject the conclusion that the trial was fair. This was the conclusion of Governor Fuller, Joseph Wiggin (the Governor's personal counsel), President Lowell, President Stratton, and Judge Robert Grant. It was based on their study of the record and on personal interviews with Judge Thayer, District Attorney Katzmann, defense attorneys, the jury, the police, and many of the witnesses. No one of these men had a motive for a dishonest decision. A compromise result (commutation of the death sentence to life imprisonment) would have served the Governor's political fortunes better than a courageous adherence to duty. It would have relieved them all from threats of violence and the abuse to which their characters were subjected for the rest of their lives and afterwards. To reject their conclusions is to abandon truthful exposition, careful analysis, and logic and substitute distortion, falsehood, and sophistry.

Sacco and Vanzetti had a fair trial, and the case would never have become a *cause célèbre* unless the Reds had made it one. Tresca and Moore started the exploitation in August 1920 and were joined by the American Civil Liberties Union in February 1921, and by the International Labor Defense in 1925. All these, with a multitude of front organizations, radical labor unions, the radical press, paid publicists, and volunteer agitators, joined in an exploitation of this ordinary murder trial for revolutionary purposes and propaganda, mass agitation, and the breaking down of the American judicial system and American institutions generally. That so many men and women of good will and supposed intelligence, not all of them eggheads or sentimentalists, should have joined in this shameful exploitation is a measure of the success of the techniques which have set a pattern of exploitation for cases of the same kind which were to follow.

My last conclusion must be a rueful one. In this volume I have told the truth about Sacco and Vanzetti, but I am not in the least confident that the telling of the truth will destroy a myth so dear to the credulous who had deified Vanzetti and so valuable to the powerful forces throughout the world who still use it for their evil purposes. The truth is mighty but it will not prevail against a Great Lie, and the Sacco-Vanzetti Myth is the greatest lie of them all.

CHRONOLOGY

1915 January 20. Bartolomeo Vanzetti, who had been employed by the Plymouth Cordage Company, voluntarily left its employment. He continued to live in Plymouth, working at occasional jobs and also, after the spring of 1919, as a fish peddler.

1916 January 16-February 15. Strike at the Plymouth Cordage Company. Vanzetti, although not an employee, took some part in it.

1917 April, May, or June. Nicola Sacco and Vanzetti with others went to Mexico to avoid being drafted. Sacco was gone three months, Vanzetti a year.

1918 October. Sacco, who had returned from Mexico several months before this, worked at Rice & Hutchins in South Braintree for eight days under an assumed name.

November 2. Sacco went to work for the Kelleys in their shoe factory in Stoughton. His first payday was November 9.

1919 May 1, *circa*. Riots in the Roxbury district of Boston and elsewhere.

June 2. Series of bomb outrages throughout the country. Attorney General Palmer's house in Washington damaged. Palmer ordered investigations of criminal activities of radicals by Bureau of Investigation of the Department of Justice (now the F.B.I.).

November 6, *circa.* A man named Mike Boda came to live in the so-called Coacci house in West Bridgewater. With him lived Feruchio Coacci and Mrs. Coacci. Boda and Coacci were alien anarchists.

December 24. Attempted holdup in Bridgewater. It was for this Bridgewater crime that Vanzetti was tried at Plymouth. Sacco was never charged with this crime.

1920 January 2. Raids in Massachusetts conducted jointly by Department of Labor and Department of Justice, followed by deportation of a number of alien Communists.

January or February. Sacco told by his employer, George T. Kelley, that he was being investigated by Federal agents.

February 25, *circa.* Arrest of two alien anarchists, Roberto Elia and Andrea Salsedo, in New York.

April 15. Murder at South Braintree of Frederick A. Parmenter, a paymaster, and Alessandro Berardelli, his guard. This South Braintree crime was the one for which Sacco and Vanzetti were tried at Dedham.

April 16. Coacci was taken from the Coacci house by Inspector Root of the Immigration Service. The next day,

April 17, Coacci was taken to New York and on the 18th he was put aboard a steamer for Italy under a deportation warrant issued by the Department of Labor.

April 17, afternoon. The Buick car used in both crimes was found in the Manley Street woods in West Bridgewater and taken to the Brockton police station.

April 19. Simon E. Johnson and his brother towed an old Overland car belonging to Boda from the Coacci house to be repaired at the Johnson garage in Elm Square, West Bridgewater.

April 20. Interview of Ricardo Orciani by Michael E. Stewart, Chief of Police of Bridgewater. Interview of Boda at the Coacci house by Stewart and State Police officer Brouillard.

April 25. Vanzetti sent by a committee to New York to learn about Salsedo. He returned on April 29.

May 2. Meeting in Boston of Sacco, Vanzetti, and others to discuss report of Vanzetti about New York visit.

May 3. Death of Salsedo in New York.

May 4. Sacco got one-way passport (*foglio di via*) for self, wife, and son at Italian Consulate in Boston. They intended to sail within a week.

May 5. Visit of Sacco, Vanzetti, Boda, and Orciani to Johnson house in West Bridgewater to get Boda's Overland car. Arrest of Sacco and Vanzetti. Interrogation of them by Stewart.

May 5, *circa*. Formation of Sacco-Vanzetti Defense Committee.

May 6. Thirty or thirty-five eyewitnesses of the two crimes brought to Brockton police station and shown Sacco and Vanzetti. Interrogation of Sacco and Vanzetti by District Attorney Frederick G. Katzmann.

May 7. Employment of John P. Vahey of Plymouth as Vanzetti's counsel. At about the same time James M. Graham of Boston was employed by Sacco.

May 18. Preliminary hearing of Vanzetti for Bridgewater holdup held at Brockton. Vanzetti held for the grand jury.

May 26. Preliminary hearing of Sacco for South Braintree murder held at Quincy. Sacco held for the grand jury.

June 11.   Indictment of Vanzetti for Bridgewater holdup by Plymouth County grand jury.

June 22-July 1.   Trial at Plymouth of Vanzetti for Bridgewater holdup. The trial judge was Webster Thayer, who afterward presided at the Dedham trial of Sacco and Vanzetti for the South Braintree murders. For the Commonwealth, Katzmann and Assistant District Attorney William F. Kane. For Vanzetti, Vahey and Graham.

July 1.   Verdict of guilty of Bridgewater crime against Vanzetti at Plymouth.

August 16.   Defendant's exceptions in Bridgewater case filed. These exceptions were never "allowed," and the case did not go to the Supreme Judicial Court. (3443-3469) On same day Vanzetti was sentenced by Judge Thayer to serve twelve to fifteen years at the State Prison.

August 19.   Fred H. Moore, a California lawyer who had been brought into the case as chief defense counsel by the anarchist Carlo Tresca and the I.W.W., received his first payment from the Defense Committee.

September 11.   Sacco and Vanzetti indicted by Norfolk County grand jury for the South Braintree murders.

September 28.   The two defendants pleaded not guilty to the two indictments.

1921 February 19.   New England Civil Liberties Committee, an affiliate of the American Civil Liberties Union, sent out an appeal for funds to aid the defense.

May 31-July 14.   Trial of Sacco and Vanzetti at Dedham. For the Commonwealth, Katzmann and Harold P. Williams, Assistant District Attorney. For Sacco, Moore and William J. Callahan (of Brockton). For Vanzetti, Jeremiah J. McAnarney and Thomas F. McAnarney, both of Quincy.

July 14.   Verdict of guilty.

October 10.   Death of Walter Ripley, foreman of the jury.

November 8.   First supplementary motion for a new trial because of newly discovered evidence filed (Ripley). A supplement to this motion was filed October 1, 1923 (Daly).

1922 May 4.   Second supplementary motion filed (Gould and Pelser).

July 22.   Third supplementary motion filed (Goodridge).

September 11.   Fourth supplementary motion filed (Andrews).

1923 March 30, *circa*.   Employment by Moore of Albert H. Hamilton as a ballistics expert.

April 30.   Fifth supplementary motion filed (Hamilton). A supplement to this motion was filed November 5, 1923 (Proctor).

October 1-3 and November 1, 2, 8,   The five supplementary motions (Ripley-Daly, Gould and Pelser, Goodridge, Andrews, and Hamilton-Proctor) were argued before Judge Thayer.

1924 October 1.   Decisions by Judge Thayer denying all five supplementary motions for new trial.

November 8.   Fred H. Moore filed a withdrawal of his appearance. On November 25 William G. Thompson filed his appearance for both defendants. On December 7 the McAnarneys also filed withdrawals.

November 17, 19.   The American Fund for Public Service (the Garland Fund) made loans aggregating $20,000 to provide funds for the retainer of Thompson.

1925 June 28.   The International Labor Defense Committee was organized and entered the case actively.

1926 January 11-13.   Argument before Supreme Judicial Court of exceptions taken at the trial and to the denials of the

Ripley-Daly, Gould, and Hamilton-Proctor motions. Chief Justice Arthur Prentice Rugg presided and the other Justices were Henry King Braley, James Bernard Carroll, William Cushing Wait, and George Augustus Sanderson.

May 12.   Decision of Supreme Judicial Court overruling all exceptions and thereby affirming the conviction of Sacco and Vanzetti. The opinion of the Court was written by Mr. Justice Braley. 255 Mass. 369.

May 26.   Motion for a new trial based on the Madeiros confession filed.

September 13-17.   Argument of Madeiros motion before Judge Thayer by Thompson and Dudley P. Ranney, Assistant District Attorney.

October 23.   Decision of Judge Thayer denying Madeiros motion.

1927 January 27-28.   Argument before Supreme Judicial Court of exceptions to denial of Madeiros motion. Thompson and Herbert B. Ehrmann for the defendants. Ranney for the Commonwealth. Chief Justice Rugg presided and the other Justices were Braley, John Crawford Crosby, Edward Peter Pierce, and Wait.

April 5.   The Supreme Judicial Court overruled the exceptions claimed to Judge Thayer's order denying Madeiros motion for a new trial and to his rulings of law in connection therewith. The opinion was written by Mr. Justice Wait.

April 9.   Judge Thayer imposed the mandatory sentence of death on Sacco and Vanzetti. The executions were set for the week beginning July 10. Governor Alvan T. Fuller granted two respites, one up to and including August 10 and one up to and including August 22.

May 4.   A Petition for Clemency dated Dedham Jail, May 3, 1927, was signed by Vanzetti and transmitted to Governor Fuller with a letter signed by Thompson and Ehrmann. Sacco refused to sign this, but the petition was regarded as if made by both defendants.

June 1.   Governor Fuller announced that Judge Robert Grant, President Abbott Lawrence Lowell of Harvard, and President Samuel W. Stratton of M.I.T. had consented to serve as an Advisory Committee in connection with the Governor's investigation of the Sacco-Vanzetti case.

July 11-12.   Hearings before the Advisory Committee.

July 27.   Report of the Advisory Committee to Governor Fuller.

August 3.   Decision of the Governor denying clemency.

August 6.   The defendants filed a petition for a writ of error in the Supreme Judicial Court based on (1) the prejudice of the trial judge, (2) findings of jury plainly wrong, and (3) findings of fact made by trial judge on motions for new trial plainly wrong. On August 8 this petition was heard by Mr. Justice Sanderson on affidavits and the oral testimony of Thompson and denied. Exceptions taken to the full bench of the Supreme Judicial Court were overruled.

August 6.   Defendants filed a motion in the Superior Court for revocation of sentence and for a new trial based on (1) prejudice of the trial judge, (2) discovery of new evidence about Sacco's cap, and (3) discovery of new evidence about the real opinion of Captain William H. Proctor. An effort to have this heard by a judge other than Judge Thayer was denied by Chief Justice Walter Perley Hall of the Superior Court, and on August 8 Judge Thayer after argument denied it. Exceptions to the denial were taken to the Supreme Judicial Court and overruled on the ground that under the Massachusetts statute a motion for a new trial could not be filed after sentence and so could not have been allowed by Judge Thayer or any judge.

August 10.   Petitions for a writ of habeas corpus were presented to Justice Oliver Wendell Holmes of the United States Supreme Court, to Judge George W. Anderson of the Circuit Court of Appeals for the First Circuit of the United States, and on August 20 to Judge James M. Morton, Jr., United States District Judge, and severally denied.

August 20.   Applications for an extension of time for applying for writs of certiorari in the Supreme Court of the United States and for stay of execution pending the applications were presented to Mr. Justice Holmes and to Mr. Justice Stone and severally denied.

August 23.   Execution of Sacco, Vanzetti, and Madeiros.

INDEX

The trial of Sacco and Vanzetti in 1921 for the murder of a paymaster and his guard in South Braintree, Mass., has been a *cause célèbre* for forty years.

Because they were professional Anarchists, it has been passionately argued by individuals and by organizations heavily financed to support the cause of the two men that they never were legally proved guilty; that they were convicted and executed for their political opinions.

In the view of the late Justice Oliver Wendell Holmes, however (as he wrote to Harold Laski), the Sacco-Vanzetti case was an ordinary murder "turned into a text by the Reds."

And in the view of Mr. Montgomery, considered one of the foremost legal minds in Massachusetts, Sacco and Vanzetti were guilty of murder as charged and were properly convicted by an uninfluenced jury. Mr. Montgomery knew many of the principals of the trial and of the final review in 1927. He has devoted years to a study of the evidence, and in his book he examines the arguments of prosecution and defense.

Further, he considers the trial in terms of the many individuals involved as witnesses, attorneys, judge, reviewers, and interested parties whose roles were unofficial but significant.

And he gives the full story of the intimidations, bribes, false confessions, threats, and propaganda on the part of supporters and defenders of Sacco and Vanzetti.

Mr. Montgomery arrives at the following conclusions, based on the facts of the case:

- that Sacco and Vanzetti were convicted solely and rightly on the evidence unfolded in the course of a fair trial;
- that proved, significant facts of the case have been distorted and suppressed by the Mythmakers;
- that judge and jury were untouched by the war